Ogimaag

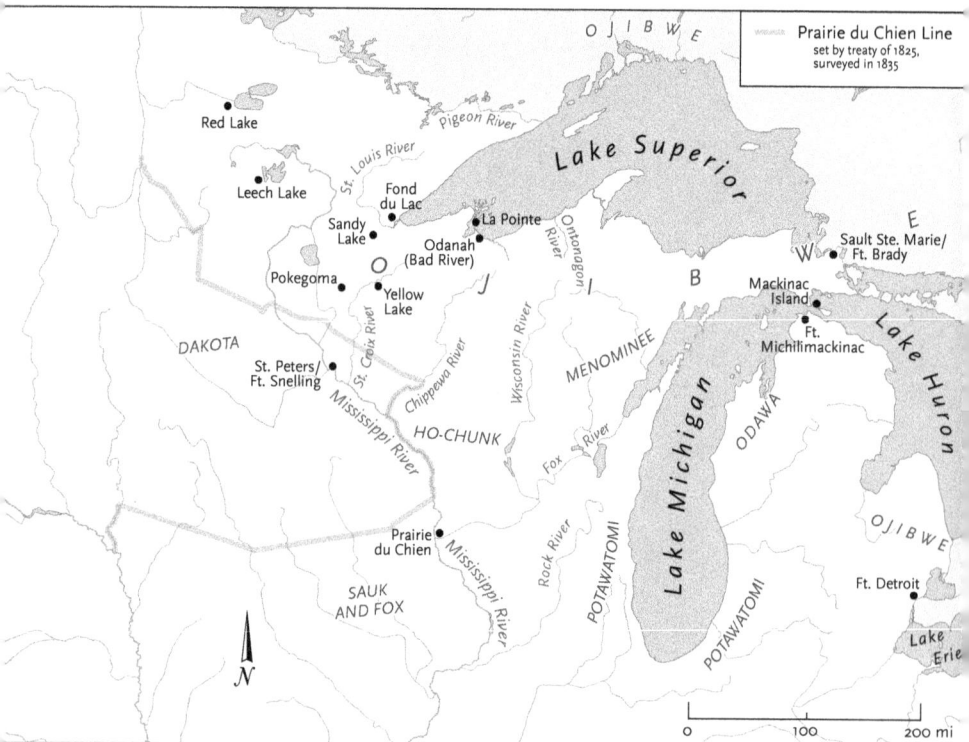

Prairie du Chien Line
set by treaty of 1825,
surveyed in 1835

OJIBWE

Pigeon River

Lake Superior

Red Lake

St. Louis River

Leech Lake

Fond du Lac

La Pointe

Ontonagon River

Sault Ste. Marie/ Ft. Brady

E

W

Sandy Lake

Odanah (Bad River)

O

Mackinac Island

Pokegoma

Yellow Lake

J

I

B

Ft. Michilimackinac

DAKOTA

Chippewa River

St. Croix River

Wisconsin River

MENOMINEE

Lake Michigan

ODAWA

Lake Huron

St. Peters/ Ft. Snelling

Mississippi River

HO-CHUNK

Fox River

OJIBWE

Prairie du Chien

Rock River

POTAWATOMI

Ft. Detroit

Mississippi River

SAUK AND FOX

POTAWATOMI

Lake Erie

N

0   100   200 mi

Ogimaag

Anishinaabeg Leadership,
1760–1845

CARY MILLER

UNIVERSITY OF NEBRASKA PRESS

LINCOLN & LONDON

Library of Congress Cataloging-in-Publication Data
Miller, Cary, 1969–
Ogimaag: Anishinaabeg leadership, 1760–1845 /
Cary Miller.
p. cm. Includes bibliographical references and
index.
ISBN 978-0-8032-3404-8 (cloth: alk. paper)
ISBN 978-0-8032-9525-4 (paper: alk. paper)
1. Ojibwa Indians—Politics and government—18th
century. 2. Ojibwa Indians—Politics and government—19th century. 3. Indian leadership—Northeastern States—History—18th century. 4. Indian
leadership—Northeastern States—History—19th
century. 5. Ojibwa Indians—Kings and rulers—
History—18th century. 6. Ojibwa Indians—Kings
and rulers—History—19th century. 7. Power
(Social sciences)—Northeastern States—History—
18th century. 8. Power (Social sciences)—
Northeastern States—History—19th century.
9. Northeastern States—Politics and government.
10. Northeastern States—Ethnic relations. I. Title.
E99.C6M48 2010
323.1197074—dc22   2010010136

Set in Scala and Scala Sans Pro.
Designed by A. Shahan.

Frontispiece:
Map of Ojibwe villages with ABCFM missions

Contents

Illustrations

Acknowledgments

I would like to take this opportunity to thank those who made this book possible by sharing their time, knowledge, and experiences with me. *Gichimiigwetch* to all the Elders who have given me advice, teachings, and guidance over the years, both before and during this project. The advice and guidance of the members of my dissertation committee—Clyde Ellis, Michael Green, Donald Matthews, Theda Perdue, and Peter Wood—were instrumental in shaping this manuscript. This book would not have been possible without the assistance of the helpful staff at the Minnesota Historical Society, the Wisconsin Historical Society (especially those at the Ashland Area Research Office), the Clarke Historical Library at Central Michigan University, Ziibiwing Cultural Center, and Harvard Library. I would also like to thank Bruce White and my Ford mentor Rebecca Kugel for their help and insightful comments at various points during this project. *Miigwetch* also to Anton Treuer for his assistance with Ojibwe language terms and spellings. Finally, I want to acknowledge the loving support of my family, both adopted and biological, as vital to the completion of this work.

Ogimaag

Introduction

*Our Father: all the warriors, women, and children compliment
you. We wish you to pity us.*—**Buffalo**

*My Father: I shake hands with you. There are as many as 1,000
warriors who shake hands with you through me. They are as
powerful as the fire.*

*My Father: All the Band and Villages who met the Governor at
St. Peters are of one mind with us. We have sent out messengers
on the right and left to learn the minds of the different Bands
and our Messengers have just brought in the messages and news
to this point.*—**Nodin**

Buffalo and Nodin were among the Ojibwe *ogimaag*, or chiefs,
gathered at Snake River in the fall of 1837 in hopes of convinc-
ing President Martin Van Buren to reassess their recent treaty.
Dutifully written down by American interpreters, the chiefs'
pronouncements were treated as ritually formulaic by American officials, who saw the ogimaag as the locus of power and
decision-making authority in Ojibwe communities. However,
when carefully examined, their statements in fact reveal a set of
underlying governing structures and assumptions about governance that are quite different from what Anglo Americans supposed. Ogimaag did not make unilateral decisions on the spot;
rather the community reached consensus before the *ogimaa*
had the authority to deliver village concerns to the Americans.
As scholar David Nichols has identified, Eastern Woodlands
communities were governed by three councils—the women, the

warriors (sometimes termed young men or braves in American accounts), and the old men (sometimes termed headmen, or chiefs)—and an ogimaa might speak on behalf of any one group or a combination of these groups.[1] Ogimaag always clearly identified the constituents on whose behalf they spoke, sometimes even expressing that they did not necessarily share the views of those who had asked for their concerns to be voiced. At the same time, these leaders were not just representational spokesmen. They possessed forms of authority in their own right. Such authority arose from two sources, an inherited or hereditary claim and a charismatic religious claim. Regardless of the origin of the chief's authority, he (and occasionally she) had earned the trust of the people and thus the right to lead through demonstrated results.

The ogimaag who gathered at the 1837 meeting stand in stark contrast to the common narrative of Indigenous government, which suggests that American Indian leadership systems were weak, had no conception of land ownership, and were separate from religious authorities. European colonial observers judged Native power among the tribes of the western Great Lakes according to the political notions of More, Locke, Rousseau, and absolute monarchy. These cultural interpretations of power and authority led them to critique tribes for the lack of totalitarian chiefly control and the absence of monumental constructions at static locations, citing these missing social elements as evidence of an anemic authority. Yet these same colonizers many times found themselves negotiating at the mercy of Indian aims and objectives. The organization of massive war parties against the Iroquois during the seventeenth century and Pontiac's revolt in the eighteenth demonstrated that Great Lakes village leaders, when pressed, could act in very powerful ways. Indeed, such events demonstrate that even if Indigenous governance was somewhat inscrutable to Western military, administrative, and fur trade personnel, it was strong, decisive, and effective to Anishinaabeg eyes.[2] For Indigenous people, leadership was enacted and validated on a daily basis that required leaders to bring to bear social, economic, and religious authority to address the issues and concerns of everyday life. While the contribution of kinship and gift exchange to social order in Indigenous societies has received increased attention in recent scholarship, the role charismatic religious authority played in augmenting the influence of hereditary leaders has not been fully explored.[3]

This religious dimension of Indigenous political authority in daily governance and in external diplomacy forms the central concern of this book. Not only does this perspective help in the revisionist process of seeing Native societies of the past as active, powerful, complex peoples, but it also leads us to important conclusions about the nature of Indigenous governance that helps us to understand more fully the demands tribal leaders made at treaty gatherings, reflects the reasons Christian conversion could bolster or weaken chiefly authority, and explains the rapid decline of Indigenous systems of leadership in the latter part of the nineteenth century. Further, studies such as this are necessary in light of the current interest of Native nations in reviving strategies of the past to cope with the problems of the future, which our Indian Reorganization Act governments cannot always address.

Because such a prodigious body of archival and scholarly sources exist on the social organization and leadership of Anishinaabeg people, this study is focused on Anishinaabeg leadership from the Seven Years' War through 1845. Anthropologists have termed societies like the Anishinaabeg *band-level* societies or acephalous societies, communities with a heightened degree of egalitarianism marked by weak and/or fluid leadership.[4] Throughout the world, anthropologists theorize, leaders of such societies gained and maintained power through hereditary authority, skillful implementation of systems of gift exchange, and displays of religious power.[5] However, defining acephalous systems as having "weak guidance" and "diffuse sources of power" poses problems because it both ignores the long history of orderly political activity among these various peoples and uncritically embraces old colonial justifications for replacing Indigenous political systems with more "stable" (controllable) Western models. Acephalous political systems were neither weak nor random but highly organized and deliberate. The flexibility they display must be understood as a strength, supporting a complex and dynamic social system that could easily respond to environmental changes or intertribal conflict. Many historical moments supply critical windows to the past through which to examine how Anishinaabeg peoples constructed, used, and transferred leadership. Viewed anew through Native eyes, these moments can recast the debates about the nature of band-level societies.

For the Ojibwe this characterization of acephalous leadership rests in part on erroneous assumptions about Ojibwe social structure and the village community. In the early to mid-twentieth century many anthropologists characterized the Anishinaabeg as having a limited social and political structure, which scholars have labeled atomism.[6] This interpretation stems from a literal reading of European sources. Fur traders, missionaries, and military personnel assumed that Anishinaabeg people were aggressive individualists who lived isolated lives in small nuclear or minimally extended family groups. They also believed that Anishinaabeg people met in larger aggregates so rarely that such gatherings, let alone any social or leadership structures related to them, were anomalies rather than the rule.[7] Accepting such a depiction of Anishinaabeg society overlooks its complexity and marginalizes the social organization necessary for the degree of intervillage and intertribal contact, trade, and warfare with other peoples that occurred in the region both before and after Europeans arrived.[8] Rather than being a weakness that demonstrated a lack of organization, or worse, some sort of "primitive" condition, fluidity strengthened the Anishinaabeg, not only helping them to survive but also binding their villages more tightly together.

Some scholars have begun the work of suggesting a more complicated view of Indigenous leadership. Richard White changed the paradigm with *The Middle Ground*. He described how Great Lakes leaders pressured Europeans into cultural accommodations, an assertion that casts enormous doubt on the atomistic contention that tribal governments were weak.[9] Rebecca Kugel further questions this view by demonstrating that factionalism within community governance could function in negotiations with external groups as a strength that resulted in greater concessions or at least successful delaying tactics. Her work also shows that women formed a distinct caucusing body within the village.[10]

Scholars have also studied Indigenous religion, but without fully grasping the symbiotic nature of religious and political authority in Anishinaabeg life. Yet scholarship has not completely alienated religion from Native leadership. Anthony F. C. Wallace identified the importance of religion to sociopolitical revitalization movements while Gregory Dowd emphasized the unifying role of such revitalization in the intertribal military mobilizations associated with Pontiac and Tecumseh.[11] However, with the exception of the role of revitalization movements defined as a somewhat extraordinary occurrence caused by societal stress, the role of religion in validating daily political authority within Indigenous societies has largely been marginalized or misunderstood.

This misunderstanding derives mainly from Western assumptions that a belief system can be classified into a polarity between sacred and profane elements. This distorts the Indigenous interpretation of the world by forcing it into ill-fitting alien categories. Power is not a cultural absolute; rather it is culturally constructed. All human societies, as part of their adaptive strategies for understanding and interacting with their local environments, develop a world view that creates the basic rules of cause and effect, provides explanations for everyday phenomena, defines the cognitive system for organizing information and experience, and provides the rules for moral social interaction and leadership. A society's world view defines "not just our physical environment but the structures of meaning and value which describe reality."[12] The way that a society formulates its explanations determines the manner in which a people live and interact with that environment. This creates a philosophical system that does not necessarily contrast sacred or profane, a person or nonperson, real or imaginary. Further, these cognitive categories define how authority is claimed, maintained, and morally exercised.

Individuals born into a given society are instructed in these abstract categories through simple socialization. For most, religious texts or oral tradition provide a road map to appropriate or inappropriate behavior and inculcate explanations for why and how things are. Religious performances and testimonies of religious experience or phenomena constitute additional empirical sources of knowledge and authority that further reinforce a particular perception of the cosmos.[13] From exposure to such sources of information during their formative years, individuals gradually become convinced that the way they have been taught to view the world is the way the world really is.[14]

Eventually even a society's language itself adapts to the categories of perception expressed by the people, thus linguistically reinforcing the perceived parameters of reality. In other words, "we see and hear and otherwise experience very largely as we do because the language habits of our community predispose certain choices of interpretation."[15] Although societies with related languages usually share similar or at least mutually intelligible world views, societies with languages from distant linguistic families generally interpret lived experience very differently. Even basic nouns may not have a one-to-one translation, let alone abstract concepts.[16] For example, the concept of *manidoo* (or *manitou,* plural *manidoog*) lies at the center of Anishinaabeg religious understanding yet cannot be directly defined in English.[17] This is due to the misinterpretation of the term as a narrow one-to-one translation for the English word "spirit." Anishinaabeg elder Basil Johnston notes that this interpretation of *manidoog* distorts what the Anishinaabe people express with this term.[18] He defines *manidoo* as "spiritual, mystical, supernatural, godlike, or spiritlike, quiddity, essence. It is in these other senses that the term is often used and is to be understood, not just in the context of manitou beings. Manitou refers to realities other than the physical ones of rock, fire, water, air, wood, and flesh—to the unseen realities of individual beings and places and events that are beyond human understanding but are still clearly real."[19] This means that primary European sources from the eighteenth and nineteenth centuries pertaining to Anishinaabe culture need to be read with the mediating process of cultural translation in mind. Indeed, the very use of English to discuss Anishinaabe culture can distort our understanding of it. Nonetheless, the attempt must be made in order to provide a context within which a broader audience can understand Anishinaabe leadership roles and the expectations Anishinaabeg communities had of United States fur traders, Indian agents, and missionaries.

But lest we depict world views as rigid and static, we must also recognize that some variation occurs within these systems of belief. An individual's status in society, age, gender, intelligence, interests, and temperament shape personal interpretations of the culture's world view. Despite this, "the cultural world view channels, limits, and inspires individual thought and outlook" and "provides a fund of generic notions from which the culture's members severally draw."[20] In other words, cultures and the world views that define them can be understood best in biological terms. Like species they have discernible characteristics that are carried by most of the members but which all individuals do not manifest in equal degree. Both species and cultures contain properties characteristic of the group that some individuals do not seem to have at all.[21] Taking this comparison further, culture and world view themselves evolve and change over time in an organic, adaptive manner, leaving room for local and individual variations that can be carried on to the next generation.[22] They evolve in a symbiotic relationship with the social and economic resource needs of a culture, the availability of those resources, and the technology available for obtaining them.

Because world view forms the matrix through which members of human societies perceive and interpret their world, these systems illuminate internal sources of power and define internal forms of legitimate authority. Any study of traditional Anishinaabeg leadership at the turn of the nineteenth century must therefore begin with an understanding of their world view and the concepts that define supernatural as well as temporal power and authority. To this end, this study is focused on the ways that Anishinaabeg peoples understand religious power as inseparable from political power; it also defines and uses Anishinaabeg terms for leaders and their sources of authority within the Anishinaabeg language itself.

The Anishinaabeg understood themselves to be part of a populous world in which the spiritual definition of personhood extended far beyond the human sphere to animals, birds, plants, natural forces, and all manner of life. These manidoog entities each had important and special gifts that helped them to survive. They shared these gifts with humanity on a reciprocal basis developed through personal relationships initiated in dreams and visions. Such relationships were considered so important to survival that an individual who failed to form ties with at least one manidoo could hardly be regarded within the community as an adult, let alone as an individual of power. Thus interaction with the sacred was a necessary and expected ingredient of living for even the least politically important person in the community, and much more so for those who claimed to be able to help others.

Given that Indigenous societies freely accepted open, direct, and personal communication with manidoog beings, new religious ideas could easily be brought in and incorporated if they proved beneficial to the lives and desired ends of an individual or community. As such, in Anishinaabeg communities, adherence to Christianity and assertion to leadership authority based on this adherence could be made on the same basis as similar claims of Indigenous religious leaders or nativist prophets of revitalization. The Anishinaabeg believed that the religions of all peoples had some truth and power to them—it must be so in order for those communities to survive and prosper—and did not decry the beliefs of others, whether of other tribes or the colonial powers, as false and without basis. The Anishinaabeg recognized that Americans had power. The Americans had beaten the British and driven them from the land. American authority must therefore have a strong spiritual basis, according to Anishinaabe definitions of power.

The presence among the newcomers of missionaries, spiritually powerful men, only reinforced this belief. In 1832, when Henry Rowe Schoolcraft made his most extensive trip through Anishinaabeg territories as Indian agent, he brought with him ABCFM missionary William T. Boutwell, introduced him to the Ojibwe ogimaag, and asked them to accept missionaries into their communities. Many of the leaders agreed. They had long sought to have American representatives closer to their communities than Schoolcraft's far-off station at Sault Ste. Marie, Michigan, and expected the missionaries to function as representatives of the United States. Since the missionaries clearly received assistance and deference from both fur traders and

Indian agents as persons of religious authority, Native people determined that they must be powerful individuals whose spiritual connections could help the communities in which they lived. This suggested to some that Christianity could perhaps serve as an additional or even a new basis for authority within the community. Unfortunately, the introduction of Christianity led to increased factionalization in Indigenous communities, as described by Robert Berkhofer in *Salvation and the Savage*, but it did so precisely because it allowed ambitious individuals in the community another avenue to power and authority outside of traditional pathways for such ambitions.[23]

For a proper examination of what leadership meant to Anishinaabe people themselves, we must first ask how they defined power and authority. In an April 1833 letter to the home office, American Board missionaries Sherman Hall and William Boutwell observed: "If any one can acquire a reputation for a conjurer or a dreamer, he is sure to pass for a great man among the Indians, and at once gains an influence."[24] Heredity was an important factor in attaining chiefly status, but leaders needed the ability to guide the community successfully through any crisis it faced, whether the crisis was famine, disease, or foreign invaders. For Native Americans, power meant the ability to live, to grow crops, to court lovers, to slay animals, to heal the sick, and to defeat enemies, none of which could be successfully accomplished without aid from manidoog. Only with the aid of spiritual power could one make beneficial choices on a consistent basis. In other words, individuals who demonstrated success in life concurrently demonstrated their access to religious sources of power even if not directly observed using them. Positive political outcomes served as further proof of a person's religious power. Continued successful decisions by leaders led to more influence. The more influential someone became, the more powerful the community assumed that person's spiritual associates to be, and the less likely they were to disagree with that individual's judgment. Anishinaabeg understood that when ogimaag made alliances, it brought to their aid not only the economic or military resources of other peoples but spiritual resources as well.

Although all Anishinaabeg people had relationships with manidoog forged through fasting or other means, leaders had a privileged link, sometimes enhanced through rituals or bundles passed down through the family, and could call on this powerful form of help for the whole community in times of need. Many if not all village leaders were also members of the Midewiwin, the traditional religious organization of the Anishinaabe people. In English this religious body is often referred to as the Grand Medicine Society, a clear reference to its healing abilities. Historically and today many aspects of the Midewiwin are considered protected knowledge not to be disbursed to the uninitiated.

Some scholars have sought to label Midewiwin ceremonies a revitalization movement, but core aspects of their performance call this notion into question. These seasonal rituals involved songs, dance, feasts, sweats, gifts, and tobacco offerings and were conducted in the spring to encourage the gardens to grow and in the fall to help the wild rice to mature. The ceremonies were acts related to subsistence and life-renewal rather than cultural revitalization in reaction to external pressures. The Anishinaabeg people consider this to be the religion of their people and assert a pre-contact origin for these ceremonies in their oral tradition.

The Midewiwin also had a political dimension. Midewiwin ceremonies united Anishinaabeg communities. The largest gatherings of the Anishinaabe year in the spring and fall included Midewiwin ceremonies. All leaders, from the headmen of the small winter encampments often numbering no more than six families to those claiming chieftainship over one or more bands, were members of this society. Since nearly all Anishinaabeg leaders were members, ceremonial gatherings also provided the opportunity for political gatherings where leaders discussed issues of war and diplomacy and resolved disputes over sugarbush, hunting, and ricing claims, both among themselves and with newcomers.

Unfortunately uncovering the daily transactions of government for Indigenous societies prior to the treaties is difficult. Self-generated documents for Anishinaabeg communities are extremely rare in archival collections prior to the twentieth century. As a result, the documentary sources that form the core of this study were written by cultural outsiders during the historical moments described. To turn the lens of these sources in upon itself so that it reveals Anishinaabeg views of their world necessarily requires the scholar to move beyond standard historical methodologies. This book combines an examination of the available Western archival sources, such as missionary records, fur trade documents, captivity narratives, government documents, and travel narratives, with ethnographic data, material culture, and Anishinaabeg oral literature in an attempt to interpret Indigenous actions within their own cultural context. This methodology, known as ethnohistory, includes using the various documentary sources to cross-check one another and cautiously using ethnographic and oral sources to evaluate the historical descriptions through the anthropological tools of "upstreaming" (interpreting the documentary record in light of more recent oral histories) and "side-streaming" with generalized ethnographic models of northeastern woodlands societies. The result is a far deeper interpretation of the available written sources.

Yet even cross-referencing sources in these various ways improves the focus of the clouded historical lens only slightly. On those rare occasions when multiple letters or diaries are available for the same fleeting event, they are obscured by the deep-seated cultural biases of their non-native authors—not to mention any personal or professional motivations that caused authors to spin the narrative of events for their own reasons. Upstreaming, when not carefully applied, can lead to another stereotype—a timeless, frozen, changeless Native society somehow unaffected by historical pressures, colonial and otherwise, retaining instead a "pure" Indigenous essence. Such uniformity not only ignores change over time but downplays village and even personal variation within a society. Yet we also assume that cultures maintain some inheritance from their past, or they would have lost their identity as a people. Verifying past actions or interpretations by use of oral history demonstrates such continuities in the midst of other changes. Side-streaming of course risks overgeneralization despite demonstrated cultural and linguistic similarities. Anishinaabe oral tradition, however, provides grounds for cautious use of this methodology. Migration stories identify historical links between Ojibwe, Potawatomi, and Odawa peoples, and further suggest that all three groups originated from among other Algonquian peoples of the Eastern Woodlands—the Abenaki perhaps, or the Lenni Lenape. As with all methodologies, the key is moderation. Use them to improve and sharpen the image, but beware of abusive excesses that only fog our understanding.

As in other American borderlands, the initial arrival of European forces, the French and British in the case of the Great Lakes region, brought enormous economic and social change for Anishinaabeg communities south and west of Lake Superior. The period from contact through the eighteenth century represents a time in which these Indigenous societies incorporated Europeans and their goods and political aims into existing systems of kin, trade, and negotiation. Europeans did indeed pressure Anishinaabeg peoples to trade specific goods, to fight in their wars, and to allow Europeans to define their alliances. However, it was also an era in which Europeans were far from controlling the relationship. Native people chose to accept Europeans as sons-in-law to expand political and trade alliances.

They chose to accept or reject European goods and terms of trade to improve their ways of life for their own purposes. They chose to accept, reject, or syncretize missionaries and their theologies. And they chose to aid Europeans in their wars even as they drew Europeans into their own Indigenous conflicts. It was a period of change around the western Great Lakes—but a period of change directed by Indigenous motives, choices, and actions for Indigenous purposes, much as Pekka Hämäläinen suggests for the Comanche during the early years of colonial interaction on the southern plains.[25]

Even the American Revolution brought little externally directed change to these communities and their political systems prior to the 1830s. Anishinaabeg communities, as before the exit of the French, maintained relations with at least two non-Indian powers, now the United States and Great Britain, whose representatives resided in small, isolated military forts or trading posts or made their way individually through the country peddling their wares and diplomacy. Anishinaabeg peoples still attempted to negotiate with American officials using the language, customs, and political forms developed during the height of the colonial fur trade. As late as the 1830s Anishinaabeg leaders such as Zhingwaakoons of Sault Ste. Marie and Eshkibagikoonzh of Leech Lake still negotiated with both American and British officials as they attempted to steer their communities through increasingly troubled waters.[26]

The close of the Revolutionary War left political boundaries in the Great Lakes country uncertain, and Jay's Treaty in 1784 allowed British traders to continue to operate on American soil in a clause allowing Native, British, and American individuals to cross the borders freely for the purposes of trade. In some ways it was not much of a concession. In 1784 the United States did not yet have its own fur trade industry and certainly did not have the military capacity to close the borders in the western Great Lakes region. As a result, regional tribes continued to practice

Indigenous gift-exchange diplomacy with both powers despite American intentions to the contrary.[27]

The War of 1812 ended overt competition between the British and United States citizens in the fur trade south of the Great Lakes, but the semi-nomadic subsistence patterns of the Anishinaabe people continued to ignore international boundaries and trade agreements. The Indigenous perception of village sovereignty further meant that Anishinaabeg leaders did not recognize the right of American or British governments to delineate political boundaries or trade or alliance ties in the region. Many bands simply continued to maintain connections with both powers, seeing the widest possible alliance network as the strongest economic and political position. Anishinaabeg leaders from Wisconsin, Minnesota, and Michigan still traveled to British posts at Malden, Drummond's Island, and Fort William to receive British gifts and advice. This only fueled American fears in the 1820s and 1830s that the British would renew warfare and once again recruit Indian allies to achieve their ends.

To demonstrate a military presence that might hold this threat in check, American officials devised a strategy for the defense of the northern frontier with a line of small forts at Sault Ste. Marie, Detroit, Mackinac, Green Bay, St. Peters, Chicago, and Prairie du Chien.[28] As supplying these forts from the produce of eastern farms proved cost prohibitive, the soldiers cleared and planted their own fields, raised livestock for meat, and traded with Anishinaabeg communities for surplus foods such as maple sugar and wild rice, as had the fur traders before them. The soldiers cut down trees for fort construction and also as fuel for cooking and heating. They represented an assault on the natural resources the Anishinaabeg needed for survival, both by consuming part of the gathered foods Anishinaabeg communities utilized and by destroying habitats for animal and plant resources claimed by Anishinaabeg communities. Yet they also represented increased opportunities for the Anishinaabeg to expand social networks and perhaps levy pressures on British allies. In the early days these forts presented annual gifts to Native communities for the materials they took from the land, much as occupants of British and French fortifications had done in earlier times. To Anishinaabeg leaders, this created a fictive kinship relationship with newcomers who wished to reside among them and compensated with goods the community members who gave up their hunting and gathering sites to the new residents.

Although Americans initially appeared to have the same objectives as the French and British, within a decade of the War of 1812 it became clear to the Anishinaabeg that these newcomers had different goals. The established tribal strategies the Anishinaabeg used to incorporate outsiders during centuries of alliance diplomacy began to falter in the face of American cultural intransigence. Native peoples had long approached Europeans much as they approached their tribal neighbors—with requests for food, clothing, or other items to emphasize mutual alliance and reliance through dependence between the parties, and expected such requests to be made of them in return.[29] Americans, however, gradually withdrew from gift- and kin-based diplomacy over the course of the 1830s and 1840s, as they needed less and less from the tribes. This weakened the effectiveness of Indigenous leaders and challenged their time-tested methods of negotiation.

Such American efforts to distance themselves from Native peoples were not yet in evidence in 1825, when the United States held a treaty council at Prairie du Chien with the various tribes of Minnesota, Wisconsin, Michigan, Iowa, and Illinois to formalize their loyalty to their new political "Father." Besides this change of alliance, the treaty aimed at ending intertribal warfare, which limited American returns from the fur trade and impeded white settlement of the region. The chiefs of various warring nations agreed to set boundaries between their territories with the U.S. military as guarantor of peace. Those Anishinaabeg leaders who were present negotiated with their enemies the Dakotas a boundary that all the Anishinaabeg villages embraced at the Fond du Lac treaty council the following year.[30]

Anishinaabeg leaders likely wanted beneficial interactions with the new American government. The Americans had not used the fort at Sault Ste. Marie to kill neighboring bands, as had been feared, nor did the treaties with the United States in the 1820s at Prairie du Chien and Fond du Lac specify any land cessions. The treaties probably appeared to the Anishinaabeg much like the earlier alliances with the French, who had mediated and settled intertribal disputes among allied Indian nations by giving gifts to "cover the dead."[31] General William Clark, one of the commissioners of the 1825 Prairie du Chien treaty, had promised that the president would take the various tribes and bands under his "protecting wing" to "protect the weak from the strong" and "prevent any bad people from crossing" territorial lines "to do mischief."[32] This language echoed the diplomatic speeches given in the French and English eras, further enabling the Anishinaabeg to view their new relations with the Americans as part of an ongoing political tradition.

Unfortunately, the peace between the Dakota and the Anishinaabeg established via the treaties of Prairie du Chien and Fond du Lac held for only two years. The Anishinaabeg increasingly believed that the United States had failed to fulfill the stipulated peace-keeping responsibilities promised in these treaties. The western Ojibwe ogimaag, whose villages bore the brunt of this warfare, complained that their Indian agent at Sault Ste. Marie was too far away for them to visit regularly and that he failed to act swiftly and decisively against Dakota treaty violators.[33] Nevertheless, community leaders continued to use the diplomatic customs of the past to pressure American agents to honor their promises, but with little result.

The 1830s brought important observable changes to Anishinaabeg communities. Where American settlers had constituted a largely unobtrusive presence in Anishinaabeg territories heretofore, the logging industry that emerged during this decade brought more white settlers and increased the stress on Anishinaabeg ecosystems.[34] There were few roads cutting through the northern forests, so the easiest way for loggers to transport timber was to use the extensive waterways of northern Wisconsin and Minnesota to float logs to market. Utilizing these waterways to transport logs often required redirecting water flow and using dams to maintain water levels. This interfered with Anishinaabeg wild rice stands either by flooding them or by siphoning off their water. These changes increased Anishinaabeg conflicts with both Native and white neighbors over subsistence resources and forced Native peoples to rely more on hunting game or trading furs to meet their subsistence needs.

The 1830s also saw the first American Christian missionaries in Anishinaabeg villages, a situation that brought many unintended sociopolitical consequences, including community political factionalization.[35] Anishinaabeg viewed the missionaries much like other prophets of the period and measured their power on the same basis: by their ability to bring about beneficial political and economic developments for the village. Most historical and anthropological studies have examined missionaries in this period as either religious or political actors, reflecting Western assumptions about separation of church and state and the resulting role of religious authorities in a society. Early nineteenth-century Anishinaabe society did not make this distinction or sharply differentiate the religious and political roles of the missionaries. Nor were Anishinaabeg nativist and accommodationist leaders exclusively political: both had strong religious feelings and experiences. Power came from many sources, and leaders exercised authority in many arenas simultaneously.

This brings us to the heart of the issue: how did Anishinaabeg peoples erect and define the daily exercise of power differently from what Western observers recorded, and what did this mean for how they constructed their leadership and evaluated its effectiveness? For the Anishinaabeg the clearest demonstration of power was the lack of dependence. Hence the animal and plant beings had more power than humans, since they could exist independently of humans with little difficulty, while humans were exceedingly dependent upon them for food, clothing, shelter, and medicine. As A. Irving Hallowell wrote of the Anishinaabeg, "Human beings are conceived of as being in constant need of help, from birth to death. So essential is such help that no performance of any kind is interpreted as due to an individual's own abilities or efforts."[36] This created an odd paradox within Anishinaabeg social organization in which individuals aspired to independence but considered it achievable only through the establishment of the widest possible networks of mutual obligation with both human and manidoog partners. Leaders often had the grandest of these networks at their disposal and used these physical and spiritual resources both to meet the needs of the community and to influence the political process of consensus building that directed community action. The chapters that follow explore these sources of power and demonstrate how they supported hereditary, military, and religious leaders within Anishinaabeg communities.

1

Power in the Anishinaabeg World

*Power is manifest in the land . . . and in the vision and deeds
of spirits, ancestors, and living people.*—**John A. Grim** and
D. P. St. John, "The Northeast Woodlands"

When the creator Gichi-Manidoo made the universe, "that one"
imbued the manidoog beings and forces (defined in the introduction) with immortality, virtue, and wisdom and implanted
them, to various degrees, into beings and objects.[1] Gichi-Manidoo had a vivid vision of the universe, which "that one" brought
into being. This act is the ultimate selfless gift, a use of the creator's power purely to benefit others, and a gift so awesome that
it can never be fully reciprocated. In honor of this first gift all
beings in creation emulate the selfless sharing of Gichi-Manidoo. The manidoog give gifts to needy humans, and humans
give gifts to aid others of their own kind and show respect to
those manidoog and humans who have aided them. The creator did not bring into existence a predetermined creation but
rather entrusted all beings not only with purpose but also with
free will. Those who shared their gifts or blessings did so out
of free will, and on the same basis, they could also withhold
their presents.[2]

Defining power and its uses according to the parameters of
Anishinaabeg systems of belief is central to understanding Anishinaabe leadership. While on the simplest level one might
say that power is what makes some strong in comparison to
others defined as weak, this still leaves much room for interpretation. What constitutes strength? Is that strength derived from

economic, intellectual, religious, or physical sources? How can that strength be used morally and legitimately? The answers to these questions at first seem obvious—certainly the early French, British, and American explorers who met the Anishinaabeg all believed that they knew how to define these concepts correctly. However, Europeans and Anishinaabeg of the fur trade era held very different conceptualizations of power defined by their own stories, economic systems, familial relationships, religions, social relationships, and technologies. Examination of the Anishinaabeg world view and its relationship with subsistence practices and social structures demonstrates the high degree of sociopolitical organization that gave rise to Anishinaabe leadership and defined why and how they used power. Anishinaabeg beliefs about their relationship to the natural world, their relationships with one another, and the complexity of the subsistence tasks that supported their relationships all combine to demonstrate the need for the structured yet versatile leadership system the Anishinaabeg developed.

Oral tradition frequently described power as flowing from one entity to another, with the more powerful ones bestowing part of their own power as gifts or blessings to those who were in need. These stories portrayed the basic human state of being as one that evoked the pity of other humans and other more powerful manidoog beings who shared these gifts and blessings with people. Even after the gift was bestowed, power fluctuated. The giver could withdraw aid or reward a virtuous individual with more power.[3] The unequal distribution of power made appearances deceptive. A braggart could turn out to be bluffing, while a young child could be the most powerful individual in the village.[4] These beliefs in the unequal distribution of power and deceptive nature of apparent form encouraged each individual to treat all others with respect. One never knew whose help one would need in the future or who might respond to jealousy or insult with secret sorcery. Mary Black-Rogers has summarized Ojibwe beliefs about power in the following manner:

1) power is necessary to live and all living things have some; 2) there is no division between natural and supernatural power, or sacred and ordinary, although there are specific kinds; 3) the source of power is different for human beings, who must derive or receive it from inherently powerful nonhumans; 4) however derived, power is unevenly distributed, both as to kind and as to amount; the intersection between these is elusive and ambiguous—and must remain so for the system to work; and 5) validation of power rests with the observation of events consequent to its use, thus it exists only in concrete actions and is not dealt with in the abstract.[5]

In the Ojibwe world the clearest demonstration of power was lack of dependence for food, safety, health, and material goods. Hence the manidoog had more power than humans, as they could exist independently of humans with little difficulty. In contrast, humans were exceedingly dependent on them to the point of being "in constant need of help from birth to death."[6] Ojibwe oral tradition instructs that survival is such a precarious and dangerous business that only with the aid of spiritual power given by manidoog could the individual expect to achieve a long and successful life. Every Ojibwe tale mentions some use of supernatural power, suggesting that Ojibwe peoples considered relationships with manidoog and the blessings and gifts that flowed from them to be a regular part of everyday experience.[7] Such help was perceived as so essential that no performance of any task, whether in the service of subsistence, war, peace, or even love, was interpreted as due to an individual's own abilities or efforts. This view represents a complete inversion of the sense of human domination over the natural world presented in western religion and philosophy.[8]

This inversion is largely due to the Ojibwe extension of the category of personhood beyond human beings, seeing the world as populated by plants, animals, and forces who had similar needs to those of humans and an equal if not greater claim to the gifts bestowed by Gichi-Manidoo at the time of creation. Understanding the category of persons in the broadest sense is fundamental to understanding Anishinaabeg determinations of causality as well as their interpretations of, and responses to, events.[9] This concept is so central to the way that the Anishinaabeg understand their surroundings that it forms the foundation of how they express ideas and relate information. The most basic categorization in the Ojibwe language is between animate and inanimate things and actions. Although scholars do not fully understand the category of animate in Algonquian languages, it seems to indicate "a potential for both movement and the exercise of volition."[10] All living things have spirit and are animate, and many things that westerners categorize as nonliving, such as rocks, the Ojibwe can define as animate beings imbued with spirit.[11] What persists, animates, and gives life to a being is its spirit, regardless of its apparent physical form.[12] In other words, the Ojibwe do not perceive human form as a requirement for identification as a person nor for the use of supernatural abilities.[13] Not only did common occupants of their everyday surroundings wield power, but the utensils made from the skins of animals or the bark of trees did not lose the power inherent in the living being, so that the terms for such things as canoes and snowshoes retained their animate status within the Ojibwe language.[14] For the Anishinaabeg, physical form is deceptive, as human, animal, and even plant forms are interchangeable.[15] In fact, the ability to change one's outward shape is one of the most reliable hallmarks of power in oral tradition.[16]

Although spiritual power in the Anishinaabeg world is not evenly distributed, the creator imbued all living beings with certain gifts from birth.[17] Anishinaabeg received four: the Anishinaabe language, freedom of choice, purpose, and a personal spirit name. After the birth the family gave gifts to an elder who had the ability to learn a child's name through dreams. These initial gifts disbursed by the family on the child's behalf started the individual on a lifelong journey of forming relationships with the other beings that occupied the Anishinaabeg world. This elder would hereafter be considered family to the named, with all the obligations that entailed, and the manidoog who aided the elder would help protect the child as well. Through these relationships human beings became conduits for the power of the manidoog persons who aided them, rather than bearers of power in and of themselves.[18]

Anishinaabeg peoples sought social relationships established through gift exchange with human and manidoog that promised to aid them in basic subsistence and to achieve the Ojibwe moral ideal, *mino-bimaadiziwin*, or life lived well, consisting of longevity, good health, and freedom from misfortune.[19] Mino-bimaadiziwin "involves not only prescribed behaviors but commitment to relations with the other persons of the cosmos [manidoog], for only under their tutelage can one find the strength one needs to live well."[20] However, the Anishinaabeg lived in a harsh environment. Starvation in the late winter months always threatened mino-bimaadiziwin. The only way to ensure mino-bimaadiziwin in all seasons was through establishing relationships of interdependency as widely as possible, including extended family in neighboring communities and manidoog. Anishinaabeg individuals approached both human and manidoog beings with requests for pity or to receive a blessing: "to be pitiable . . . seems to be the correct state for a person who wishes to receive a gift of power—a promise of help in getting through life. . . . Such gifts consisted of specific powers, abilities to perform life's jobs both great and small; in short, they consisted of the requisite 'necessaries' in order . . . to survive."[21]

Anishinaabe oral tradition suggests that manidoog blessings most frequently come in the form of dreams, fasting visions, or encounters with manidoog while in the midst of dire situations often related to illness, imminent starvation, or exposure to sorcery. As a result the relationships with manidoog beings were among the only things considered personal property.[22] The more desperate the circumstances, the closer the individual or community believed they were to earning the pity and therefore the assistance of the manidoog.[23] Those who elicited pity deserved aid whether from manidoog or other human beings.[24] Here dreams functioned not as escapes from reality but as important events that gave human beings increased self-confidence and determination in the face of adversity. Where western culture and world view makes a sharp distinction between dreaming and waking experience, the Anishinaabeg world view considers both equally tangible and real. In the Ojibwe language the same word, *inaabandamowin*, is used for both experiences.[25] Both existed in a cause and effect relationship with future events in either realm.[26] Such communication, however, was not without danger. Dreams were one instance in which the soul left the body to communicate with other spirits and sometimes traveled to their various realms. Permanent separation of the soul from the other parts of one's being produced insanity, catatonia, or death.[27] The ability of a person's being to travel or interchange increased the mystery and danger inherent in surviving the natural world. Leaders routinely trod these dangerous grounds on behalf of their community's subsistence, health, and safety.

Even when dreams did bring blessings, there were conditions for using them.[28] Those who received them had to exercise them appropriately without wasting the gift and had to maintain a proper attitude of respect and gratitude for their benefactor's benevolence.[29] Others who mimicked songs or actions that connected one to power without the proper permission or instruction received no power and often made fools of themselves. Even worse, those who used improperly the gifts flowing through them could expect their actions to backfire and injure either the user or members of the user's family.[30] This attitude of respect included not being greedy. One could be greedy for power, just as one could be greedy for material objects, and both these foibles constituted inappropriate moral and social behavior. Overfasting to obtain connections with more powerful manidoog is consistently portrayed in Anishinaabeg oral tradition as another form of greed that generally resulted in negative outcomes. Such actions, for example, could bring people so closely in touch with the spirit realm that their humanity became altogether lost.[31]

By granting a blessing, the manidoog entered an individual's family network of exchange. The Anishinaabeg addressed them using the same kinship terms as those commonly used among their human family. Use of these titles indicated a respect for and intimacy with these beings and their inclusion into the regular social milieu of the Anishinaabe community. This surrounded the Anishinaabeg with a very personal experience of the natural world, in which random forces of nature were totally foreign to Anishinaabe thought.[32] Their use of kinship terms indicates respect and intimacy with the divine and reveals the Anishinaabe belief that manidoog communities have the same social construction as those of humans, as demonstrated in their oral tradition.

Relationships with manidoog fall into two different familial categories. The terms *brothers* and *sisters* referred to the animals and plants of the natural world and their manidoog. This close relationship is likely due to the Anishinaabeg perception that animals were similar to human beings not only in terms of inner essence but also in terms of social ties and mode of life. Like the Anishinaabeg, these beings have families and subsist on the gifts of this creation. In the oral tradition animal brothers and sisters often live in wigwams within villages comprised of extended family members. Each species of animal within a given area had its own chief or head being who had authority and made decisions similar to those of Anishinaabeg leaders.[33]

Above them is an additional level of spirit beings referred to by some scholars as the various "owners" or "masters" of plant and animal species, plus the four winds and the thunder beings and other forces of nature.[34] *Owner* and *master*, however, are problematic terms for two reasons. First, they suggest a separation between these manidoog and the plant, animal, and mineral beings whom they are. Second, they suggest an owner-servant relationship between the two types of spirits that does not reflect Anishinaabe spirituality. Like Anishinaabeg leaders in the human world, they do not possess the coercive authority that such terms suggest. The Anishinaabeg address these beings as grandmothers and grandfathers out of respect for their greater spiritual power, yet the kinship reference also incorporates the respect and love shared with such family members. The Anishinaabe language thus supports a world view teeming not only with living, sentient beings but also with relatives who communicate with people on an intimate level.

When addressing specific manidoog with whom a relationship had been established through fasting or dreaming, Anishinaabeg people used the term *aadizookaan* (plural, *aadizookaanag*), a more formal term for "grandfather" than the commonly used *mishoomis*.[35] Further, this term was also used to identify the class of stories in which they appeared, suggesting that the myths themselves were considered conscious, powerful beings.[36] The relationship between a human child and a human grandfather is functionally the same as the relationship between a human being and his or her manidoog grandfathers.[37] The more powerful elder provides the needy youth with advice, teachings, and instructions on subsistence that will help the beneficiary to be successful. Examples of this familial relationship with manidoog abound in Anishinaabe oral tradition and historically documented speeches.

Oral traditions reinforced the world experienced in dreams and the benefits of gift exchange to individual, family, and village.[38] The interaction of human persons and manidoog in these stories validated Anishinaabeg subsistence activities, economic strategies, social organization, and world view. The following quote from a traditional Anishinaabeg story demonstrates several core aspects of this world view: the importance of reciprocal social relationships that extended the notion of kin far beyond biological relatives, the need for gifts or blessings from manidoog beings outside oneself, the permeable line between animals and manidoog, the moral obligation of those with power to assist others, and the close relationship between the Anishinaabeg and the natural world around them, which provided more than simple subsistence. The bear in the story especially demonstrates many aspects of manidoo power and identity. These basic components of Anishinaabe world view fundamentally define the nature of the leadership structures and sources of authority the Anishinaabeg developed to help their communities meet their various needs.

And presently, while running along through a balsam grove, very close by he [the boy] saw a bear. Thereupon was he seized; and the boy, becoming alarmed, cried out with a loud voice. "Iya!" he exclaimed. While calling aloud, he thereupon lost the memory of his father and his mother; accordingly then, instead he became fond of the bear that had come to take pity on him; he was not slain by it. Thereupon he was carried away into the forest, very much was he loved (by the Bear). "My grandson" continually was he called. And so all the while, when roaming about, he was ever in the company of the bear; various kinds of things they ate, all kinds of things in the way of berries that grew in the ground they ate. . . . All winter long slept the bear, with him slept the boy. Sometimes would (the boy) be addressed: "My grandson, are you hungry?" "Yes," he would say to him. "Just you look there at my back." So slightly over would the Bear turn. And when the boy looked, very nice was the food he saw. Everything which they had eaten during the summer before was all there. "Do you eat, my grandson!" he was told. Truly did the boy eat. So that was what (the Bear) did throughout the winter when feeding (the boy). Sometimes the bear would say: "Even though I take pity upon people, yet I do not (always) give them of my body. Too much harm would I do you if I should be killed." . . . Now once he was addressed by his grandfather saying: "Well my grandchild, now therefore will I take you back home. Too sorrowful are your parents. Come, thither let us go by where they are!" Accordingly was he then carried away. By and by he was addressed (by the Bear) saying: "Now, nigh to this place is a lake, and there dwell your father and mother." Along the edge of the water traveled the Bear. He continued straight up to a certain tree that stood by the edge of the water. Now, this (the boy) was told (by the Bear) from behind the tree, this he was told: "If at any time you are in need of food, then do you call upon me. I will feed you."[39]

One of the more interesting questions raised by this story is its context. Is it dream, vision, story, or lived experience? Do Anishinaabeg draw these distinctions in their world the same way that they are drawn in the western tradition? Clearly this young person has met something more than the average bear. Did he meet the bear while running through the woods on a warm summer day, or only dream that he did so? Most Anishinaabeg understood themselves only to achieve communication with spirits through certain methods to which the senses of the soul are attuned.[40] These senses perceive all of time as concurrent, or concurrently accessible, and gather data through communication with the other-than-human beings, which the Anishinaabeg sense all around them in the natural world. Since the spirits and the souls of human beings are not subject to physical time, time becomes meaningless in this form of communication. Through the senses of the soul, the Anishinaabeg receive information from powerful beings that exist across both space and time, including the age described in the oral tradition.[41] This means that from their perspective, knowledge cannot be permanently lost and will be returned at the right time to receive it.

The primary source of information open to the senses of the soul is that of dreams and visions, yet everyday lived experience also passed through this filter.[42] Among the Anishinaabeg, the world of the self and the world embodied in the oral tradition are continuous by virtue of their link in dream experience.[43] Dreamers and mythic heroes experienced similar phenomena, making the time described in oral tradition also part of the simultaneous past, present, and future rather than a period separated by time from current experience. This conception of time is not a thing of the past. Elders today report that the past and its customs are recoverable for the Anishinaabeg through dreams.

The concurrent perception of time among the Anishinaabeg firmly shapes their understanding of the world. Western linear perceptions of tradition as derived from a single point in time and passed down through successive ages do not apply to cyclical or concurrent time. Orientation with the realm of the other-than-human spiritual beings known as manidoog takes on a higher importance. When direction from the divine is perceived to be ongoing and continuous and the instigator of change is divine, there is less need to maintain an ancient set of rituals and doctrines, or the commemorative temporal framework within which these rituals and doctrines reside. The defining element of tradition then ceases to be a continuity of doctrine over time and instead becomes a continuity of contact with the sacred. The modes of continuous interaction with manidoog—dreams, feasts, songs, dances and tobacco—thus become the most central teachings of Anishinaabe spirituality. Authority rests in the realm perceived by the senses of the soul, populated by ageless manidoog that act both in the oral tradition and in everyday life, and with those Anishinaabeg who have most successfully interacted with these beings over time.

The gifts exchanged between human beings and manidoog were mirrored in the social lives of Anishinaabeg people. Gifting was the cornerstone of kinship, and kinship organized society. Gift exchange even served as a means to incorporate newcomers into the community.[44] If an individual, family, or community could not establish some form of real or fictive kinship, then social interaction could not take place, much less trade, and the outsider would be treated as potentially hostile to the individual or community. In place of hostile relations the Anishinaabeg preferred the extension of kinship ties renewed and reinforced through gift exchange. Adoption and other methods of creating fictive kin could incorporate an individual into the community, but marriage created a stronger bond. Families arranged marriages specifically to extend the web of relatives with whom they conducted exchange. Many fur traders chose to marry into the communities with whom they traded, because they recognized that this intensified the obligation of their wives' relatives to bring furs to their posts.

Deeply ingrained social expectations for respect and obligation framed these exchanges. "Reciprocity was necessary to keep the system functioning . . . without gifts and respect, the system would cease."[45] There was as much a right and obligation to receive as to give, an idea embedded in the ascription of familial relationships to all parties in the exchange. The closer the kin relationship, whether actual or fictive, the greater the implied obligation as well as the assumed trust.[46] Anishinaabeg oral tradition makes it clear, however, that as "pitiable" as one may have been, when one accepted a gift from a human or manidoo, one had to fulfill promises made to perform appropriate ceremonies or use the gift in appropriate ways lest the individual become ill or the gift be withdrawn.[47] By the same token, when accepting gifts, whether as a leader receiving gifts from another polity or as an individual getting gifts from the leaders they supported, a recipient acquiesced to the political messages and agreements that accompanied the gifts. Similarly, rejection of gifts demonstrated rejection of the messages proposed at their distribution. Accepted gifts became physical reminders, embodying the alliance itself, and recipients symbolically used them to show satisfaction or discontent with the results of current agreements and, on occasion, the need to renegotiate them. The presence of the items in a person's lodge served as a record of the terms agreed to, and the holder accorded them the same respect that he felt for the agreement.[48] Politically, keeping the agreement became another form of reciprocity and respect for gifts received.

This form of reciprocity was not defined by separate discrete economic transactions. Need determined repayment and was not necessarily equivalent. The social obligation to assist and to accept such assistance was more important than equalizing and canceling out the obligation. In fact, a perception or acknowledgement of "debt" is actually required to keep the system in operation.[49] This explains what nineteenth-century observers found confusing and irrational—the Native practice of giving away more food as it became increasingly scarce. Essentially Anishinaabeg gift exchange functioned like an insurance policy. Sharing food with several families balanced the unevenness of production and fulfilled the needs of the community.[50] The more families you shared food with, the more would reciprocate when they had plenty and you did not. Further, the more families you shared food with, the more likely one of them would have manidoog relationships that would aid in locating animals when they became scarce.

The importance of these networks and their continuous renewal contradicts the beliefs of some that the Anishinaabeg lived isolated lives in small nuclear family or uni-clan groups.[51]

However, Anishinaabeg societies equated being alone without anyone else to rely upon as a situation of the utmost peril, as illustrated by the case of John Tanner. He was an Anglo American abducted as a young child just after the American Revolution and adopted into an Anishinaabeg community, where he was raised and married. One year due to a falling-out with his in-laws he decided to winter on his own with his wife and children as a nuclear unit with himself as the only hunter. Community leaders intervened and strongly advised against his choice of action.[52] The perception of isolation is easily gleaned from the papers of fur trade factors and missionaries, who did not venture far from their posts but instead depended upon employees or the Indians themselves to provide meat. Their sense of social and physical isolation reflected their cultural perceptions of Indian life. Lack of local travel while residing at their posts, lack of consistent interaction with others of their social class, and their physical distance from their own culture's social centers appeared to them as isolation.

When the distances are broken down, it is evident that even during the winter, hunting camps were not located far from one another. Although an estimated hunting area of two hundred square miles sounds large, in reality, it is only a ten- by twenty-mile plot of land and is easily traversed in a single day. On those occasions when missionaries did travel between missionary stations in the winter, they rarely slept in the open but were usually able to find a hunting camp at which to spend the night, especially if they had a local resident as a guide.[53] When the need arose, for example, to heal a sick child, it was not too difficult for a family at their hunting camp to track down community members whose expertise and or presence was needed. Hunting groups also remained in constant communication with each other so that they could combine quickly for defense or other purposes.[54]

These hunting groups of twenty to forty individuals were

generally made up of a single extended family led by the old-est male and so tended to be more uni-clan in composition.[55] While these hunting groups usually contained a group of brothers and their sons, they could also include young men of other clans doing bride service. These hunting groups were referred by the Anishinaabeg term *indinaakonigewin*, translatable (from a leader's point of view) as "that which I am in charge of."[56] *Indinaakonigewin* is a flexible term that refers to anyone who falls within the sphere of influence of that individual and does not preclude the possibility that the individual may be a follower of someone else within the Ojibwe political structure at other times.[57] Further, the older a man is, the larger in number his family and kin relations become, so that the eldest males in the community would have the broadest indinaakonigewin and hence the broadest political influence.[58]

Likely it is these leaders of the indinaakonigewin, also referred to as *gichi-anishinaabeg*, or "great men," who serve on the village councils. The roles of the hereditary leaders and gichi-anishinaabeg are primarily discussed in the following chapter. Pertinent here is how historical sources reveal that a great deal of the respect these individuals earned from family and community came from extensive engagement in gift exchange. Time and again leaders impoverished themselves to provide for their supporters and dependents. Fur traders and Indian agents granted them large amounts of gifts, which leaders quickly redistributed among their people, often before the trip home. A reporter for the *Minnesota Daily Pioneer* wrote about one such occasion when Bagone-giizhig (Hole-in-the-Day the younger) received several blankets at Fort Snelling. The headman immediately gave the blankets to the men who had accompanied him until "Hole-in-the-Day placed the last blanket upon the shoulder of the old Chippewa soldier, who was deeply affected by this act of generosity," leaving himself unsupplied.[59] The community did not accord leaders any special favors; instead, chiefs had to provide for themselves and their families just as did any other man in the village. To expect deference and keep surplus would have marked them as antisocial and caused them to lose influence.[60] Yet these are the very markers Western observers looked for to fulfill their definitions of rank and privilege.

Rather than seek strong distinctions, Anishinaabeg leaders saw themselves as part of the village community. The Anishinaabeg formed political structures based on their world view. According to oral tradition, the ogimaag and council who together made decisions for the community were modeled on the council Gichi-Manidoo organized with the manidoog to address conflicts and issues of concern. As a result, the ethic of noncoercive reciprocity that organized individual and personal relationships also organized all other levels of society.[61] Local village-level leadership, while no more coercive than any other relationships among the Anishinaabeg, did in some ways earn people's obedience or at least compliance, but leaders gained this through respect and obligation based on ability as demonstrated through manidoog connections and the distribution and redistribution of gifts. Even relationships with the manidoog were not based on coercion. Every request came with a gift, and every gift came with a reciprocal obligation of some kind. There was no conception of anyone having the right to order rather than to request an action.

Explorer Jonathan Carver, who was in the western Great Lakes in the late 1760s, suggests that each family appointed a member to the village council.[62] This means that while there is little archival evidence specifically for clan leadership, the gichi-anishinaabeg who formed the council of the community likely represented the groupings known as *doodem* (plural, *doodemag*).

Doodemag also served as a way to identify members of a community and distinguished specific individuals in the pictographic representations the Anishinaabeg made to communicate with one another prior to the twentieth century. The Anishinaabeg used these representations not only to sign treaties but also in the daily messages they left for one another, as groups separated during travel or had to move camp before a traveling loved one could return. Henry Rowe Schoolcraft stated that such messages were "a common custom" in the western Great Lakes, a fact echoed in the numerous explorer, Indian agent, fur trade, and missionary descriptions.[63] Ojibwe missionary George Copway indicated that there were more than two hundred images commonly used in communication among the communities where he lived.[64] Native people also commonly hung these communications at encampments, either to tell visitors where the owners had gone or to leave the owners a message if one stopped by while they were not at home. For instance, Joseph Nicollet related that on August 5, 1837, he and his party encountered a campsite where the family had left a bark message on the door for visitors. The message conveyed that the family—a bear clan man, catfish clan wife, two boys, and three girls—had moved to Lac Courte Oreilles.[65] Likewise, John Tanner reported that he arrived back at his camp one morning to find a birch bark missive that showed a rattlesnake with a knife sticking into a dead bear. Near the rattlesnake was the mark of a beaver with one of its dugs. From this he was able to understand that his brother had killed a rival, and he hastened to the main village to learn what was transpiring as a result.[66]

These messages also conveyed information across tribal lines, even between the Ojibwe and their enemies the Dakota. Charles C. Trowbridge, a government employee accompanying Governor Lewis Cass on a tour of Wisconsin, Michigan, and Minnesota in 1820 indicated that two of their guides brought to their attention another such bark message as the party drew near to St. Peters, which lay in Dakota territory. This one depicted the Mississippi and Minnesota rivers, with Fort Snelling at the mouth of the latter, and a Dakota chief with a weapon in one hand and a pipe in the other. Along the Mississippi River in the direction of Ojibwe settlements the author had inscribed the locations of nineteen lodges and the numbers of persons who had stayed at them, along with the American flag. The guides explained to Trowbridge and Cass that the American officer at Fort Snelling had encouraged the Dakota to seek peace with the Ojibwe and had taken great pains to find them for nearly three weeks before turning back. The party was then able to expect that the Dakota sought a treaty and would not disturb the Ojibwe traveling with Governor Cass prior to St. Peters.[67]

Ojibwe ogimaag even used these doodemag images to convey powerful messages to the United States government. Seth Eastman recorded that Buffalo, the ogimaag of La Pointe, carried one such missive to Washington, D.C., in 1849 when he arrived there to petition the government for a revision of the 1842 treaty boundaries. The image showed the clans of the ogimaag of the Lake Superior bands of Ojibwe with lines joining their hearts and minds to that of the crane, Buffalo's doodem, who carried their words to the president. The image demonstrated their agreement as a group to the message Buffalo delivered and sanctioned Buffalo to speak on their behalf.[68]

Political agreements between Eastern Woodlands tribes could also be confirmed with a belt made of wampum beads. On such belts Native people wove purple and white beads into hieroglyphic patterns that stipulated each article in the agreement between the parties involved and allowed chiefs to refer back to them, as explorer Jonathan Carver put it, "with as much perspicuity and readiness as Europeans do their written records."[69]

Doodemag not only functioned to communicate identity but also served a variety of important functions within the village and, through ties of kinship, bound villages together. A society based on the need for establishing social networks of reciprocity likely places greater value on and defines itself in terms of its larger social units rather than its smaller parts. Like clans among other Algonquian peoples, the Ojibwe doodemag were corporate bodies that provided lineage identification, indicated appropriate marriage partners, and expanded kinship obligations beyond the more immediate extended family. Each Ojibwe doodem bears the name of an eponymous ancestor that emerged from the Great Water to originate the doodemag.[70] These animal, fish, and bird clans told the creator that they would take care of the Ojibwe, and oral tradition teaches that the doodem spirits teach and protect each person from birth to death.[71] Ojibwe give all individuals from other villages or even other tribes who bear the same doodem the same hospitality as close relatives, and they refuse to marry people of the same doodem. Assumed relationships with doodem members are established based on generation. When two or more doodem members meet; those of the older generation become fathers and those of the same generation brothers and sisters.[72] Although some inter-doodem politics derived from doodem mythology, nearly all scholarly sources agree that doodemag served primarily a social and not a political function.[73]

In contrast, Ojibwe oral tradition suggests that each doodem had a specific role in the community. Of those scholars embracing the political role of clans, most agree that the Crane and Loon clans were involved in political leadership, with the Loon serving as speaker for the Crane. However, many of these scholars obtained this information from William Warren's nineteenth-century book *History of the Ojibwe People*. This may mean that a narrow interpretation of the roles of doodemag at the La Pointe community have been over-generalized to represent the doodem organization of all the Ojibwe villages. As Warren himself descended from chief Waabojiig of La Pointe, and was a politician serving in the legislature of Minnesota Territory, he may well have been interested in promoting the political role of his bloodline for his own ends.

However, others have also suggested that the doodemag

served specific roles in the community. In *Mishomis Book*, Edward Benton-Banai related that in addition to the chiefly bird clans, there was a fish clan of intellectuals and philosophers who would settle disputes between the chiefly doodemag when necessary. In addition, the bear doodem served as village police and were also known for their medicinal plant knowledge. Martin doodem served as the warriors of the community, and the remaining bird doodemag, such as the eagle doodem, served as spiritual leaders for the people.[74] Since the doodemag of individuals besides chiefs were seldom recorded in the historical accounts of fur traders, missionaries, and explorers, the documentary evidence can neither confirm nor deny that doodemag served in these capacities. Evidence exists for many additional named doodemag, such as the wolf, mermen, thunder, catfish, and bull-head doodemag, some of whom provided the hereditary chiefs for various villages. Doodem-linked political leadership was largely connected to hereditary chieftainships passed down in specific lineages. Yet the historical record suggests that not all villages took their leaders from the same doodem, and when the primary hereditary leadership of a community changed from one lineage to another, it did not necessarily stay within a specific doodem. Hereditary chiefs might have led the dominant doodemag within their community and held responsibilities in this regard that are now lost to history.[75] The opinions of a leader's doodem, however, probably had a great deal of influence with him, and larger doodemag within a village had a greater political voice. Although within the Midewiwin certain responsibilities, such as that of doorman, fall to members of specific doodemag, the Midewiwin does not restrict overall lodge leadership to any specific doodem lineage.

Despite the prominent role of doodemag in Anishinaabe communities, the village appears to have been the largest and most meaningful social, political, and economic entity. Given the choice, Anishinaabeg people at any given time of the year congregated in as large a group as the ecosystem would sustain. Bishop Frederic Baraga, Catholic missionary to a number of Ojibwe communities in the early nineteenth century, reported in 1847: "The Indians are very social and would live in great bodies together, were it not for the difficulty of their mode of living, by hunting and fishing."[76] Although each hunting group had a headman, the entire village council of headmen, or gichi-aninshinaabeg, together with the ogimaa, allocated to families areas available for hunting, ricing, gardening, making sugar, and fishing.[77] Neighboring communities respected these usage rights and did not infringe upon them without consent.[78] As environmental conditions varied year to year, the allotments of these areas, although prejudiced toward past usage, altered to fit the needs of the changing environment and village population.[79] This annual discussion also took place because individuals were free to circulate in and out of the village to live with either the husband's or the wife's family, depending upon changes in the subsistence base, the political winds, or extended familial needs.[80]

Village populations, despite shifts due to political or other factors, remained remarkably stable. A comparison of Schoolcraft's village population statistics in 1830 with those recorded by the French in 1670 reveals that in both cases, the average Ojibwe village had a population between one hundred and one hundred and fifty.[81] Villages near the Dakota that had greater defensive needs averaged larger populations, the largest at Pembina with a population of 884 and Leech Lake with 730.[82] Larger populations also clustered around particularly influential chiefs. James Doty reported to Lewis Cass in 1820 that a chief named the Brachu was not only ogimaa of the people at Sandy Lake but also "the first emperor of these tribes," presiding over a community of 363 individuals.[83] In the 1830s more than three thousand Ojibwe lived in seven major centers within the territorial United States (Leech Lake, La Pointe, Sandy Lake, Lac Courte Oreilles, Lac du Flambeau, Yellow Lake, and Fond du Lac) and about a thousand more in small villages on the Dakota frontier.[84] The carrying capacity of local subsistence resources also affected population. Pembina and Leech Lake were both located in wetlands with many lakes providing habitat for abundant wild rice, ducks, and fish.

Anishinaabeg people, however, understood the concept of village differently than Europeans. They saw the village not as a location where permanent houses were erected but rather as a group of people with whom one chose to reside and to whom one had familial or other reciprocal ties.[85] Families, although in many ways self-reliant, depended for their existence on affiliation with a village.[86] This village association was so ingrained in one's identity that even today, when Anishinaabeg people introduce themselves in the Ojibwe language, they state their name, doodem, and the community to which they belong. These villages were social, economic, and political centers whose subsistence activities in the summers made possible semi-sedentary life along lakeshores, rivers, and arable bottom lands.

Socially the village served as "the nucleus of political organization . . . composed of closely related families."[87] These villages exhibited political solidarity in intertribal relations, relations with agents of colonial governments, and relations with traders and missionaries.[88] Villages south of Lake Superior were more rigidly organized than those to the north due to the rigors of warfare with the Dakotas.[89] The viability and reliability of summer gardens in the village ranges of these southern groups as compared to those of their northern neighbors made these communal areas all the more important. Households were never discrete autonomous political units but depended on adherence to a village for all claims to land use for sugarbush, cultivation, gathering, and hunting. Marriage, gift exchange, and defensive needs in turn made villages socially and politically dependent on each other.[90] The village also served as the locus for the celebration of full Midewiwin ceremonies.

Had villages not been central to Anishinaabe social life, there would have been little reason for the missionaries of the American Board of Commissioners for Foreign Missions to establish permanent mission stations in Ojibwe country. While attendance rates for their schools and services fluctuated seasonally as children were more likely to be absent during wild rice and sugarbush seasons than during the winter hunts, the Leech Lake village where William T. Boutwell established his mission post from 1833 to 1837 always had some inhabitants. Over the course of the winter the active men hunted in their hunting grounds and periodically returned to the village to bring meat, to trade, and to meet in council if any political concerns emerged.[91] When an entire community did go away from their homes, they left them as modern Americans would when taking a vacation. Henry Rowe Schoolcraft described such a village in late July of 1831, when the inhabitants were probably away harvesting wild rice: "We found eight large permanent bark lodges, with fields of corn, potatoes, pumpkins, and beans in fine condition. The lodges were carefully closed, and the grounds and paths around cleanly swept, giving the premises a neat air. The corn fields were partially or lightly fenced. The corn was in tassel. The pumpkins partly grown, the beans fit for boiling. The whole appearance of thrift and industry was pleasing."[92]

These villages formed the largest segment of Anishinaabeg society with vital political and economic functions. Externally, the same chiefs who dealt with the day-to-day issues of allocating sugarbush and wild rice beds negotiated with other villages, with Dakota leaders, and with agents of colonial governments. Or, when necessary, they solicited or led war parties made up of members of the entire village against their enemies. At treaty gatherings, leaders identified themselves by community affiliation and attempted to negotiate on this basis, thus demonstrating the importance of the village to the Anishinaabeg themselves. Further, when the chiefs negotiated for final reservation sites in the 1850s, they chose the village sites where they raised gardens and harvested rice, again demonstrating the perceived importance of these places and activities to their communities. Internally the Anishinaabeg also preferred to act as a village. Missionary and fur trade records consistently report that village leaders deferred requests made to the village during the winter until spring, "when many more of the Indians would be together."[93] Whether this preference for full village participation represented the need for all gichi-anishinaabeg to be present for the council or the need for the entire community to caucus until they formed a consensus on the issue, Anishinaabeg political and economic lives centered on community.

As a part of maintaining gifting relationships with extended family in other villages, Anishinaabeg people regularly visited neighboring communities throughout the year. In particular, acknowledged leaders were not stay-at-homes but traveled widely, visiting village members at dispersed winter camps, calling on Indian agents, and journeying to other summer villages. In the 1840s Bishop Friedrich Baraga commented that the Ojibwe continuously visited one another, and ABCFM missionary Edmund Ely mentioned several occasions during the 1830s when Eshkibagikoonzh, the leader at Leech Lake, came to visit at Fond du Lac or passed through on his way to see the Indian agent at La Pointe.[94] Explorer Father Pierre François-Xavier Charlevoix. who traveled through the Great Lakes in the early 1720s, wrote that the Indians were "eternally negotiating . . . some affairs or other . . . such as the concluding or renewing of treaties, offers of service, mutual civilities, making alliances, invitations to become parties in a war, and lastly compliments of condolence on the death of some chief or considerable person."[95] This suggests that the political culture Baraga and Ely described had been the norm for at least a century. The consensual nature of Anishinaabeg politics meant that families, clans, and villages needed continuous contact with one another to discuss options and persuade others to courses of action when faced with greater concerns, such as peace, war, hunger, and treaties. The opinions and preferences of others in the community's social network were important and deserved respect; leaders did not make decisions out of hand without full consultation and deliberation. That many of the chiefly families from various communities intermarried with one another likely also contributed to frequent visitations between tribal leaders.

That villages were the most significant political units of Anishinaabeg society did not preclude them from forming strong alliances with one another. Villages throughout the Great Lakes worked together in Pontiac's Revolt. Once the Americans had won the Revolutionary War (1776–83), the Algonquians of the Ohio Valley and Great Lakes regions regularly continued to act in concert in diplomacy and war until Anthony Wayne defeated them in 1798. Tecumseh's movement drew on these ties once again. In fact, intertribal cooperation continued as late as the Treaty of Prairie du Chien negotiations in 1825, when an Iowa chief named White Cloud told William Clark: "My fathers the Socs, Foxes, Winnebagoes, Menominees, Chippeways, and Potawatomies are links of the same people. I speak for them as well as for myself my father, you see people here apparently of different nations, but we are all one. . . . You Socs, Foxes, Winnebagoes and Menominees—we are but one people. We have but one council fire and eat out of the same dish."[96] The idiom "to eat from a common dish" commonly appeared as a metaphor of peace, alliance, and friendship among Algonquian peoples.[97] Although this ceased to be a political reality with the treaty of Greenville following Wayne's victory, a continued sense of unity and common interests probably resonated with the assembled chiefs. These peoples continued to be allies who spoke Algonquian dialects, intermarried, exchanged information, and shared resources with one another.

In particular the Ojibwe, Odawa, and Potawatomi continued to embrace origin stories that recounted their common migration to the western Great Lakes.[98] Like members of a doodem, this teaching linked all Anishinaabeg peoples together as blood relatives on some level. The Three Fires, as they termed themselves, "represented a complex web of acknowledged symbolic kinship relations that bound the three tribes together."[99] This alliance kinship was also reflected in the terms *older brother* and *younger brother* used among these tribes at both the 1821 and 1833 Treaties of Chicago in much the same way that tribes farther east used such terms to denote relative strength between partners. At the Chicago treaty gatherings, Ojibwe representatives gave their advice before the assembly as the "elder brother" but ultimately allowed their younger brothers the Potawatomi and Odawa to decide what to do with their own lands.[100] While the leaders of these tribes met with one another to discuss trade, diplomacy, and war as well as to hold Midewiwin ceremonies, their decisions to act collectively or independently remained on the conscience of each village leader and council—not in the authority of a central leader. As a result, the terms *confederacy* and *league* do not really apply to this alliance, as they suggest a more formal and permanent structure of leadership among these three tribes.[101] However the fact that their leaders did meet to discuss important decisions affecting all the people is reflected in the words of the Odawa leader Chambler at Prairie du Chien in 1825, when he stated: "We three nations, Chippewas, Potowotomies, and Ottawas have but one council fire."[102]

For centuries these communities maintained primarily peaceful relationships with one another throughout the western Great Lakes region. Their common interest depended primarily upon real or fictive kinship ties strengthened through the exchange of goods. The majority of these goods were subsistence products gathered during the seasonal activities of Anishinaabeg families utilizing village territories. The complexity of these activities not only supported the need for the leadership structures the Anishinaabeg developed but also demonstrates why women served as one of the three important constituencies that leaders represented. Women provided Anishinaabeg communities with the majority of the staple foods they survived on throughout the year and produced surpluses for trade. Although both Indian and French men complained when they lacked meat, they seldom starved because of what women had harvested to feed them.

Unfortunately the gendered bias and economic interests of seventeenth-, eighteenth-, and nineteenth-century observers led them to ignore Native women's work and focus instead on men's work as the economic basis of society. In reality, Native women produced a wide variety of gathered and harvested foods including corn, wild rice, and maple sugar that fulfilled the majority of Anishinaabeg dietary and material needs. To obtain or produce these foods the Anishinaabeg congregated in much larger numbers from late spring to early fall. Of course by spring most fur traders were on their annual voyage back to Montreal, Albany, or Detroit to resupply and missed opportunities to observe women's considerable work.

In these seasons Ojibwe women planted and gathered a large variety of vegetable and grain products that not only fed them during the long and uncertain winter but also generated a surplus. Fur traders who filled their canoes with trade goods needed to purchase rice, corn, meat, and other products from Anishinaabeg communities, particularly from the women, in order to survive their winter sojourns. However, instead of participating in the credit system established between Anishinaabeg men and the male fur traders, women engaged primarily in direct trade and refused to allow their food products to be counted against the debts incurred by their husbands.[103] Although further analyses need to be done, Bruce White's work with Michel Curot's 1802–3 fur trade journals demonstrates that standard interpretations of the fur trade have not reflected the balance of products produced by men and women. If Anishinaabeg families did indeed receive as many or more products from fur traders and other exchange partners through women's trade of food products as through men's trade of furs, then the larger social networks involved in women's labor need to be taken into account as equally significant to Anishinaabeg social organization as the men's smaller hunting groups and territories. Anishinaabeg society viewed men's and women's contributions to family and community as balanced with one another, requiring that women's concerns be acknowledged in the political system.

By the late eighteenth century the Anishinaabeg had merged the demands of production for the fur trade with their sophisticated seasonal subsistence regimen. The expertise necessary for their way of life varied from intense knowledge of the flora and fauna of a given region to awareness of the effects of widely varying weather patterns and the development of techniques to thresh, preserve, and store these foods for use throughout the year. This system, while to some extent governed by the seasons, required numerous decisions about land use, travel, and trade—decisions just as important to Anishinaabeg survival as those pertaining to war and peace. These systems were not static across the region of Anishinaabeg settlement but varied from village to village based on the accessible resources in their recognized territories. Anishinaabeg leaders knew the weather conditions that were beneficial or detrimental for the growth of wild rice, maple sugar, and berries as well as those that would help or hinder the hunts and fishing expeditions. They knew the number of members in their band, where they camped in each season, and the general boundaries of the area their band occupied. They anticipated and planned for seasons of scarcity despite the assertions to the contrary made by colonial observers.

As Anishinaabeg communities expanded westward, they encountered different local resources and other cultural groups that produced changes in the ideal seasonal round as communities in different ecological regions maximized use of resources available in their area. The seasonal movements of Anishinaabeg peoples embodied the most sophisticated and reliable use of subsistence resources available in the region. The following represents how this seasonal round was practiced in Wisconsin and Minnesota between the American Revolution and the reservation era.

Spring thaws brought maple sugar, the first gathering crop following the harsh northern winters. Each extended family had its own maple stand, known as its "sugarbush," to which it returned annually.[104] Families who were new to an area had to search for an unclaimed grove of maple trees or obtain permission from local leaders to harvest in a village territory.[105] In village territories, the council allotted maple groves to the women.[106] The sugar camp, although occupied for only a few weeks of the year, had permanent sheds to hold sugaring utensils when not in use as well as the frame poles for a large lodge for boiling the maple sap.[107] The stored vessels varied in size from a small duck's bill to those that, when filled, would hold one hundred pounds of sugar or more. The sheds also contained carved wooden spoons and ladles for dipping sap and stirring syrup as well as the granulating ladles for working the boiled sap into sugar.[108]

While it was a women's occupation prior to the reservation era, sugaring was very labor-intensive. Women and children tapped hundreds of trees and daily collected their sap, also gathering and chopping firewood to keep the fires burning day and night to boil the sap into sugar. When the maple sugar was ready to eat, Anishinaabeg families held a "first fruits" feast where they offered the initial portion to Gichi-Manidoo. At such a feast the host made a long prayer petitioning for safety, health, and long life for himself and his family. All gathered for the feast then received a portion of this "first fruit" and participated in the general feast. They often prepared this food in a special kettle used only for this purpose, and the Anishinaabeg usually placed some sugar on the graves of departed relatives.[109] Following this feast, the women often cached their sugar cakes and syrup in birch bark containers in the ground during the summer to keep them cool and unspoiled, and left them there through the winter to prevent freezing.[110] However, they ate much of the sugar as it was made.[111]

The sugarbush and the tools used there was the woman's domain, and the sugar produced there was her property. She most often used the granulated sugar and sugar cakes as gifts or trade items, and the community regarded a woman with a large supply of maple sugar in its various forms as someone who planned ahead for the needs of her family. Trapping and sugaring often overlapped, with the women producing sugar while the men trapped for beaver and other furs.[112] In other words both genders spent this season obtaining products that not only benefited their families immediately but that they also exchanged for additional goods from traders. Trade records show that women often traded the products of their labor—wild rice, maple sugar, tanned hides—for the goods and utensils that they needed to produce these products more easily, such as kettles. These women sought goods that they wanted for themselves and their families and were just as capable as their husbands of playing one trader off against another.[113] They got their tools from the trader with the best goods at the best price. Sugar became an even more important item of trade as settlement advanced. In 1865 alone, the Keweenaw Bay village sold 453,252 pounds of maple sugar.[114]

Toward the end of the sugarbush season the fish runs began, and people from many camps gathered at sturgeon fishing sites along the shore of Lake Superior during the three- to four-week spawning run.[115] The spring gathering was the largest annual meeting of Anishinaabeg groups, with camps as large as one thousand persons. Sturgeon, a very large fish of two to four feet in length, easily fed dense human populations during the spawning run.[116] Anishinaabeg people invested significant corporate labor in these fishing sites. Communities that had access to the larger rivers flowing into Lake Superior during the sturgeon run, such as Rainy Lake and the Ontonagon River, constructed elaborate wooden weirs that allowed fish to travel upstream to spawn but trapped them as they returned downriver.[117] The sturgeon weir Anishinaabeg people used on the Ontonagan River existed for decades if not far longer. It was observed by Alexander Henry in 1763, Henry Rowe Schoolcraft in 1820, and Lieutenant James Allen in 1832. As Allen described it:

> The weir or sturgeon dam is in the same place Alexander Henry found it . . . and is built with poles stuck in the mud of the bottom, close together to prevent the sturgeon's passing between them, inclined a little down stream and kept in place at the top by transverse poles to which they are bound by bark, the transverse poles being supported by forked braces placed below and inclined up stream. The Indians stand on supports attached to the weir and catch the fish with hooks fastened to long poles, which they move about in the water at the base of the weir, until they feel the fish against them, when the fish is hooked by a sudden jerk of the pole. The weir is placed at the foot of the first rapid and when the fish are ascending, has an opening made in it to allow them to go up, but is closed when the fish are descending and it is at this season that most of them are taken.[118]

Schoolcraft had reported earlier that the weir spanned the entire width of the river and that the opening that allowed the sturgeon to pass upriver to spawn also allowed canoes to navigate the river.[119]

For the Ojibwe families who gathered at these sites, these

weeks were filled with activity. They traded goods and information. Gathering in councils they discussed the availability of game and other resources, decided whether to accept or reject invitations to war parties, and resolved any land-occupancy issues, such as where each family would spend the following winter. Midewiwin ceremonies also took place at this time.[120] These week-long ceremonies reinforced group cohesion and allowed leaders to meet to voice their concerns for the spiritual well-being of the people. They made decisions affecting the entire village. For example, in 1836 they rejected the school that missionary Frederick Ayer of the ABCFM proposed to build at Yellow Lake.[121]

In other areas men used spears, gill nets, traps, trolling lines, fish hooks and toggles, decoys, ice fishing, and seines to catch a variety of fish, including pickerel, white fish, lake trout, walleye, pike, catfish, gar, perch, black and white bass, tullibee, and herring, which the women preserved by drying them on racks.[122] Outside the seasons when various species of fish spawned, Native people also used gill nets.[123]

After the fishing season families moved to their gardens, which were usually close by at the site of the summer village.[124] The community built the village in a circular clearing or along a river or lakeshore with the lodges located on elevated ground away from the surrounding trees. The village also contained a grassy area where councils often met, providing the basic governance of the community, and dances took place including Midewiwin and other ceremonies, with fields variously located around the outside of the community.[125]

While farming was mainly conducted by women, the process of preparing the field for planting fell to the men. They expanded gardens each year by girdling trees, burning underbrush, and breaking new ground. The women then planted potatoes, corn, and pumpkins as their primary crops. Notably, Anishinaabeg people claim to have grown all of these foods prior to European contact.[126] Once all the gardens had been planted, the *midewijig,* or initiated members of the Midewiwin (see glossary), held a feast and asked the manidoog to bless the garden.[127]

An important activity often neglected in discussions of Anishinaabeg agriculture is controlled burning. This is partly due to lack of historical sources and the assumption on the part of historical observers that any evidence of burning must be accidental or from natural causes. However, recent scholarship has identified the used of controlled burns as a primary cause for the distribution of grasslands and forest in Wisconsin and the Midwest generally. Aboriginal peoples in the Midwest routinely modified the landscape with fire to clear village and agricultural lands, assist in fuel-wood cutting, improve visibility and overland travel, manage pests, facilitate hunting and warfare, and return carbon and phosphorus essential for agriculture to the soil. Burning on a regular basis increased the preferred browse of large game such as deer and elk as well as game birds such as turkeys and grouse. Many of the plant resources used by midwestern Native peoples also depended on regular fires for habitat regeneration and reproduction. Native settlements tended to be near natural fire barriers, suggesting a general pattern of frequent fires.[128] Taken collectively, selective tree felling combined with controlled burning created groves of trees and plants tailored to the gathering needs of Anishinaabeg people. These activities required careful community cooperation and the direction of practiced leaders.

Historical records suggest that controlled burns took place in the early spring and the late fall after the first frost, the very times when the whole village community of men and women were gathered together. The few recorded instances witnessing controlled burning in Anishinaabeg communities support this. Zebulon Pike, on his expedition to determine the sources of the Mississippi River, remarked that on October 20, 1805, he discovered the prairie on the opposite side of the river to be on fire. His Dakota guides informed him that the Anishinaabeg living there had set the blaze.[129]

The most important aboriginal agricultural innovation in Wisconsin was that of ridged fields, usually referred to in the historical literature as garden beds. This innovation improved cultivating conditions by draining water, minimizing temperature fluctuations, and mitigating the spread of disease and insect pests. Ridged fields broadened the region in which Native people could expect reliable yields, including some areas that average fewer than ninety frost-free days annually.[130] Lieutenant James Allen in 1832 described the gardens he saw on the island in Cass Lake as "slightly undulated by little hills and valleys," suggesting this form of agriculture.[131] Allen further attested to the high crop yield induced by this technique, stating: "The whole quantity under cultivation is about eight acres, producing potatoes, corn, and vines now growing beautifully; and the great extent and abundance of the crops, in proportion to the number of Indians, conveyed an idea of providence and comfort."[132] Former garden beds of this type are still identifiable on the Bad River reservation near Ashland, Wisconsin.[133] This was where the Anishinaabeg who lived on Magdalen Island went every summer to plant their gardens before they settled there permanently under the treaty of 1854.[134] In the state of Wisconsin alone, scholars have identified more than 175 aboriginal garden bed sites.[135]

Once the women had planted their gardens, berries soon ripened. Schoolcraft observed (and probably tasted) ripe strawberries at Keweenaw Bay and the Ontonagon River during the last week of June.[136] As the summer advanced, blueberries, gooseberries, June berries, raspberries, huckleberries, chokecherries, and other berries ripened. Since berries were one of the staples of the Anishinaabeg diet, Anishinaabeg women collected them quite systematically—yet because this was a group activity, it was also a social and political event. While at these collective activities, women likely discussed political, social, economic, and religious concerns facing the community, just as did men. Women carried birch bark baskets called *makakoon* attached to their belts. When the baskets were filled, the women emptied them into strategically located larger containers also made of birch bark. Anishinaabeg women dried large quantities of these berries for future use. Four containers of fresh berries usually filled one container when dried.[137]

Anishinaabeg women also collected other plant products needed for survival, following a few common sense rules. They picked roots in the spring and fall, when the cool weather kept the sap concentrated there. Conversely, they collected bark materials such as birch bark, basswood bark, and cedar bark in the late spring and early summer, when the sap was in the tree.[138] For example, on July 20, 1820, explorer Henry Rowe Schoolcraft observed nine Indian canoes ascending the river freighted with rolls of birch bark and bundles of rushes for mats.[139] This journey likely also gave the women the opportunity to check on the wild rice to determine when it would be ripe and to estimate the size of the harvest. Indeed, two days earlier Schoolcraft encountered a couple of Ojibwe women in a canoe who had come down the river "for the purpose of observing the state of the wild rice, [and] at what places it could be most advantageously gathered."[140]

Anishinaabeg women gathered most other plants, such as nettle stalks for twine, in August when the plants had developed to their fullest extent, observing certain ceremonies before gathering these plants, especially those that had a medicinal use. The person gathering the substance offered tobacco to the cardinal points, the zenith, and the earth and told the plant that it was intended for a good purpose, that they would take no more than necessary, and asked that its use be successful. Men who gathered plants for medicinal purposes showed similar respect.[141]

In early August the women went to their family's wild ricing beds and bound the sheaves of rice together in small bunches with basswood fiber twine to protect them during their final ripening.[142] William Boutwell observed this activity at Rice Lake on August 1, 1832.[143] Binding the rice not only marked the stand for a particular family but also maximized yields by preventing loss of rice kernels to predators and storm damage. Stakes marked out each family's claim, which the women had confirmed when they bound up the stalks of rice.[144] Around early to mid-September the wild rice ripened. Once again Anishinaabeg people moved their camps to family-designated wild rice beds.[145] Ricing was the final social gathering of the year prior to dispersal to winter camps. Although each family group harvested its own patch of rice, depending on the size of the lake or river several family groups often camped near one another as they harvested adjoining rice beds.[146]

Anishinaabeg people considered a canoeful of rice to be a day's harvest.[147] Then they poled the canoe to shore, where the women spread the rice evenly on sheets of birch bark to dry.[148] After the rice dried in the sun, the Anishinaabeg parched it either by roasting it slowly on a scaffold over a low fire or by placing the rice in a large kettle propped in a slanting position over the fire, so that a woman sitting beside it could stir the rice continually with a paddle.[149] Because a hull enclosed the rice kernel when harvested, it next had to be threshed. Then the women winnowed the rice either by tossing it in a tray or by pouring it slowly from a tray on to a sheet of birch bark placed on the ground to allow the breeze to blow away the chaff.[150]

As with other harvests, families held thanksgiving ceremonies when they finished processing the first rice. Communities, fearing future retaliation from offended spirits, never considered eating new rice without this ceremony.[151] Traditionally, the Anishinaabeg attributed any weather patterns or pests affecting rice maturation to supernatural causes.[152] Thomas Vennum reports that fall Midewiwin ceremonies coincided with the time when the rice ripened and was harvested because Anishinaabe people believed that this helped the rice to mature.[153] Midewiwin theology thus taught that the rice was a special gift to the Anishinaabeg people to help them achieve long life.[154]

After the rice harvest the women stored excess wild rice as well as dried potatoes, corn, berries, acorns, squashes, and other foods for recovery later in the winter.[155] Once preserved, these fruits and vegetables if properly stored could be used for up to two years.[156] After placing the dried food in woven basswood or nettle fiber bags or in birch bark containers, the women placed the food in caches, pits dug into the ground that were about six feet deep and lined with birch bark, with the water-repellant white side facing out to keep the food safe and dry. On top of the containers the women added a final level of straw or birch bark before laying across the hole wooden beams, which were then covered with a mound of dirt.[157] This method of securing goods for future use was so effective that traders quickly adopted the practice for storing their excess goods, especially rum, and stored foods.[158] They could bring goods into the country only once a year and needed to space out the availability of their merchandise.

Storing foods for future use was an important survival strategy for Anishinaabeg peoples. Not only was it a method to ensure that nourishment would be available in times of scarcity, but the size of the caches governed how much time the men could devote to the hunt for trade pelts as opposed to the hunt for edible game.[159] Anishinaabeg people also stored wild rice above ground in fawn skins, perhaps for ease of transport, as wild rice was frequently sold to traders in these containers.[160] The women, who did much of the gardening and gathering of wild edible plants, determined how these resources would be distributed throughout the year, perhaps caching more of one food source to compensate for the loss of another due to changing weather patterns and water levels.[161] Women also preserved seed for corn, potatoes, and pumpkins to be planted the following year. They did this even in years with severe famine, although once fur traders arrived, the Anishinaabeg sometimes purchased additional seed for crops from the fur traders.[162] Caches ensured that food would be available later in the year, both to hedge off winter starvation and to barter with traders, who often depended upon Native people for a significant portion of their subsistence. The decision of Anishinaabeg communities to fast periodically in the winter when the hunt was poor was not necessarily based on the absence of these food caches but rather on frugality. Caches were especially important for the laborious process of making maple sugar at the end of winter, when other sources of nourishment were scarcest.

While the women harvested and cached the produce of their gardens, the men visited the trading posts to receive their fall credits and annual gifts. Credits commonly included the shot, powder, and traps that the men would use for the winter hunt. Hunters gradually paid off these credits over the winter with food and furs. Women also traded their wild rice, maple sugar, and corn, without which the fur traders could not survive the winter. These food products were so valuable that in the 1760s a bushel of corn sold for 40 livres, while a pound of beaver fur was worth only 60 sol.[163] In late July 1775, Alexander Henry the Elder purchased about one hundred bushels of rice left over from the previous year's harvest from a village of only one hundred persons.[164] This meant a poor rice or garden crop endangered both Indian and white populations.

In late fall Anishinaabeg communities also caught large numbers of fish, which they dried or froze. In Sault Ste. Marie, Anishinaabeg fishermen took as many as five hundred white fish in two hours. These fish supplied a great deal of the winter provisions for the Sault Ste. Marie community.[165] For villages located on the shores of the Great Lakes, fishing remained primarily a men's occupation, but for inland communities that fished smaller lakes, such as Nett and Leech lakes, women often took care of spreading gill nets each morning and hauling in the catch at night.[166] Of course both hunting and fishing, though seasonally intensive, were engaged in year-round as well.

When the ice froze on the lakes, villages broke up into smaller units of about six families to begin the winter hunt.[167] In addition to cooking and drying meat, women spent their days chopping wood, tanning hides, and mending clothing.[168] Dried meat was light to carry and remained edible for long periods.[169] The women rehydrated dried meat in stews, pounded it into a powder and stored it in this form, or mixed it with fat to make pemmican. Women tanned hides with the hair on and spread them on the cedar boughs along the edge of the wigwam to dry. These were either traded or made into winter suits for the men or overcoats for the women and children. Each man had two or three leather suits for winter use that required considerable mending due to very hard wear.[170] Women also supplemented the food regimen by snaring small birds and animals near the camp, such as rabbits and partridges. The women froze any of this meat that was not immediately used.

Men hunted every day that the unpredictable winter weather permitted.[171] Cold temperatures with little snow left the ground frozen, making game difficult to track. On the other hand, too much snowfall could make it difficult for deer and other animals to obtain food, which caused them to move to other areas rather than starve. A good hunter under good weather conditions would often take one or two deer a day, and it was the custom to give a feast when a man killed his first game of the season. Each family of the winter camp would give such a feast.[172]

Hunters had to maintain a special relationship with the animals they sought. Like all other social connections in Anishinaabe society, this relationship was reciprocal. The hunter did not ask for the life of an animal unless he was in need. The animal then gave itself to the hunter to nourish his family. In return the hunter performed ceremonies that honored the gift he had received and ensured a continued supply of prey. Schoolcraft describes such a ceremony observed after finding a bear caught in a log-fall trap: "As soon as the bear fell, one of the Indians walked up, and addressing him by the name muk-wah [the Anishinaabeg word for bear] shook him by the paw, with a smiling countenance as if he had met with an old acquaintance, saying, in the Indian language, he was sorry they had been under the necessity of killing him, and hoped the offense would be forgiven."[173] Hunters always extended such thanks to the animals they killed and often presented them with a gift of tobacco.

Beyond seeking big game animals to feed their families, winter was also the season when men hunted for meat and furs to exchange for European goods. Accepting trade goods that made hunting more efficient obligated hunters to commit not only to pursuing large game animals to feed their families but also to pursuing the smaller less meaty animals with pelts Europeans desired. Hunting for fur during the sparse winter months likely represents an adjustment to their European neighbors, who preferred thick winter pelts and gave more goods for them. For Anishinaabeg hunters, the trade was still a viable source of goods well into the 1830s. In 1832 the Anishinaabeg traded about seven thousand dollars' worth of furs at American posts as well as an additional unknown quantity of furs at British posts along the Canadian border.[174] The most intensive period of trapping specifically for the trade occurred during maple sugar bush season in early spring, when families were not as dependent on the outcome of the daily hunt for food.

Only two things superseded the reciprocal obligation between hunters and fur traders. The first was severe hunger, which necessitated concentration of time and resources on large game hunting or else resulted in the hunter's consumption of pelts previously intended for exchange. The second was the presence of a third party—often a competing fur trade company—who convinced the Anishinaabeg that their competitor's gifts were stingy, misleading, or otherwise suspect on some level. This meant that the competitor had already reneged on the obligations or promises embedded in the gift exchange, releasing the Anishinaabeg from the obligation they represented.[175]

Although men used traps and guns obtained from traders to hunt with in the early nineteenth century, traditional hunting methods persisted. Anishinaabeg hunters usually carried a deer call made from wood and reeds that imitated the sound of a fawn calling to a doe; various hunting charms, including herbs that were said to attract the deer by scent; and birch bark torches to "shine" for the eyes of game animals at night.[176] Men encouraged young boys to learn to shoot with bow and arrow, particularly since the supply of balls and powder from traders was unreliable.[177] Knowledge and experience also assisted the hunter. Some animals followed certain patterns when fleeing the hunter; their reaction could be anticipated. For example, boys could catch partridges by sneaking up behind them and slipping a basswood noose over their heads. The partridge would then attempt to take off, strangling itself.[178]

All these subsistence sources were subject to annual variations in weather and other natural cycles. Rice failed if water reached levels too high or too low. Heavy snows made it difficult for animals to find food, resulting in starvation deaths among deer, elk, and moose herds. Winter thaws made the fall harvest of frozen fish inedible and lowered the sugar content of maple sap. Gardens were susceptible to drought, short growing seasons, and pests. All of this made the world a difficult and unpredictable place in which to live, a place where an individual alone had little chance of survival without establishing contingencies for times of scarcity. Occasional reliance on bark and lichens to survive when other subsistence sources failed provided a constant reminder of the Anishinaabeg's utter dependence on other beings. Such events prevented them from growing complacent or taking the gifts of the creator for granted.[179]

The Anishinaabeg seasonal subsistence cycle "was not simply a movement of humans over a natural landscape" but movement within a world that was at once spiritual as well as physical.[180] The Ojibwe world view and the exchange and kinship networks it supported helped the Ojibwe establish systems to adjust and provide for these extreme situations. They continuously sought to create and extend relationships of mutual obligation and reliance with other villages and tribes and by developing similar relationships with the manidoog. In other words, the Anishinaabeg believed that the inherent need and weakness of human beings was the cause of crises, for which the only remedy was the intervention of powerful allies.[181]

The gifts and blessings that passed between family members, between leaders, between humans and manidoog, between all "persons" in the Anishinaabeg universe, wove the fabric of society together. They defined relative power between the parties, established reciprocal obligation, protected against times of scarcity or adversity, and gave individuals the confidence that whatever the odds, they did not face these odds alone. As we enter into discussion of traditional Anishinaabeg leadership in the next chapter, we must remember the context within which that leadership functions. The basic needs of society structured the kinds of decisions required of leaders, while leaders' connections with manidoog and other social groups maintained through reciprocal gift exchange impacted the success of their actions and decisions. The social construction of Anishinaabeg communities defined the extent of their influence and how it could be expanded or lost. Anishinaabeg communities evaluated their leaders on rules shaped by the world view in which they lived their daily lives.

Given the importance of managing the subsistence base and exchanging gifts to expand networks of interdependence, the fur trade impacted this system in a variety of ways. While intertribal gift exchange can be documented in the western Great

Lakes as early as the 1646 feast of the dead ceremony described in the *Jesuit Relations*, the types of objects given and the occasions on which they were exchanged evolved somewhat over time. The development of a negotiated *bon marché* between the tribes and their French neighbors, while still in the realm of diplomatic exchange, began the process of introducing market forces into this alliance system.[182] Still, perhaps partly because alliance perpetuated by systems of exchange was situated within the religious as well as worldly activities of Anishinaabeg people, gifting remained at the core of the Indigenous sociopolitical system until treaty payments transmuted internal interdependence into dependency upon United States goods and rations. Although some Anishinaabeg signed land treaties prior to the 1840s, it was not until the majority of Anishinaabeg had begun receiving annuities from the federal government that the Indigenous governing system described in the following pages shifted into crisis. The treaty annuity distributions and micromanaging efforts of United States Indian agents significantly undermined existing Anishinaabeg governance, disturbing the balance of power that supported Indigenous leaders.

To return to the perspective of John Grim and D. P. St. John with which the chapter opens, in the Anishinaabeg world view, "power is manifestly present."[183] It is present in subsistence success, in dreams, in gifts and blessings that passed between family members, between leaders, between humans and manidoog, between all "persons" in the Ojibwe universe. Gifts wove the fabric of society together. They defined relative power between the parties, established reciprocal obligation, protected against times of scarcity or adversity, and gave individuals confidence that they did not face a difficult world alone. The world view and basic needs of society structured the kinds of decisions required of leaders as well as the sources of power upon which they drew.

2

Ogimaag

*I want to do all I can for my children so that they can say when
I am gone, "My father worked in my interest and guarded my
interest, and for that reason his life was sacrificed."*
—**Mezhucegiizhig**

*Before I left my country every Indian gave me counsel, and told
me what to say to you and to our Great Father, and when I return
they will look to me for a reply. . . . These wampums were present
before many chiefs, and the words that I now speak are the words
they wished me to say.*—**Crossing Sky**

Anishinaabe leadership arose from two sources: charismatic
and hereditary. Charismatic individuals who led through demonstrated ability might lead war parties, emerge from the ranks
of the Midewiwin, or direct the actions of hunting groups. These
leaders are addressed in chapters 3 and 4. Before looking at
such roles, we must examine the types of leadership embedded
within Ojibwe social organization. This chapter, then, explores
the position and role of the hereditary ogimaag as well as the
appointed officers who assisted them. The right of hereditary
ogimaag to lead, to negotiate with outside groups, and to manage land and resources within the community through redistribution and allocation descended to them through patrilineal
lineages; however, the extent of their actual influence and authority, particularly outside their own communities, was based
on reputation and ability. Although discussion of hereditary

ogimaag may at first seem a purely secular project, the Anishinaabeg understood the authority of these chiefs to flow from the networks of mutual obligation that these individuals had established with manidoog as well as human communities.

Although some contemporary Anishinaabeg doubt the historic presence of hereditary leadership, records from the period frequently include the transition of the position of village chief from father to son. It is spoken of by explorers Jonathan Carver and Giacomo Beltrami, American Indian agents Henry Rowe Schoolcraft and Thomas L. McKenney, and fur traders William Warren and Peter Grant as well as missionaries Frederick Baraga and George Copway, who along with Warren was of Ojibwe descent.[1] En'dusogi'jig, a hereditary chief at Mille Lac, told ethnomusicologist Frances Densmore in the first decade of the twentieth century that "a chief was respected for his personal characteristics, and that anyone who wished to join his [village] was at liberty to do so. . . . The duties of a chief included the presiding at councils of his [village], the making of decisions that affected their general welfare, and the settlement of small disputes. He represented the [village] at the signing of treaties, the payment of annuities, and any large gathering of the tribe."[2] However, the ogimaa never made decisions alone, as there were significant constituencies within the village with whom he had to consult. Eastern Woodland Indian societies in the eighteenth century had three political classes: women, warriors (sometimes referred to as young men), and chiefs.[3] At any large gathering, leaders were always careful to assert whether they had the consent and support of these constituencies.[4] In an oral society it was always vitally important to clarify whom you spoke for in any given situation.

Despite the fact that both oral tradition and written sources document that men predominantly held the position of hereditary leader, this did not mean that women were excluded from the political process. Little in the historical record refers to women in leadership positions or the existence of women's councils among Ojibwe women, but there are clues indicating that women played influential roles. While women had more visible authority in matrilineal societies, the Ojibwe still recognized and honored women for their generative power as mothers of the nation and their ability to grow crops.[5] Work within the female domain of planting and gathering work was done communally, and the absence of men while they engaged in this work implies the supervision of these tasks by senior women. William Johnston described such a situation when he wrote to his sister Jane Johnston Schoolcraft while serving as an interpreter for Leech Lake on September 24, 1833. "On visiting the lodges," Johnston noted, "I found only women as occupants, busey [sic] in putting up the corn for the winter; Almost every lodge had a surplus of ten sacks of it for sale."[6] Even amidst pressure from American officials to assimilate to the cult of domesticity in the latter half of the nineteenth century, Ojibwe women continued to use the work group as the "forum in which they discussed community issues and formulated their opinions," developing a consensus position from among their ranks just as did men's councils.[7] When discussing political issues, any woman could rise and make her opinions known and would receive the respectful attention of all those present.[8] The *ogimaakwe* or chief woman then reported the women's consensus to the men's council in the presence of all the women.[9] Occasionally we see in chiefly speeches the influence these women's councils had, as when a chief told English fur trader Alexander Henry that "our wives and children came to us crying, and desiring that we should go to the fort to learn, with our own ears," whether the English were planning to trade guns and merchandise with tribes the chief considered to be their enemies.[10]

Women's councils also had input on decisions concerning warfare. Explorer Jonathan Carver related in the late 1760s that while small war parties could act without full community support from either men's or women's councils, "when war is national, and undertaken by the community, their deliberations are formal and slow . . . balancing with great sagacity the advantages or inconveniences that will arise from it . . . [and] the advice of the most intelligent of their women is asked."[11] Once war was settled upon, women could also play a role in encouraging the men to brave deeds. Indian agent Henry Rowe Schoolcraft observed a war dance in 1831 where an old woman "sitting in a ring of women . . . rose up, and, seizing a war-club which one of the young men gallantly offered, joined the dance. As soon as they paused, and gave the war-whoop, she stepped forward and shook her club towards the Sioux lines, and related that a war party of Chippewas had gone to the Warwater River, and killed a Sioux, and when they returned they threw the scalp at her feet."[12]

On other occasions women leaders worked to forestall conflict. When negotiations between Michigan Territorial Governor Lewis Cass and the Ojibwe community at Sault Ste. Marie nearly degenerated into armed conflict in 1820, Ozhaagashkodewikwe —the wife of the English fur trader John Johnston and the daughter of the chief Waabojiig at La Pointe—sent her son to call together the local chiefs. The leaders assembled in response to her call because her father was one of the most influential leaders of his day, and they respected her kin connection to him. Possibly they respected her own abilities as a mediator as well, yet Ozhaagashkodewikwe also spoke on behalf of her absent husband, clearly indicating to the local chiefs that the English fur trader would not support hostility toward the Americans. In his memoirs her son George Johnston stated that his mother "with authority commanded the assembled chiefs" to suppress the bellicose intentions of the young men of the community.[13] Indian agent Thomas McKenney later commented that he believed no chief in the Chippeway nation exercised authority, when it was necessary for Mrs. Johnston to do so, with success equal to hers. Seven years after the incident McKenney also corroborated that she had "sent for some of the principal chiefs" and convinced them not to attack the American delegation. McKenney stated that he had "heard Governor Cass say that he felt himself then, and does yet, under the greatest obligations to Mrs. J. for her co-operation at that critical moment; and that the United States are debtor to her, not only on account of that act, but on many others."[14]

In taking such actions Ozhaagashkodewikwe may also have been stepping into a role assumed by other elite Ojibwe women —that of representing absent husbands, fathers, or brothers in community political affairs and at treaty meetings. Thomas McKenney attended two councils in 1827 where other women acted in such roles. These wives attended wearing their husbands' medals and bearing gifts.[15] Despite pressures from colonial and American authorities to restrict political representation to men, as late as 1889 at least three Ojibwe bands had women serving as hereditary chiefs, only one of whom was standing in for a relative, in this case her brother, who was absent in Canada. American documents indicate that the collected hereditary chiefs requested that these women be allowed to sign official documents on behalf of their communities.[16]

That wives might be called upon to represent their husbands likely played a role in how carefully chiefs weighed the decision of whom to marry. As with other Algonquian nations, Ojibwe ogimaag generally married women from other elite families, increasing the kinship bonds that obligated these communities to one another, while at the same time ensuring that a wife was respected in her community and had learned the responsibilities of a leader's wife.[17] Women from elite families were more likely to supervise work groups and learn the skills to build consensus on political concerns among the female members of the band community.[18] Further, these wives participated in gift giving that bound elites together through the products that they produced for their families and communities. McKenney noted that the wife of Bizhiki gave him a *makak* (a bark container, likely containing food) and a terrapin shell at a chance meeting when McKenney and Bizhiki passed each other in canoes on the river.[19] On another occasion John Tanner, traveling with his mother, an elite woman referred to in his memoirs as an ogimaakwe, or leading woman, in her own right, also received particular hospitality from the leader's wife when visiting a new village. He stated that when they entered the lodge, "the women immediately hung a kettle over the fire" to cook them food. Tanner added that "the woman who appeared to be the principal wife of the chief, examined our moccasins, and gave us each a new pair."[20] Clearly wives played an important role in demonstrating the hospitality and generosity of their communities.

Women of course also played important roles in the family, and while they were otherwise not present at councils of war, there is evidence the Ojibwe women, as in other eastern tribes, were present when councils made decisions concerning the adoption of captives. Alexander Henry, a fur trader captured at Michilimackinac during Pontiac's Revolt, stated that his adopted sister-in-law was present at the council when his adopted brother stepped forward to ask the band to recognize his kin claim to Henry. This woman also assisted her husband with the distribution of gifts to the warriors who had captured him.[21]

The most influential leaders proved adept at brokering marriages for themselves and their children that extended their authority as far as possible. As fur trader Peter Grant noted, in 1804 an ogimaag's "consequence and respectability in society are generally esteemed according to the nature of their alliances and the number of their children."[22] While divorce was not difficult, Baraga reported that families seldom separated once they had two or more children: "Children are strong links which keep the two parties together."[23] Children became physical embodiments of bonds between kin. For those seeking influence beyond the borders of their home villages, Hickerson has suggested that "relationships through marriage undoubtedly contributed to cooperation in broad spheres of political and military activities."[24]

Judicious marriages not only strengthened ties between villages but also allowed leaders to be influential in more than one town, extending political boundaries beyond the limits of any one village.[25] Broken Tooth, the Sandy Lake chief from 1753 to 1832, gained wide influence due to the married connections of his prodigious family. His three daughters married fur company managers Charles Ermatinger (Northwest Company) and Charles Ashmun (American Fur Company) and ogimaa Hole-in-the-Day the elder, or Bagone-giizhig I, of Gull Lake, while his son Loon's Foot married into the chiefly family at Fond du Lac. These connections alone bound three villages together in close alliance while gaining steady access to British and American goods. His grandson Hole-in-the-Day the younger, or Bagone-giizhig II, skillfully deflected opposition from within the Ojibwe nation by marrying into families of former or potential opponents. By doing so he not only acquired six wives; he also converted antagonism into kin loyalty and mutual obligations.[26] Through his marriages and leadership, Bagone-giizhig II gained preeminence among the Mississippi Ojibwe, numbering about twelve hundred persons in his band in 1852.[27] Similarly, Majigaabaw of Leech Lake connected himself to several families of influence by marriage.[28] Families seldom declined proposals from powerful men, as the Anishinaabeg feared that doing so denied them important connections and commonly engendered sorcerous attacks on the family.

Marriage connections to powerful men benefited families, and they regularly offered their daughters in marriage to men of high standing.[29] Still, Bagone-giizhig's choice to marry six times was excessive. Few men took more than three wives: Eshkibagikoonzh, the influential leader from Leech Lake, for example, had three wives, and the prominent Waabojiig of La Pointe only two.[30] Ogimaag entered into such marriages to form important kin connections with other ogimaag lineages and with fur traders and Indian agents to improve and expand the social capital available to the community from those sources with the most perceived power.[31] Younger sons of village ogimaag married daughters of powerful families in neighboring villages in hopes of acquiring influence. Loon's Foot, a younger son of Broken Tooth of Sandy Lake, is one such example. He married the daughter of Zhingob at Fond du Lac and became the Fond du Lac speaker and a man of influence there when such positions were not open to him in his home village.[32]

Of course such ties went both ways. Ogimaag had obligations to those with whom they had marriage connections, a circumstance that fur traders quickly realized and capitalized upon.[33] While marriage to those outside the Anishinaabeg world often ensured conduits for elite gifts, it also obligated ogimaag to speak to their communities on behalf of those outsiders, a prospect that brought them increasing antagonism from within the villages in the nineteenth century as the costs of alliance with American interests became apparent.[34]

While the positions of the hereditary leader and lineage headmen were permanent, there were also short-term civic appointments, such as that of "rice chief" during the rice harvest. Temporary chiefs provided leadership in matters for which that individual had demonstrated past expertise. The title and position lasted only until the completion of that task.[35] The temporary nature of the position, however, made the title available to many and perhaps led to the assumption that Anishinaabeg society was politically egalitarian. Although egalitarianism was perhaps a philosophical ideal and an economic expectation, it was not a political or social reality. The prestige individuals gained through their ability to provide and protect as well as to heal and call on manidoog assistance became grounds for enduring distinctions in social rank and political influence between families and individuals.[36]

Of course authority, rank, leadership, and influence do not mean the same thing in all societies. The English language is imperfect for discussing Anishinaabeg leadership for at least two important reasons, the first involving issues of translation and the second about usage. The Anishinaabeg used different words for hereditary and charismatic leaders, a distinction most European and American visitors did not grasp. The Anishinaabeg term *ogimaa* (plural, *ogimaag*) referred to hereditary leaders.[37] Headmen and elders were called *gichi-anishinaabeg*.[38] The term for a war leader was *mayosewinini* (plural, *mayosewininiwag*), and a Midewiwin member of high degree was called a *gechi-midewid* (plural, *gechi-midewijig*).[39] When *chief* became the general term that Europeans used for any individual in any tribe or culture group who exercised influence, it masked the rich variety of leadership structures developed by the original peoples of North America. Looking at the disparate societies of the Cherokee, Iroquois, Ojibwe, and Comanche, for instance, the differences among them that the word *chief* obscures become even more vast.

The French, as the earliest Europeans to develop relationships with Anishinaabeg communities, provided no clear sense of Ojibwe leadership in their early reports. They used the term *chief* so often in reference to any Indian who had any influence within a community that the word in their records is not a reliable determinant of whom the Anishinaabeg considered their own leaders.[40] Because leadership seemed so unstable to these French outsiders, their early missionaries went so far as to suggest that Algonquian peoples had no real government at all because their leaders "obtained everything by eloquence, exhortation, and entreaties."[41] Of course, the extremely authoritarian nature of French society in the seventeenth century gave them little frame of reference for understanding how Indian nations applied and used authority in a persuasive rather than coercive context.

When the English arrived in the eighteenth century, they applied the term *chief* as used in the British Isles to what they thought were similar circumstances in North America. In English usage, *chief* originally referred to certain types of political associations, particularly in Ireland, where the English applied the term to the proprietor of a moderate landholding who held tenancy from the Lord Paramount and to whom the local occupants paid rent or tribute.[42] Furthermore, the English, like the French, also randomly affixed the term to anyone they believed had some sort of influence in any Native community. Such careless usages underscore that Europeans not only misunderstood the origin and exercise of chiefly power but also failed to understand the nuances of how this authority was held, transferred, and wielded differently throughout Native American societies. In particular, colonial authorities usually expected chiefs to be more authoritarian than their societies actually allowed, because they wanted chiefs to carry out colonial wishes using a dictatorial authority that Native leaders did not possess. We see this sense of the word echoed in modern English usage, where *chief* refers to someone with direct authority, one who is a leader, as in chief of police, commander in chief, or chief executive officer. In these cases the term carries with it an implication of solitary decision-making power, coercive authority, and obligatory obedience that is entirely absent from Anishinaabeg conceptions of leadership.

Not surprisingly, the Anishinaabeg described their leaders quite differently. Although he did not refer to their hereditary origin, Ojibwe scholar Basil Johnston defined an ogimaa as "a man or woman who counted many followers and one on whom many people relied."[43] This individual the Anishinaabeg looked to for leadership "so as to derive the benefit of that person's continued success and kinship with manitous."[44]

Ogimaag were people of influence—individuals who could persuade by elegant oratory and presentation of gifts but who could not demand compliance without placing their positions in the community or even their lives in jeopardy. Johnston further emphasized that ogimaag never asked their people to take risks they themselves did not bear. For instance, they broke trails through forests and swamps in all seasons, undertaking the same types of hard physical labor as many other community members. At the same time, if ogimaag became too reckless and took risks that endangered village members or even caused loss of life, they lost influence and followers.[45]

Not only did ogimaag not make solitary decisions; they would be criticized for making decisions alone. Instead, ogimaag made decisions in consultation with village councils. The village council acted as a "panel to judge wrong-doing, settle individual and family disputes, allocate hunting and fishing territories, decide where and when to move the community with the seasons, and make decisions on issues of peace or war."[46] The council included the gichi-anishinaabeg and all the mature males of the community. Gichi-anishinaabeg best translates as great man, and this term applied to respected elders.[47] As explorer Jonathan Carver noted in the 1760s,

Each family has a right to appoint one of its chiefs to be an assistant to the principal chief, who watches over the interest of his family, and without whose consent nothing of a public nature can be carried into execution. These are generally chosen for their ability in speaking; and such only are permitted to make orations in their councils and general assemblies. In this body, with the hereditary chief at its head, the supreme authority appears to be lodged; as by its determination every transaction relative to their hunting, to their making war or peace, and to all their public concerns are regulated.[48]

In council the gichi-anishinaabeg sat in a circle close to the ogimaag, and "next to these [sat] the body of warriors, which comprehends all that are able to bear arms, hold their rank. This division has sometimes at its head the chief of the nation, if he has signalized himself by any renowned action, if not, some chief that has rendered himself famous."[49] At times, the women sat around the outside of the group.[50] Women also sent representatives to village councils to represent their concerns and were often present during council deliberations and treaty meetings.[51] Carver goes on to assert: "In their councils which are held by the foregoing members, every affair of consequence is debated; and no enterprise of the least moment undertaken, unless it there meets the general approbation of the chiefs."[52]

Without diminishing the importance of councils and collective deliberation, ogimaag held more authority, or at least greater responsibility, than other community members. W. T. Boutwell and other missionaries in the early nineteenth century reported that decisions concerning the permanency of their missions in Ojibwe communities depended upon the presence of the primary ogimaa in camp. When he arrived at Cass Lake in 1832, Boutwell asked the highest ranking man in camp if the village would allow a missionary to settle in their community. The principal man replied, "Neither myself nor any one present can answer the inquiry as the chief is absent and many of the young men are very vicious."[53] Although the ogimaa consulted the community and council, he "replies for the whole, and you may understand that the whole are bound by his reply as much as if each one had spoken for himself."[54] For this reason, ogimaag had to be very careful to determine the consensus of the community before speaking in a manner that would commit the whole village to a particular action. His authority depended as much on his respect for their will as on their respect for his proven leadership.

The administrative structure of Ojibwe society consisted of

large villages of several hundred members in which the hereditary ogimaa served as the ultimate arbiter in internal disputes and as the emissary with external groups, both human and manidoog. Three councils assisted him in making decisions: the gichi-anishinaabeg (or headmen) of each extended family, the women, and the young men (or warriors) advised the ogimaa. The most visible of these councils to outsiders was that of the gichi-anishinaabeg. These headmen held prestige rankings under the ogimaa based on oratorical skill, right decisions, and fair dealings. If the ogimaa were away, minor disputes could be handled by the second or third in influence within the village, whom outsiders sometimes identified as second or third chiefs. This distinction was not externally derived. Bishop Baraga notes in his 1853 Ojibwe language dictionary that the Anishinaabeg referred to the second chief of the village as *aanikeogimaa*.[55]

In everyday life, little distinguished the ogimaa from the rest of community in the eyes of outsiders. An ogimaa publicly demonstrated his status in only a few ways, but distinct symbols usually signaled the presence of a chief in the community. The lodge of Waabojiig at La Pointe had "a center post crowned with the carved figure of an owl, . . . [which] was neither his own nor his wife's totem."[56] When Waabojiig left for the winter hunt, his family shut up the lodge and took down the owl.[57] In the nineteenth century British or American flags flew from most ogimaag' lodges, indicating the rank of their occupants and demonstrating their alliance with colonial powers.[58]

While ogimaag and their representatives did not mark themselves from other members of the community in dress or action on a daily basis, they did do so on political and ceremonial occasions.[59] Baraga observed that "the chiefs don't distinguish themselves in dress from others, except on public occasions, when they wear a white shirt, a red coat, the silver medal [chief's medal] and a hat with galoons and plooms."[60] As a symbol of their role within the community and their centrality to diplomatic relations, ogimaag wore the military coats and other items that traders and Indian agents gave only to them, but they also wore traditional Ojibwe symbols of chiefly authority. Grenville Sproat described the ogimaag gathered for the 1842 treaty: "They appear in full dress covered with ribbons and silver trinkets, their faces painted . . . [and] with enormous head-dresses of feathers, otter skins, bear claws, some of them wear a pair of horns projecting on both sides."[61] These accoutrements likely referred to war honors, clan patrons, and manidoog that assisted these leaders. In any case, they clearly identified the ogimaag as such at formal council meetings.

Although outsiders recognized little meaning in Ojibwe clothing, dress in fact reflected a deeply symbolic and performative side of Ojibwe leadership roles. Gechi-midewijig (Midewiwin leaders), for example, did not wear European clothing on public occasions. Treaty Secretary Verplanck Van Antwerp reported that Majigaabaw, a third degree midewid, appeared at the treaty council of 1837 "in true Ind costume to wit naked except as to his leggings breech cloth & flap; his full head of hair ranging loosely upon his shoulders; a sort of crown upon his head made for the occasion & filled w/ feathers of the Bald Eagle, placed there by the chiefs; & the medals of several chiefs hanging around his neck."[62] As a speaker, Majigaabaw likely did not have access to European frock coats, but as a gechi-midewid, he probably would not have worn them even if he had had them. On such occasions, Baraga wrote, "the sacrificers and juggers never dress differently from other Indians."[63]

Dress also conveyed political meanings. Eshkibagikoonzh (also known as Flat Mouth or the Guelle Plat), for example, alternated between traditional and American clothing in order to make political statements on the occasion of Indian agent Henry Rowe Schoolcraft's visit to him in 1832. When he invited Schoolcraft to breakfast at his lodge, Eshkibagikoonzh wore only an old, worn, breechcloth. Later, when delivering an explosive speech before the entire assembled community condemning American negligence following the 1825 treaty, he wore traditional Ojibwe clothing. However, when the nervous agent Schoolcraft prepared to leave the community immediately afterward, fearing increased hostility, Eshkibagikoonzh "came down to the lake shore, to bid us farewell, dressed in a blue military frock coat, with red collar and cuffs, with white underclothes, a linen ruffled shirt, shoes, & stockings, & a neat citizen's hat."[64] Schoolcraft interpreted this attire as a sign of respect for the American government, but such an interpretation ignored the chief's diatribe against the United States government during the council earlier that day. It further ignored the Native cultural practice that predated European arrival of clothing exchange to indicate fictive kinship. By not wearing American clothing earlier in the day Eshkibagikoonzh embodied the imperiled state of the alliance, but when Schoolcraft left so abruptly, he made the gesture of recreating the alliance, perhaps fearing his blunt words had not left the door open to further negotiation.

Wearing the dress of one's allies, particularly when that clothing was presented as a gift, demonstrated commitment to that alliance as well as acceptance of fictive kinship obligations established by the gift. A number of examples of clothing exchanges between the Ojibwe and Dakota suggest that this means of cementing an alliance was an ancient cultural practice, rather than an indication of subservience to colonial powers. For example, in 1833 William Johnston wrote to his sister Jane Schoolcraft that at Leech Lake an ogimaa and two of his men returned from a hunting expedition in Dakota clothing: "while hunting they met the Sioux, who came up and extended the hand of friendship; and to ratify it, as it is their custom they exchanged all there [sic] articles of clothing."[65] Such an exchange not only confirmed peace between the two parties; it also conferred fictive kinship. At the 1825 treaty gathering at Prairie du Chien, ogimaa Ogimaakewid exchanged garments with a Dakota, an act that made them brothers.[66] Such exchanges provided very visual symbolism to the new recognition of kinship, and therefore alliance, that the transaction confirmed. Such exchanges of clothing to denote friendly status also occurred between the Ojibwe and Europeans, as exemplified through the actions of Majigaabaw in 1836. The war leader closed a speech to William Boutwell, in which he apologized for misadvising the warriors, with a request for a shirt, a gift that symbolized a renewal of friendly relations.[67]

Because ogimaag did little to distinguish themselves from the community on most occasions, demonstrating their authority when it mattered involved a variety of visual cues in addition to clothing. Reflecting the ordered seating in family lodges, the ogimaa sat at the designated place of honor at formal meetings while the other men sat in a complete circle around him.[68] Further, the initial ceremonies of council gatherings usually included the recitation of genealogies to demonstrate the legitimacy of the ogimaag's authority.[69] European observers usually dismissed this event with the phrase "the meeting began with their usual harangues," but American Board of Commissioners for Foreign Missions documents contain examples of these genealogical recitations.[70] This formality that Anglo Americans dismissed as unimportant "harangues" not only validated the ogimaa's authority but also established the ogimaa's right to represent the people and preside over decisions about such critical community concerns as usufruct of village territory.

Nevertheless, ogimaag succession seldom went outside the hereditary lineage. Charles Trowbridge, assistant to Captain Douglas during Lewis Cass's expedition in 1820, related that the Ojibwe never deviated from the practice of hereditary leadership except for the occasional individual "who usurped authority, holds the tribe in awe by his ferocity or the influence of numerous relatives devoted to his interest."[71] However, Trowbridge went on to note that such individuals were soon deposed, further suggesting the tenuous nature of leadership outside the hereditary line. According to Catholic missionary Frederick Baraga, who served among Anishinaabeg communities in Michigan, Wisconsin, and Minnesota in the 1830s and 1840s, the first-born son always succeeded his father as hereditary ogimaa except in cases of inability or continual sickness and infirmity. In such instances the ogimaa designated another of his sons to succeed him upon his death.[72]

The installation of a new ogimaa involved feasting and ceremonies known as Aanike-ashangewin.[73] Examples of such feasts appear in the *Jesuit Relations* dating as far back as 1640.[74] The *Jesuit Relations* for the years 1670–72 note a gathering at the Island of Ouiebitchiouan of "fifteen or sixteen hundred Savages of various Nations assembled, to perform certain superstitious rites which they are accustomed to render to the departed" who had been a noted chief of the Amikwons, or Beaver Nation.[75] The visitors included a large number of ogimaag from surrounding communities who had come to observe and participate in the rituals that would confirm the new ogimaa due to his father's past victories against the Iroquois. This shows that even in the seventeenth century, community chiefs knew each other, supported one another, and had established ceremonies for transferring their authority to the next generation that were widely recognized across the region. Further, the gathering at which these ogimaag met and jointly participated in ceremonies was not called by the Jesuits or the fur traders, but rather was one that drew the French to the Indians. This was not a succession confirmed at a French trade fair, or a leader the fur traders raised up to do their bidding, but a large gathering organized by the Native people themselves for their own cultural purposes, to which the French decided to tag along.

The succession of less famous leaders was a more local affair where the council of lineage headmen or gichi-anishinaabeg performed a brief ceremony recognizing the transference of ogimaa authority to the appropriate inheritor. This demonstrates that not only did the previous chief have the option to appoint his successor, but the community had the right to ratify the appointment, so that such transitions involved a democratic element. Indian Agent Henry Rowe Schoolcraft asserted that the "right [of hereditary rule] was, however, ascertained to be nugatory only when not supported by the popular voice of the clans; which act virtually bestowed upon it all the force of a representative system."[76] If the gichi-anishinaabeg approved of a candidate, they invited him to a meeting and offered him a pipe, which, if accepted, signified the acceptance of leadership.[77] That said, the position remained within the immediate lineage whenever possible. Sherman Hall, who visited Lac du Flambeau in the fall of 1833, recorded that the ogimaa he met there received the office after his brother had died the previous winter.[78] These checks and balances must have given strength to the system, as fur trader Peter Grant related that despite the lack of "established laws to enforce obedience . . . such is their confidence and respect for their chiefs, that instances of mutiny or disobedience are very rare among them."[79] The practice of some hereditary ogimaag adopting their father's name when assuming his position may have added to the stability of the office.[80]

Despite several attempts by the federal government to raise a pliant individual as a single leader over all of the Anishinaabeg peoples, the Anishinaabeg preferred their aboriginal organizational structure. Fur traders and American agents consistently failed to dominate Anishinaabeg politics by giving medals and other accoutrements to individuals who had not already received community sanction as leaders. Here again the lack of coercion as a means of social control within Anishinaabeg societies emerged as a bulwark against outside political domination rather than a weakness within the community. Not until the reservation system undermined the authority of ogimaag in land and resource allocation were outsiders able to begin to subvert the traditional political system.

Even though they lacked coercive authority, ogimaag did have a variety of official assistants to help them administer their governing and diplomatic responsibilities. *Giigidowininiwag* or *aanikanootaagwininiwag*, or speakers, *oshkaabewisag*, also called pipe bearers, and gechi-midewidijig all appear to have been important figures in village politics, though the available sources have difficulty classifying or ranking these offices.[81] Other sources mention a *miishinoo* (plural, *miishinoog*), who served as an ambassador or secretary for the ogimaa.[82] Part of the scholarly confusion over tribal officials stems from the fact that these offices were not mutually exclusive. A person could serve as oshkaabewis and giigidowinini, or be a miishinoo and serve in either or both of the other two positions.

William Warren provided a rare picture of these offices in his description of the Fond du Lac community, stating that under the ogimaa Giishkimin "was a chief of the warriors, whose business it was to carry out, by force, if necessary, the wishes of the chief. Next in rank to the war-chief was the pipe bearer, or Osh-ka-ba-wis, who officiated in all public councils, making known the wishes of his chief, and distributing amongst his fellows, the presents which the traders occasionally gave to the chief to propitiate his good will."[83] The only observer whose writings clearly distinguished between oshkaabewis and miishinoo is the explorer Nicollet, who visited Leech Lake in 1836. He suggested that the oshkaabewisag assisted the ogimaag in political councils and the mayosewininiwag (war leaders) in councils of war, while the miishinoog assisted gechi-midewijig with their ceremonies. Nicollet went on to observe that if the oshkaabewisag were away on other business, the miishinoog stepped in for them at war councils.[84] Scholar Michael Angel describes miishinoog as "'stewards' responsible for ensuring the ceremonies were carried out correctly," which also distinguished them from the oshkaabewisag, who often served as messengers.[85] In his dictionary missionary Frederic Baraga defines miishinoo as a steward or administrator.[86]

The office of miishinoo also reflected a more intimate relationship between leader and assistant. A miishinoo apprenticed himself to an ogimaa, gechi-midewid, or gichi-anishinaabe, forging a lifelong relationship between the two through a fictive kinship bond akin to adoption but with a different set of responsibilities that focused more on instruction and training. Certainly this instructional role was the focus for those associated with gechi-midewijig. When a hereditary ogimaa took on a miishinoo, this individual served as his oshkaabewis and in some cases as his giigidowinini, or speaker, as well. Peter Grant in 1804 described the "michinawois" as persons "who act as secretaries or ambassadors on great public occasions," second in rank only to the ogimaa.[87]

Childless hereditary chiefs, such as Curly Head of Sandy Lake, at times adopted individuals as heirs, and the miishinoo could fill this role. Curly Head, who became so ill at the 1825 treaty gathering at Prairie du Chien that he died on his way home, called his two pipe bearers to his death bed and formally constituted them as his successors.[88] Because the sources do not use Anishinaabeg language, it is difficult to determine whether Strong Ground and Hole-in-the-Day I were his miishinoog or oshkaabewisag, but these two men became prominent leaders among the Anishinaabeg people at a critical time in their history. Eshkibagikoonzh, hereditary chief of Leech Lake, also developed a close relationship with a miishinoo. Eshkibagikoonzh had lost his sons in warfare with the Dakota, a fact he brought up quite pointedly with Schoolcraft at their contentious meeting in 1832. He believed that the United States shared some of the blame for their deaths for shirking responsibilities it had assumed under the 1825 Treaty of Prairie du Chien to maintain peace between the Ojibwe and their Dakota neighbors. The loss of his sons might be what prompted Eshkibagikoonzh to invite or accept Majigaabaw as his miishinoo. While descended from renowned orators, Majigaabaw was not a Leech Lake village member by birth, although he had been raised among them.[89] In any case, both Schoolcraft and Boutwell refer to this important relationship between the two men.[90]

The relationship and its importance were both clearly demonstrated at the previously mentioned explosive meeting between Eshkibagikoonzh and Indian agent Henry Rowe Schoolcraft on July 17, 1832, at Leech Lake. Schoolcraft quickly delivered his message and rudely announced his intention to leave without giving the assembled ogimaag the expected opportunity to confer and offer a consensus response. Eshkibagikoonzh replied with an impassioned impromptu speech demanding that the United States honor its agreements lest the Ojibwe feel forced to seek more constant friends among the British. Despite his harsh words, when it looked as though Schoolcraft was really going to leave these issues unresolved, Eshkibagikoonzh embarked in a canoe with his family, an indication of his peaceful intentions, and followed the Indian agent upriver. Yet to assist him in these delicate negotiations, the Leech Lake leader also brought his miishinoo. In his description of this second meeting, Schoolcraft indicated that this companion was Majigaabaw, who served Eshkibagikoonzh as "his Indian Secretary" and as "his companion and pipelighter," the English terms often used to identify the oshkaabewis.[91] On this particular occasion, Majigaabaw must not have served as giigidowinini, since Schoolcraft conversed directly with Eshkibagikoonzh, and a "quiet and passive" Majigaabaw "uttered not a single expression that implied passion or vindiction."[92] Since Majigaabaw did not on this occasion serve as giigidowinini, yet had clearly been brought along by Eshkibagikoonzh for a specific purpose, he must have fulfilled the responsibilities of miishinoo or oshkaabewis, as Schoolcraft described him. In his position as miishinoo, therefore, Majigaabaw must have assisted Eshkibagikoonzh in a number of other capacities depending upon the situation, another indication of the flexibility in Anishinaabeg leadership.

As a messenger and helper to the ogimaa, the oshkaabewis, or pipe carrier, carried his words to others or delivered them through the village as a crier. He was also responsible for lighting and passing the ogimaa's pipe at council meetings and other diplomatic occasions. Kohl related that "Indians rarely visit another person's wigwam alone, and the chiefs, more especially, usually take with them their 'shkabewis,' adjutant or speaker, whom they allow to speak for them and send on errands."[93] Some sources suggest that an ogimaa generally chose two such assistants from among the warriors of renown within the community. As warriors, they also served as physical protectors of the ogimaa's person.[94] This description mirrors Curly Head's selection of Strong Ground and Hole-in-the-Day I to assist him.[95] Frances Densmore described the oshkaabewis acting in his role as the village crier, the individual who carried messages for the ogimaa:

> When everyone had retired and the camp was quiet an old man walked around the camp circle, passing in front of the dark tents. This man was a crier and he made the announcements for the next day, telling whether the people would go hunting or what would be done in the camp. He also gave good advice to the young people who were taught to respect him and obey his words. Only a man who was known to embody in his own life the excellent principles he uttered was allowed to act as crier. He usually announced that it was time for the young men who were calling upon the young maidens to go home. He spoke impersonally of the conduct of the young people, describing incidents in such a manner that those concerned in them would know to what he referred. He taught sterling principles of character and gave such advice as he thought necessary.[96]

As direct accusations were considered highly impolite if not dangerous in Anishinaabeg society, reference to general situations or stories that included courting lovers would have been enough to remind the young people of their responsibilities. The ogimaa and gichi-anishinaabeg often appointed a giigidowinini, especially if the ogimaa himself did not happen to be gifted with eloquence or was not fluent in the language of a given group of visitors. Strong oratory was an important leadership skill in a consensus-based society that relied on verbal persuasion and interpreted eloquence as credibility.[97] As such, if an ogimaa feared that his oratory might prove weak, he asked another to speak his meaning for him so that his ideas might have a better opportunity for acceptance. At the 1837 treaty gathering at Fort Snelling, for example, Peter Garrioch observed that only two or three individuals delivered speeches during the negotiations: "the rest of the chiefs, about twenty in number, did not appear to take any part in the way of speaking, but spent their time in consulting with each other, and dictating to those who addressed the governor and the assembly."[98]

The giigidowinini also delivered the decision of ogimaa and council to waiting community members. In some cases this could be a dangerous job. In 1820 when the senior ogimaag of Sault Ste. Marie sent Zhingwaakoons to tell Sassaba and his warriors to disband their war party and permit the American delegation to proceed in peace, Zhingwaakoons took several blows from Sassaba's war club before the war party laid down their arms.[99] Because of the hazards inherent in crossing or offending other people, giigidowininiwag emphasized their role in communicating the words of others in order to mitigate any potential retaliation. Bezhig (The One Who Stands Alone) of Snake River, after telling the Americans at the 1837 treaty gathering that the Anishinaabeg wanted more tobacco and gifts than they had received, insisted that "I have been told by the warriors and chiefs to say what I have said to you. I do not say it of my own accord."[100] At the same gathering Majigaabaw made a similar pronouncement: "I have but few words to say, but they are those of the chiefs and are very important."[101]

One of the most consistently mentioned giigidowininiwag in the 1830s was Majigaabaw, giigidowinini for the Leech Lake community, who also served in this capacity for all the assembled ogimaag at the 1837 treaty gathering at St. Peters.[102] At this gathering he revealed that his authority as giigidowinini had hereditary origins: "My brother (the Wind) stands beside me, and we are descended from those who in former days were the greatest orators of our nation."[103] In most of his recorded speeches or messages, Majigaabaw specifically stated that he was only a messenger for a specific group of ogimaag.[104] This may indicate that giigidowinini could be a temporary office, although Majigaabaw's reference to his genealogy indicates that it was certainly customary to call upon members of his family to fulfill such duties. As a further reminder of his representative status, at formal treaty gatherings he wore medals belonging to those ogimaag whom he had been asked to represent.[105] Majigaabaw must have been a very eloquent man to receive this responsibility for such a large community. However, he might also have been a wise choice due to his reputation as a gechimidewid of high rank.[106] Few would have dared to react impulsively to the messages he delivered, no matter how unpleasant. He had the force of the manidoog behind his words.

With the arrival of Europeans and Americans, the office of giigidowinini became the source of some confusion. Americans, who consistently sought to identify one head ogimaa of all the Ojibwe people, focused attention on the giigidowinini's office because this was the individual with whom they interacted. As a result, they often mistook the giigidowinini as the chief because he delivered the decisions of ogimaa and community to the Indian agents. This mistake led in some cases to colonial representatives awarding chief's medals to giigidowininiwag rather than the hereditary ogimaag.[107] Although some giigidowininiwag used these awards to attempt to increase their rank and stature within the community, without the proper credentials or the ability to provide gifts, they could not succeed. At the Fond du Lac community in the 1830s, a giigidowinini named Loon's Foot, son of a hereditary chief in a neighboring community who had married the daughter of the Fond du Lac ogimaa, attempted to assert his claims to the ogimaa position following the death of his father-in-law. However, the deceased chief's son, who had just reached his maturity, challenged this claim. While Loon's Foot had received medals from the American government in the past, was of a chiefly family by birth and marriage, and was the appropriate age for the job, he lost his bid for authority to his much younger brother-in-law, whose hereditary right the community was unwilling to deny. The community did, however, reaffirm Loon's Foot's status as giigidowinini, and he continued to be a respected man of status within the community.[108]

In addition to dealing with foreign powers like the United States, ogimaag adjudicated intravillage conflicts, which required mediating quarrels without becoming partisan to numerous petty squabbles.[109] For example, families sometimes requested ogimaag to intervene in private affairs such as divorce proceedings. Although the Anishinaabeg recognized divorce with little ceremony or stigma, marriage was an important tie between two kin groups, which the parties that had negotiated the marriage usually hoped to keep intact. Extended families resisted divorce more strenuously when children were involved. On such occasions, they asked the ogimaag and gichi-anishinaabeg of the village to do all in their power to persuade the couple against separation. If, however, the couple remained resolute in their decision to separate, the ogimaag had no power to force them to remain together.[110]

Ogimaag also served as judges in matters of civil concern. In cases of nonfatal violence, ogimaag had great jurisdiction, and on occasion they ordered a person's gun destroyed or his livestock shot.[111] Dispensing justice generally took place only after consultation with the gichi-anishinaabeg of the village unless the situation demanded an immediate intervention that could not be avoided. Nicholas Perrot, a French fur trader, official, and explorer in the mid-seventeenth century, noted that when quarrels erupted, individuals "seldom refuse to accept the decision of any prominent man who intervenes in the affair."[112] Such intervention involved risk to the ogimaag. William T. Boutwell recounted one incident in which an ogimaa attempted to end a fight at Leech Lake: "fists and clubs were used to settle their troubles, but on one occasion they actually resorted to their muskets and took the open field. The chief as a pacificator stepped between the parties and received a wound from which he never recovered."[113] Still, instances such as Boutwell described were rare. The community preferred decisions based on consensus of the ogimaag and council of gichi-anishinaabeg.

Such policing of the community was a responsibility ogimaag shared with doodemag and gichi-anishinaabeg, depending on the severity of the crime. For minor transgressions, such as stinginess, laziness, or neglect of a relative, sarcastic humor could be used by any member of the community to remind individuals of their responsibilities. Employing jocular songs and cutting remarks, everyone played a role in encouraging conformity to those basic expectations that kept life in harmony and balance within the village.[114] Ojibwe minister George Copway stated in the early nineteenth century that for misdemeanors, such as theft and adultery, the perpetrator "is brought before the chief, who reprimands him before the crowd."[115] Thieves were then "clothed as such," while adultery was punished by having one's hair or nose cut off as a mark of public disgrace.[116]

Major crimes consisted of spouse stealing, sorcery, and murder.[117] Bishop Baraga noted in 1847 that the Anishinaabeg perceived willful murder as the greatest crime, as the murderer committed an offense not only against the individual murdered but "more yet to his relatives and friends."[118] All individuals in traditional Anishinaabeg society were part of a web of re-distributive obligations with others, particularly those of their lineage. Consequently, when someone committed murder, he not only harmed the victim but also diminished the redistribu-tive network of everyone with whom the victim had obligations. Doodemag rights superseded the ogimaa's authority in these instances, although ogimaag often played a role in persuading the families to accept more peaceful solutions. Under doodem custom, the relatives of a murdered man had the right to avenge his death by killing the murderer or adopting him as a member of their own family.[119] As a result, those who committed mur-der seldom attempted to conceal their guilt but went to their homes and awaited discovery.[120] If the murderer himself could not be located, the aggrieved doodem could exact vengeance on any one of the murderer's doodem and consider the mat-ter settled.[121] Occasionally the lineage of the perpetrator took preemptive action and arranged to appease the lineage of the deceased by presenting them with a large number of gifts in a custom called "paying the body," although this was more com-monly practiced in situations of accidental death.[122]

Given the severity of the crime of murder and the seriousness with which lineages regarded their responsibilities for reprisal, ogimaag interfered in matters of vengeance only at their peril. Leaders became involved only when vengeance jeopardized the entire community, and in these cases, they sought community acceptance of their intervention through persuasion and the dis-tribution of gifts, particularly if they learned that the crime had been provoked. If the crime were unprovoked, the chief could execute the perpetrator in an effort to forestall further cycles of retaliation between the doodemag that would disrupt village life.[123] Ogimaag were themselves subject to this rule of doodem revenge. In his diary of 1804 fur trader Michel Curot reported that one of the ogimaag with whom he traded took refuge in the woods with one of his wives after he stabbed another member of the encampment, even though the community needed him to resolve a dispute that had arisen in his absence.[124]

The politics of kinship dominated Great Lakes villages, but the ties and obligations of kinship weakened with distance and changes in residence. Therefore, ogimaag also interceded when the bonds of kinship failed.[125] Families wishing to cover the dead with gifts often asked an ogimaa to open the negotiations not only as a neutral party but also as an individual whom others held in high esteem. When Europeans and Americans arrived, they pressured hereditary chiefs to interfere with clan prerogatives concerning murder if the victim was white. Schoolcraft related that one ogimaa offered himself to Schoolcraft in place of the actual murderer, whom Schoolcraft had requested, since the ogimaa had been unable to keep him in custody. Friends or relatives of the culprit had even attempted to murder the ogimaa. He presented Schoolcraft with gifts befitting his station, "an elegant pipe with a stem three feet long, ornamented with feathers &c.," and pledged to use all possible means to bring in the murderer the following spring.[126]

Perhaps the broadest jurisdiction ogimaag held concerned the equitable distribution of land and resources since this impacted both members of the village and outsiders, whether other Anishinaabeg tribal allies, fur traders, or missionaries who wished to join the community. This jurisdiction is attested to in multiple historical sources. From oral histories to Jesuit journeys to disputes over land use between Anishinaabeg communities and missionaries or fur traders, the mediating role of the ogimaag is evident. The Ojibwe both claimed their land as a result of warfare with the Dakota and memorialized their voluntary migration to the region in the distant past in their oral tradition.[127] These two views make more sense when we realize the Anishinaabeg did not perceive land as something to possess and govern, as Americans did, but rather as a place to live and be a part of.[128] The migration story focuses on the latter explanation, describing how various signs led the Anishinaabeg people to the western Great Lakes where food (wild rice) grew on the water.[129] Gichi-Manidoo, the Great Spirit, gave the land to the people and it belonged to everyone in the community.[130]

Although Anishinaabeg people migrated into the western Great Lakes, once they arrived they did not continue to wander aimlessly. Instead they followed a semi-nomadic pattern of returning to seasonal camps year after year. The romantic notion that these communities were so in harmony with the natural world that the Anishinaabeg had no recognition of land claims and territorial boundaries does not stand up to scrutiny. Even if such a relationship had existed between Native people and the natural environment, their fellow humans threatened disharmony. For example, with more than eight hundred residents, a community the size of Leech Lake had to have ways to prevent families and individuals from coming into conflict with one another or with other communities over the resources necessary to support themselves under fluctuating subsistence conditions. Native communities, therefore, did indeed recognize territorial boundaries and organized methods for ensuring that the usage of lands within those boundaries did not cause internal strife. Among their other responsibilities, the ogimaag and the three councils that composed the body politic of Anishinaabeg communities—gichi-anishinaabeg, warriors, and women—discussed the indicators for the year's productivity and apportioned the land among the doodem lineages annually to make the best use of whichever resources were at peak productivity in a given year.

The historical record contains numerous examples of forms of Anishinaabeg proprietorship of community lands. Despite Jesuit complaints about the nomadic nature of Algonquian communities, they also provided evidence in their *Relations* of family proprietary rights. Itinerant Jesuits reported that Anishinaabeg families in the early seventeenth century adjusted their direction of travel so as not to intrude upon the hunting areas of others.[131]

Peter Grant described this practice in detail among the Anishinaabeg at the turn of the nineteenth century: "It is customary with them in the beginning of winter, to separate into single families, a precaution which seems necessary to their very existence, and of which they are so sensible that when one of them has chosen a particular district for a hunting ground, no other person will encroach upon it without special invitation."[132] Records of the Hudson Bay Company throughout the eighteenth century indicated that hunters had discrete claims to the territories they hunted.[133] And Frederic Baraga, writing in the 1830s and 1840s, described such claims among the Ojibwe on the southern shore of Lake Superior where he ministered.[134]

Although most of the references to family land proprietorship relate to hunting territories because of fur traders' interests in this resource, historical and anthropological evidence also demonstrate proprietorship over other resources, such as fish and firewood, as well as ricing and sugarbush areas.[135] The proprietorship ogimaag inherited was not a fee-simple ownership as Anglo Americans understood land ownership; rather it was a governorship or stewardship of the usufruct resources the band lands provided for residents. The ogimaag and councils carefully distributed these resources among families in order to limit conflict both between and within their villages. Since the agricultural and game-carrying capacity of Anishinaabeg lands varied greatly from year to year with profound effects on human society, Anishinaabeg peoples learned to read the land and predict its vagaries.[136] They warned fur traders in advance, for example, that the 1833 wild rice crop would be poor following severe flooding.[137] As anthropologists such as Leo Waisberg, Diamond Jenness, and Harold Hickerson have demonstrated, hunting and gathering societies such as the Ojibwe developed methods to adjust to fluctuating conditions both before and after European arrival.[138] Rather than lock families into permanent individual land holdings that would not be consistently productive over time, villages served as the primary land-holding unit for which the ogimaa and council distributed usufruct rights to families on an annual or as-needed basis. Village communities also altered their movements as necessary within their territories based upon changes in availability of resources from year to year.[139] Ogimaa and council distribution of usufruct resources subordinated the interests of the individual to that of the village, without which families could not function. Hickerson has gone so far as to argue that land holding and distribution were the chief function of the village.[140] This means that Native villages determined their ranges and land use, not the fur traders, as some scholars have assumed. Traders had to wait until Native people chose their hunting lands before they could place posts appropriately.[141] Ogimaag and councils controlled the location of missions in a similar way. Frederick Ayer, ABCFM missionary, for example, chose to relocate his mission in 1836 when the Yellow Lake community moved closer to the Snake River.[142] Family claims to hunting districts or other resources as opposed to village distribution did not become permanent until the encroachment of white settlement limited space and, in Canada, the government instituted trapline registration.[143]

Scholars have referred to the aboriginal village land distribution system as allotment, but to prevent confusion with the United States federal policy of reservation allotment in the late nineteenth and early twentieth centuries, I use the phrase *village allocation*. Under a system of village allocation, the ogimaa discussed with the gichi-anishinaabeg, the women, and the warriors the decisions involving hunting and other land use by families and individuals before designating a tract of hunting land, sugarbush, or other resource to each lineage to be used for a single season.[144] Fur trader Jonathan Carver supports this, stating that at the time of the Seven Years' War, "it is generally supposed that from their territories being so extensive, the boundaries of them cannot be ascertained, yet I am well assured that the limits of each nation in the interior parts are laid down in their rude plans w/great precision" so that "the most uncultivated among them are well acquainted w/the rights of their community."[145] Anthropologist Frank G. Speck argued that the practice of allocating resources allowed the ogimaag to regulate hunting on their territories so as not to deplete particular populations, and also allowed some areas of the village holdings to lie fallow periodically to restock.[146]

Once the ogimaag and council allocated the land, other families did not harvest on another's claims without asking permission or receiving an invitation. Violating another family's territory was such a serious offense that it could be punishable by immediate death or more subtle revenge by sorcery.[147] Because kinship and gift exchange tied the individual into a larger incorporated group, however, kin relationships and obligations usually limited the actions families took to protect their resource rights, and trespassers were generally not killed.[148] However, the fact that they could be killed reveals how serious a crime encroachment on another's usufruct territory was. Encroachment upon village lands by groups larger than an extended family group, such as other villages or tribes, made dealing with the perpetrators in those cases a village matter. Territorial negotiations between the Ojibwe and Dakota in the early nineteenth century involved the holdings of villages and combinations of allied villages, not small family groups or individuals.[149] Examples of such resource allocation and permission for outsiders to access them appear in John Tanner's autobiography. Tanner, an Anglo American adopted by an Odawa family at the turn of the nineteenth century, lived among Odawa and Ojibwe communities from the age of eight until advanced middle age, when he returned to Kentucky and wrote an as-told-to autobiography in 1830. In his account, Tanner described at least three separate occasions on which he as an outsider migrating into the region with his family acquired harvest rights from local villages.[150]

When families needed to hunt or gather outside their designated areas due to warfare or scarcity, they generally found assistance by utilizing their kin networks to request access to the usufruct resources of another hunting group or village. Anishinaabeg values and kinship networks emphasized the need to share resources with those who lacked them. However, the needy party had to ask the hunting group gichi-anishinaabe or village ogimaa for permission to use the resources.[151] Tanner relates an occasion that clearly demonstrates the kin-based responsibilities to fellow Anishinaabeg. The Odawa family that had adopted him arrived in the Red River country following a series of events that had left them without adult men in their family unit. As Tanner relates:

> As soon as we arrived the chiefs met to take our case into consideration, and to agree on some method of providing for us. "These, our relations," said one of the chiefs, "have come to us from a distant country. These two little boys are not able to provide for them, and we must not suffer them to be in want among us." Then one man after another offered to hunt for us; and they agreed, also, since we had started to come for the purpose of hunting beaver, and as our hunters had died on the way, that each should give us some part of what they should kill. . . . The Indians gave Wa-me-gon-a-biew and myself a little creek where were plenty of beaver and on which they said none but ourselves should hunt. . . . We remained in this place about 3 months, in which time we were as well provided for as any of the [village]; for if our own game was not sufficient, we were sure to be supplied by some of our friends as long as any thing could be killed. The people that remained to spend the winter with us were two lodges, our own making three.[152]

As Tanner was a youth at this point in time, he did not take notice of how his adopted mother approached the ogimaa and gichi-anishinaabeg of that region with a request to reside among them. However, it is clear that these men recognized Tanner's group as kin and as in need. Since Tanner and his younger brother were still children, the council not only allocated usufruct territory to the family but asked for men to volunteer to hunt with the family as well.

Tanner's narrative demonstrates these interconnected practices, particularly that village members had first access to usufruct rights while outsiders had to obtain permission from the local ogimaa and council for access. Later, as an adult, Tanner further recorded that another ogimaa had granted him permission "to hunt in a little piece of ground which I had selected and a promise that none of his people should interfere with me there.[153] As Tanner would spend his life among a people to whom he had an unusually small number of kinship ties, he consistently mentions either requests to or invitations from various ogimaag to settle with a given village and share their resources.

The ogimaag's special jurisdiction over village territorial lands is given its strongest expression in Anishinaabeg oral tradition. The central hero of Anishinaabeg mythology, Wenabozho, came into conflict with the underwater beings who had killed his nephew. In his anger he proclaimed, "Whoever is underneath the earth down there, I will pull them out and bring them up on top here. I can play with them and do whatever I want with them, because I own this earth where I am now."[154] This statement expresses a powerful connection between Wenabozho and a particular place because he is the one who has taken up occupancy there. Ogimaag repeatedly made similar statements to missionaries when justifying their authority. Not only did they validate themselves by relating their descent from past ogimaag, but they specified that their lineage was the first to occupy their village's territory. For example, in May of 1835, Eshkibagikoonzh of Leech Lake visited William T. Boutwell's mission. He told the missionary, "There are some who talk much, and bad. But you must not listen to what they say. This Lake was first discovered by my ancestors, and if anyone has anything to say, I am the one."[155] Similarly, in 1836 when Edmund Ely came into conflict with Nindipens at Fond du Lac village over a planned expansion of the mission, Nindipens told him: "You ought to have asked permission of me before you began to build. This land is mine. All the land which you see around here, & all which my father has trod is mine. He gave it to me before he died. All the trees are mine also. . . . The traders have always asked permission of me, even when my father was alive & have given me something for it."[156]

The proceedings of the 1825 treaty gathering at Prairie du Chien, at which the Ojibwe were one of several tribes participating, demonstrate that while the ogimaag understood that the United States sought to define tribal territories, they still insisted on delineating their *village* territories. Each ogimaa stepped forward and identified the region within which his village claimed usufructary rights. Rivers or other bodies of water tended to bound these holdings, and distinct landmarks identified them. For example, Broken Tooth, the most influential of the assembled Ojibwe ogimaag, claimed from the Rum River to the source of the south fork of the Crow River, then to the fork of the Red River, then to the Cheyene River, and finally to Devil's Lake.[157] To make sure his claims were clear, Bezhig, whose land bordered that of the Dakota (who probably contested his title), presented the American negotiators with a birch bark map in addition to providing a verbal description.[158] Ogimaag also carefully avoided stepping on each other's claims. Despite pressure from United States agents to commence negotiations at the 1837 treaty gathering at St. Peters, Eshkibagikoonzh of Leech Lake told the agents:

I do not wish to take any further steps about what you have proposed to us, until the other people arrive who have been expected here. They have not yet come, and to do anything before their arrival might be considered an improper interference and unfair towards them. The residence of my [village] is outside of the country, which you wish to buy from us. After the people who live in that country shall have told you their minds, I will speak. If the lands which you wish to buy, were occupied by my [village], I would immediately have given you my opinion. After listening to the people whom we are expecting and who will speak to you I will abide by what they say and say more myself.[159]

Ogimaag scrupulously avoided asserting claims to the land or authority over communities outside of their jurisdiction. However, their roles in mediating actual land use among families and visitors and in conducting the ceremonies that kept the land productive and called the game made their ties to this resource strong enough that outside observers often referred to these individuals as the "land chiefs" or "chiefs of the land."[160]

Diplomatic customs for sharing land and resources with hungry outsiders originated long before Europeans arrived.[161] Native peoples adjusted their traditional land use systems to the presence of Europeans.[162] French fur trade personnel learned to ask permission from Native communities for fishing rights and other resources, especially when seeking to establish permanent posts.[163] Land disputes between Anishinaabeg communities and the American and British fur traders who took over French posts in the 1760s following the Seven Years' War often resulted from ignorance or dismissal of Indian forms of proprietorship. Annual gifts the traders gave to the community compensated the local village for land resources such as fish and firewood that the fur traders used. They also established fictive kin ties that brought outsiders into Anishinaabeg exchange networks. Gifts demonstrated a respect for Anishinaabeg rights and leadership and assisted the community to weather annual fluctuations in productivity.

When fur traders and missionaries in the nineteenth and even early twentieth centuries used Anishinaabeg resources without proper compensation, communities reminded them of their obligations. In the 1830s, the missionaries of the American Board of Commissioners for Foreign Missions ran into this problem a number of times. Edmund Ely at Fond du Lac, Frederick Ayer at Yellow Lake, as well as David Chandler at L'Anse all were challenged by local ogimaag and gichi-anishinaabeg who clearly asserted to these missionaries that the local leadership must be consulted concerning any alterations in land use. The missionaries, who understood themselves as invited into the field by the fur traders, asked only their missionary supervisors, the regional Indian agent, and the local fur traders for permission when wishing to add on to their facilities at the posts. This behavior aroused the animosity of the local villages, who insisted that the missionaries desist or enter into an agreement with the community.[164] When the missionaries ignored repeated warnings to engage in proper reciprocal and compensatory behavior, they often jeopardized their own property, especially livestock.[165] Anishinaabeg peoples leveled similar penalties against fur traders who attempted to end the credit system and institute direct market pricing. The local community at L'Anse, Michigan, for example, forbade fur trader Ambrose Davenport and his employees to fish and cut wood in 1838 until they restored the credit system, which they quickly did.[166]

As the previous examples all suggest, the key to the Ojibwe political process was the discussion of decisions facing the community. In a political environment that stressed consensus, such discourse was an ever present reality. As Sherman Hall noted in an 1833 letter printed in the *Missionary Herald*, "In any matter which shall affect the whole [village], the chief will never act or give his opinion till a council has been held with his men."[167] In addition to council meetings, the unofficial and continual discussion of issues among all residents of the village also played an important role. Schoolcraft noted "Popular feeling is the supreme law. They exchange opinions casually, and these are final. Councils generally deliberate upon what has been, beforehand, pretty well settled."[168] Most decisions in tribal politics involved much prior caucusing, negotiation, and compromise.[169] As aboriginal people visited each other, they frequently discussed major issues so that people's individual opinions were commonly known. These visits also allowed Anishinaabeg decision makers to gather the evidence they needed to support their positions in council.

Tribal leaders conducted such a fact-finding mission on September 6, 1831, when the first and third ogimaag of La Pointe came to visit missionary Sherman Hall in the company of a third member of the community, whose role Hall did not identify. Hall again took the opportunity to request a council to determine if the community would allow him to set up a permanent mission station at La Pointe. The ogimaag declined to answer definitively since many council members were still absent at their summer gardens. However, the ogimaag did take the opportunity to assess what kind of neighbors the missionaries would be. Claiming the traders gave them nothing, they told the missionaries they were hungry and requested food. Since this was harvest time when wild rice was ripe and fish and game abounded, the Ojibwe likely were not as hungry as they led Hall to believe. What they actually wanted, however, was to determine whether Hall would act appropriately as a community member and share his food when asked. Hall replied to this request in the best way possible, though he himself did not realize it. He answered that his family had few provisions and also relied on the trader for their support, but that he had a few quarts of corn he could spare. Nearly all European and American visitors appeared very rich to the Ojibwe because they seldom went hungry and had a good supply of items that were rare in Ojibwe communities, such as scissors. While Hall honestly expressed what he saw as his own poverty, to the visiting ogimaag he appeared a wealthy man acting with humility and generosity. Satisfied with Hall's performance, the ogimaag "stayed some time, conversing freely," and a few weeks later they approved Hall's request to reside at La Pointe.[170] As this example demonstrates, the distinction between political and personal conversations was often hazy, and Americans frequently misunderstood how one shaded into the other.[171]

Europeans and Americans, of course, pressured Anishinaabeg leaders to make instant decisions on topics that deeply divided Anishinaabeg communities, hampering their efforts at consensus building. Ogimaag resisted making quick decisions at treaty gatherings because of the importance of discussing the issue with kin, gichi-anishinaabeg, and other men and women of influence, such as gechi-midewijig and mayosewininiwag, before a final decision could be made.[172] This lengthy Anishinaabeg decision-making process was one of the reasons that Anishinaabeg congregated at treaty meetings in such large numbers. The will of the community had to be consulted, and in order to be able to do so, as many members of the community as could make the journey did so. Johann Georg Kohl described one such gathering at La Pointe in 1853:

> Like the women, young persons, in our meetings at La Pointe, always sat in the centre of the circle, close to the place where the American agents have their table and where the speakers stand. Some of them who were very old, were allowed chairs to sit on. The other old men sat together in the grass near them. Further out the young fellows lay about in groups. Among them were men of twenty and twenty-five years of age, but they never interfered in the discussions, save by now and then uttering a loud "Ho!" or some other cry of applause. The opinions of the Indians as to the long-lasting minority of the young men are very strict and if the latter do not act in

accordance with their views, they are very roughly reminded of their position.[173]

In other words, all members of the community ideally heard the deliberations firsthand. Certainly Kohl's observations demonstrate that all three constituencies, the women, the warriors, and the gichi-anishinaabeg were present and listened attentively to the discussions. When each ogimaa stood to speak at such a gathering, the gichi-anishinaabeg who had accompanied him stood with him, demonstrating by their presence their agreement with the words of their leader.[174] After a formal council session ended, community members were ready to discuss the day's events around campfires and share their opinions with their leaders. When multiple villages gathered together for large land cession treaties, ogimaag were similarly respectful that all villages were present to represent themselves. When the ogimaag of the Wisconsin communities were late for the 1837 treaty gathering at St. Peters, the twenty ogimaag from Minnesota declined to consider the United States government's offer to purchase a large tract of Ojibwe land because the Wisconsin villages occupied the majority of the land that the United States wished the Ojibwe to cede.[175] Ultimately George Manypenny, commissioner of Indian Affairs in the 1850s, became frustrated with negotiating treaties in Indian country as time-consuming and costly since the government, as host, was obligated to provide food to its assembled guests. He began the practice of routinely bringing tribal leaders to Washington DC, to sign treaties, an innovation that created rifts between leaders and their communities. The people keenly felt the absence of their input into such important decisions.

The ogimaa seldom made decisions without consulting the gichi-anishinaabeg of each family lineage. These men formed a governing council the ogimaag called together to discuss "every transaction relative to their hunting, to their making war or peace, and to all their public concerns."[176] As Hudson Bay Company trader James Isham has noted, "A Captn or chief comes along with a gang of Indians, in this gang they divide themselves into Severall tents or hutts, where their is an ancient man, belonging to Each family, who is officers under the Chief (alias) Uka maw."[177] Similarly, explorer Jonathan Carver stated: "Each family has a right to appoint one of its chiefs to be an assistant to the principal chief, who watches over the interest of his family, and without whose consent nothing of a public nature can be carried into execution."[178] In fact, fur trade, Indian agency, and missionary documents demonstrate that ogimaag consistently sought to delay making decisions on behalf of the community until they consulted with all community gichi-anishinaabeg or, preferably, held a formal council. Western observers erroneously saw this as a sign of weakness and indecisiveness on the part of Anishinaabeg leaders. On the contrary, it demonstrated the degree to which these leaders respected one another and chose to postpone making irrevocable pronouncements until certain that they had the weight of their community behind them. As these gichi-anishinaabeg represented lineages, they also represented doodem interests and responsibilities to the community in these councils.

To organize a larger council, an ogimaa sent his oshkaabewis with several tools of diplomacy to neighboring leaders. To ensure a timely gathering, the oshkaabewis arrived with bundles of sticks for each leader invited to the council. One stick was to be discarded each day until the day of the council was reached, a procedure that allowed the ogimaag to assemble at approximately the same time.[179] The oshkaabewis also carried shells on a cord painted red, black, green, or white to indicate whether the council intended to discuss war, peace, or other topics.[180] Finally, and most important, the oshkaabewis carried a pipe. Through the tobacco offering in the pipe, the spiritual world became involved in the invitation and observed the renewal of friendship and alliance signified when neighboring ogimaag smoked the pipe with the visiting oshkaabewis. An ogimaag could refuse to attend the gathering and return the shells with the oshkaabewis, but refusing to share the pipe indicated that the ogimaag perceived the sender and his community as enemies.[181]

In most cases, ogimaag and their attendants began to arrive days before the agreed upon date of the council to visit and discuss the issues before meeting formally.[182] Because all of these supposedly informal consultations were as important a part of the political process as the formal council itself, decisions took time to reach, a fact European and American negotiators often resented. United States Indian agent Charles Trowbridge expressed his frustration in 1833 with Ojibwe decision making: "On walking through the Indian encampment this morning, I observed a large number of old people assembled, and on enquiry found that it was a council convened to deliberate on the proposition made to them by the governor. Though such a question might be settled without any difficulty, it is characteristic of the Indians, that they duly weigh the most trivial matters before a decision is made."[183] Clark's journal of the council that signed the Treaty of Prairie du Chien in 1825 indicated that he expected about two thousand Native people to attend at a cost to the United States government of at least $10,400 in rations, presents, and interpreters. Clark explained that "it is impossible to prevent the attendance of a larger number as every chief who attends the council will be followed by a part of his village—and the assemblage of Indians may amount to a greater number than is contemplated at this time."[184] Agreement among villages required laborious discussion with constituent councils before reaching consensus on treaty issues.[185] Even when counseling among themselves, fur trader and explorer Alexander Henry related that "the Indians rarely make their answers til the day after they have heard the arguments offered."[186] This ensured plenty of time to discuss issues among those who had accompanied the ogimaag to the council.

Councils could meet for a variety of purposes. At times a council served as a mere formality, but at other times it became an opportunity for those representing various minority positions to express publicly their concerns before accepting a consensus decision. Bishop Baraga observed that "partial councils, that is, councils called by some chief in his camp or village, are frequent where they deliberate some difficulties among themselves, or some concerns with their traders, etc."[187] Even these small discussions involved set rituals. No discussion took place before the ogimaa smoked his pipe. The individual who sought a decision from the council supplied the tobacco and food necessary for their deliberations.[188] If the ogimaa called the council or broached the topic of discussion on a more intimate level, he himself contributed the required tobacco.[189] This tobacco, smoked in the pipe, created a spiritual connection with the manidoog to help guide the decisions of the council in a good way. Eshkibagikoonzh, ogimaa of Leech Lake, told explorer Joseph Nicollet that the pipe "is the instrument that drove away the bad thoughts his head has sometimes entertained."[190] Tobacco not only had a calming effect but called on the manidoog to help the ogimaag best present the needs of his community. Missionary Leonard Wheeler said of chiefs at the 1842 treaty gathering at La Pointe that they "attach importance to what they are about to say in proportion to the time they spend in smoking over the subject upon which they are to speak."[191] The ogimaag also sought the approval of the manidoog with whom they had established relationships on behalf of the community. While some communications that the chiefs carried on with the manidoog undoubtedly involved private ceremony, public ceremonies also formally invited these additional members and protectors of the community to participate.

Before a council began, a gechi-midewid ritually purified the meeting place, to keep negative or evil influences or even sorcery from affecting council deliberations.[192] Like other ceremonies, such as Midewiwin gatherings and funerals, the formal opening of the council was marked by the kindling of a sacred fire that would burn during the full course of the meetings.[193] The oshkaabewis of the ogimaag who had requested or agreed to hold the meeting then brought out the sacred pipe, filled the pipe bowl with a tobacco mixture used only in ceremonies, and lit the pipe to present to the other leaders as a gift. The pipe, like the fire, was (and remains to the present) an important step in opening communications between the manidoog and the people. Basil Johnston connected the pipe ceremony to council gatherings by referring to the oral traditions of the Ojibwe nation: "The significance of this ritual came from the smoking of the pipe performed by the spirit of Nanbush and his father . . . an act which symbolized the end of conflict and the beginning of peace between them. Thereafter, the ritual of the smoking of the pipe was an essential part of every conference, performed before deliberations began in order to induce temperance in speech and wisdom in decision. It was for this reason that councils, both general and local, were called Zuguswediwin (the smoking of the pipe)."[194] This feature is borne out in all recorded descriptions of council proceedings from the historical era.

All present at the council recognized the sacredness of passing the pipe. As the oshkaabewis prepared the pipe, the ogimaa who had invited the assembled leaders said an invocation to the four directions and, when the oshkaabewis presented the pipe, blew smoke to these directions as well as the sky and the earth. The oshkaabewis then took the pipe around the circle, presenting it to each of the assembled leaders in turn. There was absolute silence during this time out of respect for the ceremony. Next, the speaker or giigidowinini rose to his feet to relate the history of the Anishinaabeg, as was done on all formal occasions, a history intimately connected with the Midewiwin society.[195] The giigidowinini thereby reminded the leaders of the living history of which they were a part and also that, as the latest carriers of tradition, their decisions would impact the next seven generations—as their fathers' decision to follow the prophecies westward had shaped their own. As scholar Michael McNally has observed, Ojibwe people established authority in public by saying how they came to any political, intellectual, or religious authority they claimed to exercise. Such a recitation included whether the authority was based on hereditary claims or links to teachers generally acknowledged to have been authorities in the past. Part of claiming authority involved publicly defining the limits of the authority each ogimaag claimed.[196] For example, when ABCFM missionary Henry Wheeler and his wife arrived at the La Pointe community, the ogimaa Buffalo asked to meet with them and opened his oratory with "a speech in which he told us of the extent of his dominions—of the manner in which he received our first missionaries."[197] These speeches also indicated for whom the ogimaa spoke, whether the entire village community, a select constituency of that village such as the warriors, or whether his words represented entirely his own opinion.

This process for establishing one's authority took place whether the ogimaag were meeting among themselves or with officials from colonial powers. Majigaabaw took the responsibilities of performing the invocation and relating the history of the Ojibwe people at the 1837 treaty gathering. After he finished these ceremonies, each of the ogimaag present carried on the story, introducing themselves by providing their family histories, indicating who in their family had first been appointed to public office and relating each of the generations in between. Part of this recitation included the geographical areas for which the assembled ogimaag and their fathers held responsibility.[198] Following these actions, the ogimaag began to discuss the matters at hand, though never quickly. Such councils generally lasted for several days. As Nodin (the Wind) noted at the 1837 treaty gathering, "I attended a council at Prairie du Chien [Treaty of Prairie du Chien, 1825] which lasted 10 days. . . . This will last longer as it is one of greater importance."[199] Nodin's assessment of the gathering was certainly correct since it lasted for over a month.

Any interested party in the community could request the ogimaa to call a council to discuss anything of interest, but the ogimaa's role in calling the council was pivotal and exclusive.[200] When missionaries William T. Boutwell and Edmund F. Ely made requests that the community needed to discuss in council, they approached an ogimaa and asked him to convene a council on their behalf. Reflecting the ogimaa's central role, when the ogimaa was absent, others in the community informed the missionaries that no decision on the matter could be made until the ogimaa returned.[201] At the same time that only the ogimaag could convene councils, they could not make decisions on their own. Frederick Ayer wrote to David Green of the ABCFM in 1835, for example, that the Ojibwe community at Pokegoma held a council where they "confirmed the grant of land made us by the chief."[202]

Ojibwe leaders of the early nineteenth century received authority from their hereditary claims coupled with religious power they demonstrated through making successful choices and mediation that benefited the community. Basil Johnston has further argued that Anishinaabeg leadership received authority from what the community permitted them to do. He stated:

A civil leader had certain prerogatives which he exercised not constantly or permanently but only on certain occasions and only under certain circumstances. He was permitted. One of the prerogatives of a leader was to speak, but when speaking he did not purport or even presume to speak on behalf of his people without first seeking their guidance and their opinions upon the matters to be discussed. By deferring to custom and the will of the people the spokesman was seeking permission.[203]

Because ogimaag always consulted the council, the community could not hold them individually responsible if they made poor decisions that had detrimental outcomes.[204] Thus the ogimaa did not make arbitrary decisions; rather he made them in consultation with gichi-anishinaabeg representing each extended family group. As fur trade and missionary documents indicate that many communities had individuals recognized as second and third ogimaag for the village, these gichi-anishinaabeg may have been ranked. Village size did not determine the number of chiefs; even the small village on the Ontonogan River and Kabamappe's village south of Fond du Lac had second chiefs.[205]

Ogimaag demonstrated their hereditary authority and access to manidoog through right actions. They presided at village councils, represented the community at regional councils and treaty gatherings, and had assistants of various kinds who helped them conduct their duties. They led not through coercive power but through persuasion. But how do we explain those ogimaag whose leadership extended beyond their own villages? This is where the role of the ogimaa did border on the charismatic, as especially gifted individuals obtained and maintained influence over regional populations though their eloquence and exercise of the usual and expected talents and skills of an ogimaa.

Ogimaag established specific boundaries to their territories and they articulated these to one another and to American agents. They were equally scrupulous not to assert claims to the land or to assert authority over communities outside their jurisdictions. The proprietorship ogimaag inherited was not a fee-simple ownership in the Anglo American sense but rather a governorship of the resources the land provided for its residents. The ogimaag both mediated actual land use among families and visitors and conducted the ceremonies that kept the land productive and called the game.

Manidoog power enhanced the authority and influence ogimaag obtained through other sources. Anishinaabeg leaders held power not through coercive decrees but by earning respect. Respect came from being born to a chiefly lineage, from making decisions that benefited the people, and from skillfully exercising generosity to convince village members to pursue a certain a course of action. Building on this, ogimaag gained influence through marriage connections, consulted community and council opinion, and had assistants such as giigidowininiwag, miishinoog, and oshkaabewisag to assist them in their duties. Nevertheless, if they did not demonstrate successful leadership for the community, the community had the right to choose new leadership. Many of the most influential Anishinaabeg leaders also held charismatic leadership roles at one time or continued to hold them simultaneously with their other civic responsibilities. The responsibilities and authority of gechi-midewijig and mayosewininiwag augmented the influence of these men and had deep ties to the manidoog community. These additional aspects of leadership are explored in the following chapters.

3

Mayosewininiwag

*It does not devolve upon any chief in particular to make or form
a war party, but any of the braves can muster together a band of
volunteers. Those who have a desire to do so, can join these parties,
the number of each party being regulated entirely according to the
bravery of the individual who forms it.*—George Copway

*We have already taken life for life, and it is all our customs require.
Father, do not think that I do not love our people whose blood has
been shed. I would fain kill every one of the* . . . *Dakota tribe to
revenge them, but a wise man should be prudent in his revenge.*
—Ezhkibagikoonzh

The presence and assistance of the manidoog infused Anishinaabeg leadership and drew people to follow those whose beneficial decisions reflected extensive support from these very important and very revered spiritual kin. While the support of these
beings was important for ogimaag, it was crucial for leaders like
mayosewininiwag and gechi-midewijig whose authority rested
on the ability to gain followers through demonstrated success
and persuasion. Ritual demonstrations of connection to manidoog assistance through song and dance bolstered their ability
to inspire others to action. In other words, these leaders were
charismatic.

Max Weber defines charisma as "a certain quality of an individual personality by virtue of which he is set apart from ordinary men and treated as endowed with supernatural, super-

human, or at least specifically exceptional qualities."[1] Many theorists who have built upon Weber's work have suggested that charismatic authority arises in situations of social instability and tends toward the destruction or decomposition rather than the construction or stabilization of leadership institutions.[2] However, this characterization of charismatic leadership as aberrant, irrational, and distinctive to societies in transition ignores the many societies that have had orderly and stable charismatic leadership structures over long periods.[3] Societies reliant upon such structures for their group decision making would hardly have maintained them if they had not proved successful in meeting people's needs. First, in Anishinaabeg society, charismatic and hereditary leadership existed in a complex interrelationship. Second, Anishinaabeg evaluated the quality of candidates for hereditary leadership offices according to their ability to achieve and hold other more transient forms of leadership, in particular charismatic leadership roles. As a result charismatic leadership provided stability and authority rather than chaos to Anishinaabeg governance.

The Anishinaabeg world view institutionalized charismatic authority in such a way that community members easily recognized who had it and who did not. One elder informed musicologist Frances Densmore that "if a man is to do something beyond human power he must have more than human strength" and indicated that for him, songs brought this ability.[4] Anishinaabeg people individually and as a group used tobacco, songs, dance, dreams, feasts and fasts to communicate with, request aid, and thank the ever present manidoog. As discussed in the previous chapter, ogimaag used tobacco and feasts to draw on manidoog assistance and may occasionally relate a dream to lend weight to their concerns. Mayosewininiwag and gechi-midewijig show their connections to the manidoog more demonstratively, more charismatically through public rituals involving not only feasts and tobacco but also songs and dance. These additional demonstrations of access to manidoog support brought increased respect and confidence in the individual's abilities. All of the most prominent ogimaag of Ojibwe communities in northern Wisconsin and Minnesota in the early nineteenth century demonstrated their charismatic authority through becoming skilled mayosewininiwag during their youth, by becoming skilled and successful hunters, or through attaining positions within the leadership of the Midewiwin society—or by some combination of the three. These avenues to leadership were open to anyone in the community regardless of hereditary qualifications, and some of those who gained prestige through these avenues successfully challenged the authority of ogimaag who did not. However, those individuals who exerted the strongest influence in Anishinaabeg society were those who combined hereditary and charismatic leadership.

Different cultures and their world views define the culturally specific qualities of charisma. As Edward A. Shils has theorized, "the charismatic quality of an individual as perceived by others, or himself, lies in what is thought to be his connection with (including possession by or embodiment of) some very central feature of man's existence and the cosmos in which he lives."[5] Shils points out that this "central feature" in many societies is the "ruling power or creator of the universe, or some divine or other transcendent power controlling or markedly influencing human life and the cosmos within which it exists."[6] The most obvious demonstration of charismatic authority in Anishinaabeg society was (and still is) through contact with the manidoog. Although the roles of war mayosewinini and medewijig were not the only charismatic leadership opportunities open to village members, they were the most influential. Examining them in detail as examples of charismatic authority within Anishinaabeg society broadens and complicates our understanding of Anishinaabeg leadership. The sources of prestige and respect stem not only from organizational positions of authority but also from participation of their leaders in activities that continued and strengthened the social confidence of ordinary people. Religion and politics are the most logical institutional abodes of charismatic qualities and symbols.[7] In a society like that of the Anishinaabeg and other Native American peoples who do not sharply differentiate these spheres, scholars must accept charismatic authority as a stabilizing institution. This means that Anishinaabeg leadership was perhaps either more fluid than previously thought or that this fluidity had more structure than has previously been recognized. Fluidity of leadership at times functioned as a strength for Native American communities in general and Anishinaabeg communities in particular. With these new recognitions in mind, the strict dichotomy between peace and war chiefs that some authorities have maintained needs to be reexamined.

Anthropologist Charles Cleland posited that Ojibwe leadership in the 1820s and 1830s "was in the hands of peace and war chiefs. The former supposedly had purview over internal, domestic issues and the latter over 'foreign affairs.'"[8] Rebecca Kugel adopted this view, maintaining that "the Ojibwa sharply distinguished the civil or village chiefs from the military leaders; the latter, although highly valued as village defenders and protectors, nonetheless were firmly subordinate to the former."[9] Evidence suggests that the difference between war and peace chiefs or inside and outside chiefs was not as sharp in Anishinaabeg society as these and other scholars have supposed. Although only limited opportunities existed for mayosewininiwag to become ogimaag, no restrictions barred those of chiefly lineage from leading war parties. To the ranking individual of a lineage, leadership of war parties to avenge the deaths of kin was an important responsibility. Any division between the two offices of civil and war leader had little to do with the distinction between inside and outside chiefs, a concept applicable to certain southwestern tribes but one that has little relevance in the Great Lakes.

It is equally important to remember that ogimaag handled both internal and external diplomatic relations in consultation with village councils. Similarly, the Anishinaabeg did not perceive war as a constant or even a long-term state, and as a result, permanent war leaders were unnecessary. Any man had the right to organize a war party regardless of doodem or lineage affiliation.[10] A mayosewinini had only limited authority, and his power was determined largely by the number of warriors who followed him for the duration of the crisis. Explorer Joseph Nicollet relates that a mayosewinini had to indicate prior to departure "the route and direction he will follow, of the place where he will halt, and where the campaign will end by itself, if up to this point the enemy has not been encountered." He could not deviate from this plan without releasing his warriors from their pledge to follow him.[11] This episodic view placed mayosewininiwag in the category of temporary leaders whom a community elevated to office until the completion of a given task.

Although war is not generally thought of as infused with religious power, the rituals of Anishinaabeg warfare involved the manidoog at every stage from a boy's first expedition through the ceremonies a mayosewinini performed to call and conduct a war party. Mayosewininiwag who consistently demonstrated combined military and spiritual power by winning battles and honors while incurring few or no casualties gained in influence. Those who led their warriors to defeat or returned with high casualty rates lost influence. Individuals who had conducted successful war parties were subsequently able to recruit more warriors, and families who needed to fulfill their revenge obligations were more likely to invite such men to lead war parties. Kohl tells us that "if the leader of a [war] band is very influential—he will have sent tobacco to other chiefs among his friends and if they accepted it and divided it among many of their partisans, other war bands will have started simultaneously from the villages and come together at the place of assembly already arranged."[12] Like the ogimaa, the mayosewinini led by persuasion and reputation rather than coercion. Warriors fought for finite and kin-related reasons, but preferred to join the war party that had the best chance for success.[13]

Revenge motivated Anishinaabeg warfare, or, more accurately, the brief encounters that have been identified as wars among Native peoples. Frances Densmore has suggested that revenge was actually an insufficient term to embody the concept: "this motive [for war] is inadequately expressed by the word 'revenge' for it involved the idea that the death of a Dakota 'restored' the one who had been killed by a Dakota."[14] Therefore, the Ojibwe had to keep the overall kill-tally in their favor for the spiritual well-being of their communities. However, since this restoration was often accomplished through the abduction and adoption of an individual from the offending community, this often became a very literal replacement of the individual in their kin networks of social and economic obligation. Minnehwehna explained this custom to Alexander Henry in 1761: "It is our custom to retaliate, until such time as the spirits of the slain are satisfied. But the spirits of the slain are to be satisfied in either of two ways; the first is by spilling the blood of the nation by which they fell; the other, by covering the bodies of the dead, and thus allying the resentment of their relations."[15] A war party, when raised, was only authorized to kill a number of the enemy equal to the deaths their people sustained, either by taking enemy scalps or by abducting captives. If the enemy wished to forestall violent repercussions, their leaders could instead offer gifts to the aggrieved, which would also end the matter. In any case, once the death had been balanced by another death or covered via gifts, the conflict was over. The next violent encounter with the same group was a separate and discrete conflict.

Insults and injury as well as deaths could also require revenge. Indian agent Lawrence Taliaferro reported in 1826 that an Ojibwe visitor complained to him: "The Dakota met me in my lands and broke my gun and treated me roughly. Some of the Chippeways wanted to revenge it—but I told them that it was my gun that had been broken and that I was able to get another—so they must not think hard on it."[16] Warriors practiced stealth and surprise as battle tactics, and they intended to take only a few of the enemy and escape with no casualties. A single encounter resulting in one or two scalps or captives could satisfy the revenge needs of the war party and result in their return home.[17]

Leading war parties to victory was one avenue to prestige. Success indicated the favor of the manidoog whom the mayosewininini had approached in the appropriate manner for help over the course of his life. Connection with the manidoog was so important to the war party's success that warriors maintained contact through every phase of a war expedition. Prayers in the form of song formed a key connection to spiritual power, and were sung at every stage of a war expedition from the announcement of the leader's decision to form a war party to the subsequent victory celebrations. Even death itself was accompanied by songs that maintained this link.[18] Dreams and visions also played an important role in spurring an individual to organize a war party, to decide who should go, and to determine when the battle would take place. Charismatic symbols lay at the heart of Anishinaabeg society and were reflected in the relationships with the manidoog that suffused all of these activities.

At an early age youths fasted for several days at a time alone in the woods with blackened faces, hoping to invoke the pity of the manidoog.[19] The Anishinaabeg urged fasting on young men more than young women, but they did not bar young women from seeking such visions. When women occasionally did have visions pertaining to war or other traditionally male skills, the community respected those visions because their origin was manidoog. German traveler Johann Georg Kohl told of one such woman whom he met at La Pointe during his travels:

A warlike maiden suddenly appeared, who boasted of having taken a Dakota scalp, and she was led in triumph from lodge to lodge. I was told that a supernatural female had appeared to this girl, who was now 19, during the period of her great fasts and dreams of life, who prophesied to her that she would become the greatest runner of her tribe, and thus gain the mightiest warrior for her husband. . . . Thrice—so said the prophetic voice—she would join in an expedition against the Dakota, and thrice save herself victoriously by her speed of foot. In running home the warriors of her tribe would try to outstrip her, but she would, in the two first campaigns, beat everybody. . . . On the return from the 3rd campaign, however, a young Ojibeway would race with her, and conquer her, and she would then be married to him. The girl had made her first war expedition this year. She had proceeded with the warriors of her tribe into the enemy's camp, raised the scalp of a wounded Dakota on the battle-field, and had run straight home for several days, thus bringing the first news of the victory, which greatly augmented her renown. At La Pointe she walked in procession through the village, the scalp being borne before her as a banner. She was pointed out to everyone as the heroine of the day and of the island.[20]

The community fully embraced the rather unusual actions of this young woman, not only because she brought them news that their warriors were returning victoriously but also because her dream gave her the right to undertake this action. Further-more, as an omen of success—the vision predicted victory for the three war expeditions she foresaw herself accompanying—the young woman's manidoog power had proven stronger than any power the Dakota possessed to counter the manidoog gifts of the Ojibwe warriors.

Manidoog more often empowered women to fight back when the enemy attacked their own communities. A story passed down in the family of a woman named Bicaganab (d. 1892) related that when the Dakota attacked her camp, she fought back with a club. The warriors drove her down to the water and into a canoe. They continued pursuit in their own canoes and tried to draw alongside her so as to bash her head in. Using her paddle, she first destroyed their canoe and then pounded the Dakota with the paddle until they took refuge on the shore. Instead of following her retreating countrymen, Bicaganab hid nearby in the rushes and later returned to the site of the battle. There she found only the dead Dakota covered with their blankets. She collected their scalps, guns, and beadwork into a sizable pack to take with her. Then she painted her face and went to the Ojibwe camp with her acquisitions.[21]

If such power was important and celebrated for this young woman, it was even more central to the identity and function of male warriors and mayosewininiwag. Dreams not only predicted the profession of young men and the success of their war parties; they also initiated and halted expeditions. An excellent source on the experience of warriors and mayosewininiwag is a man named Odjibwe, whom Frances Densmore interviewed at the age of eighty-nine in 1909. This would put his birth year around 1820 and place his experiences of first becoming a warrior and war leader in the 1830s and 1840s.[22] As a youth, Odjibwe sought a vision to help him become a warrior after the Dakota killed two of his brothers. He shared with Densmore the dream that led him to lead war parties, a dream that, interestingly, included a powerful female spiritual being: "A party of Sioux approached and the woman gave a gun to each of the Dakota, telling them to shoot at him. The Sioux took the guns made of rushes and shot at him. Out of the guns came horseflies, which lit on him but could not harm him. Then the woman told him that he would be a great warrior and would always be protected. Odjibwe [the informant] said that what the woman told him came true, for he was never wounded by the

Sioux."[23] The woman also gave Odjibwe a song to sing when he needed to connect with or call upon this power. He could not remember the song until his first battle when the dream vividly returned to him. From that time, he could sing the song whenever he needed it.

Although as he told Densmore he had never recounted the entire vision lest it lose its power, Odjibwe had probably shared parts of it during ritual. As he grew older, his success as a warrior and his escape from personal injury increasingly demonstrated the strength and power of his vision, which encouraged others to join him when he sent out invitations for a war party. Indeed, Densmore reported that in 1909 he carried eleven war-honor feathers for deeds in battle. Three bore notches, indicating that he had killed and scalped three Dakota. The eight unnotched feathers commemorated the scalping of Dakota whom others had killed, an action requiring great bravery since the enemy attempted to take their dead with them. Dots of rabbit fur also marked these feathers, indicating the number of bullets in his gun at the time of securing the scalp.[24] Others accompanying Odjibwe to war hoped that his manidoog protection extended to them as well, but in the end this was his dream, his power, his connection to the manidoog. After singing his song for Densmore to record, he remarked that he "feared he would not live long, as he had given away his most sacred possession."[25] At the end of his life, he had given up the song that connected him to the manidoog power, kept him safe, and encouraged him to be the man he had become.

Dreams were tricky things to interpret. Warriors disclosed their dreams to the mayosewinini, who disqualified them from the war party if the dream suggested a negative outcome for the individual or the group. However, because Anishinaabeg politics were noncoercive, the mayosewinini could not prevent a truly determined man from going along. Common positive symbols in dreams included small birds, such as hummingbirds, which made difficult targets due to their size and speed. On one occasion, an older man felt confident in joining the war party because he had dreamed of a large bull buffalo. The mayosewinini and even the other warriors attempted to dissuade him from the expedition, "because the buffalo is not like a small bird. . . . It is big and can be seen easily." The old man went anyway, was shot full of arrows, and died. As the anthropologist Ruth Landes put it, "He thought he had a strong dream because he dreamed about a strong thing. He had erred in his equipment of power, not in overriding the constituted authority."[26]

Odjibwe also provided Densmore with a great deal of information concerning the ceremonies and symbols that transformed a youth into a warrior in the eyes of the community. The first step was to demonstrate courage to the community by participating in a dog feast. An old and venerated warrior announced the feast the night before the ceremony, and the next day most of the community gathered for the event. According to Frances Densmore, the ceremony began with "much singing and dancing, and many speeches."[27]

This ceremony and Odjibwe's residence in Minnesota indicate that the Ogichidaag, the Ojibwe warrior society, probably conducted the ceremony. Nearly all references to its existence come from Minnesota Ojibwe, who were more consistently engaged in hostilities with the Dakota. Such warrior societies had their own identifiable leaders, ceremonies, and prescribed rights for the group that cut across kin and village lines. The society might have existed in all Ojibwe communities in Wisconsin and Minnesota, but there is little evidence, suggesting that even if the society had a presence, its role was less prominent or political than in communities bordering the war zone between the Ojibwe and Dakota.[28]

Observers defined the society as "restricted to the men who had won war honors," and excluding "young men who had not yet distinguished themselves, but who were considered as potential members."[29] On the plains such societies also handled certain policing functions during great communal hunts that are not associated with the Ogichidaag.[30] However, since the Ojibwe did not generally hold large communal buffalo hunts in the summer months, the ogichidaag were not needed in such a role. Few contemporary observers knew much about how the Ogichidaag society was organized or what its members did besides fight the Dakota, so it is possible that they had some policing functions that were not widely visible to outside observers.

Most likely the ogichidaag policed the very white residents whose diaries serve today as source material about its existence. Nearly all ABCFM missionary reports of property damage (excluding minor thefts) coincided with the organization of war parties and might indicate attempts to settle injustice at home before settling it abroad via war. For example, Frederick Ayer reported that after he and his family left their home at Pokegoma to travel to La Pointe, "a small party of Indians returned and encamped in the neighborhood of the mission. They joined in a war-dance near the house, at the close of which they dashed a canoe of the mission to pieces as a signal to further outrages."[31] On another occasion, when the Leech Lake community, or at least its warriors, suspected William Boutwell of instructing the officers at the fort at St. Peters to deny them powder and shot, the ogichidaag confronted him: "More than forty had assembled, among this number the soldiers, or warriors, as they are called in distinction from the others. I cut each a piece of tobacco, and after smoking, their leader, the Little Buffalo informed me why they had assembled."[32] Those gathered had intended to kill his cattle, but after he boldly denied the allegations and offered many gifts to the assembled warriors, Boutwell escaped with a sound scolding: "You must obtain a great many mirrors, vermillion, and other small articles for the young men. And when your provisions came, you ought to give us a feast of something that we don't always have, and tell the young men it is to pay them for the fish you get out of the lake. And when your tobacco comes, you ought to give it to the old men. And your clothing that is sent to you—you should give it to the children that are poor. You don't do us any good at all by being here."[33] Whether or not it was a regular duty of the ogichidaag, warriors definitely had a primary role in reinforcing community norms.

Indian agents and missionaries often complained about the Ojibwe's failure to police internal "criminal" behavior. They failed to understand that they themselves became socially sanctioned targets for theft in punishment for what Ojibwes understood as their antisocial crime of hoarding resources. Furthermore, the punishment of murder lay with families, a tradition European and American outsiders considered anarchic. Once a death occurred, revenge was mandatory, but the ogimaa, gichi-anishinaabeg, and the mayosewininiwag usually sought to prevent individuals from committing nonsanctioned random violence. For example, in the late 1780s, a disgruntled Ojibwe customer at Lac Courte Oreilles village attacked trader Michel Cadotte. Hearing the discharge of the gun, the "war chief" wrestled the gun out of the man's hands and was on the point of breaking the stock over the shooter's head when the rest of the warriors intervened. The bullet had narrowly missed the trader's wife, who was the daughter of an important chief at La Pointe. The Lac Courte Oreilles community nearly executed the offender, but Cadotte intervened on his behalf, and the warriors spared his life.[34] Here the warriors took the lead in protecting the community from escalating vengeance by restraining the actions of one of their own and subjecting him to community jurisprudence. One assumes that this was one of the ogichidaag's regular duties—to defuse potentially violent situations.

Zhingwaakoons's actions in 1820 at Sault Ste. Marie present another example of local internal community policing. A local influential warrior named Sassaba had taken offense to territorial governor Lewis Cass, who had come to demand tribal land for an American fort. Sassaba, who had lost a brother to American forces in the war of 1812, broke up the meeting with Cass and began to gather a war party. The village council met a second time and decided to send Zhingwaakoons to order Sassaba's war party to stand down: "My friends and relatives, I am authorized by our chiefs and elders to stop your proceedings."[35] The elegance of Zhingwaakoons's oratory and his steadfastness in the face of Sassaba's violence convinced Sassaba's men—and eventually Sassaba—to give way.[36] In this case a larger diplomatic matter, peace with the Americans, was at stake, and the civil chiefs sent one group of warriors to remind another that their role in diplomacy superseded the warrior's right to revenge. And in March of 1835, one of the Leech Lake civil chiefs warned missionary William Boutwell that "when the Indians are all here in the spring, they [the ogichidaag] mean to invite old and young to assist them, but in what, I cannot say. One thing I am certain of, that the subjects are the traders, because the Indians have suffered so much want from ammunition and tobacco."[37] Apparently the ogichidaag had considered punishing the trader for the crime of hoarding.

The "Begging Dance" may also hold clues to the wider purposes of the Ogichidaag society. In this dance the warriors presented themselves in full war dress before new arrivals to the community, shared a pipe of tobacco with them, and then expected a distribution of presents. Missionaries who built their stations in villages rather than at fur trade posts commonly experienced this sort of greeting. Edmund Ely reported it at Fond du Lac, and Sherman Hall at La Pointe. William Boutwell described in detail the performance of this dance when he and the Indian agent Henry Rowe Schoolcraft arrived at Fond du Lac Post in June of 1832:

This morning the drum was the first thing heard; and at eight, thirty or more, who joined in the dance, headed by their chief came before our door, where they exhibited for an hour. Their approach was the most comical—a half-hop, turned by the beat of two drums, accompanied by a monotonous sound of the human voice—each holding his musket in a presented position, which as they came near, was discharged—two American flags were borne at the right of their column. The pipe was now lit, and first presented to Mr. Schoolcraft and next to myself, then to Mr. Johnston, and finally went the rounds, when they commenced their dance, accompanied with the monotonous drum and the voices of a few [women]. At short intervals all united in a yell. The bodies of the principal part of the men were naked, except the cloth about the loins and leggins, and painted in a manner to exhibit the most hideous spectacle possible. Their heads and the bodies of many were ornamented with the feathers of the eagle. After the dance had proceeded a short time, one of the warriors began a sort of Phillipic to the young men, recounting his exploits, in which he was careful to tell them how many of the Sioux he had killed.[38]

Lieutenant Allen, who commanded the military escort with the Schoolcraft party, noted that Schoolcraft gave gifts to the participants following the dance.[39] Despite their disdain for the ritual, outsiders honored its purpose in the interests of peace.

This description resembles one that fur trader William Johnston described a year later at Leech Lake, though he termed it the "pipe dance":

A party of sixty warriors, almost all young men came to our village and honored us with a dance, they were accompanied by a train of old men, women and children; Nothing was new or strange in their dancing—only the appearances of the men who were painted and dressed as if going to war, with a profusion of eagle's feathers dyed of beautiful colors and worked with different colored porcupine quills. And I never saw a more manly and better set of men; they kept dancing the pipe dance and striking the post; and told of their warlike exploits.[40]

In an ogichidaag dance, each warrior who had earned eagle feathers had the right to tell how he had earned them. This recitation stirred up the courage of those within the society and encouraged youths who were thinking of embarking on their first war expedition.

These men from a number of communities needed provisions for their journey to Dakota territory, so following the dance, they expected noncombatants to provide gifts to those who were about to fight on their behalf. These gifts also explain the presence of the elderly, women, and children following behind the ogichidaag. If the warriors were undertaking obligations to avenge the dead, they were not hunting, fishing, or otherwise providing for their families. The gifts the ogichidaag received on such occasions also went to support their families during their absence. Europeans scorned and misunderstood the economic purpose and social significance of the dance. A good indication of how badly they misunderstood the dance can be seen in the name they applied to it, the "begging dance."[41]

The ogichidaag likely also played a strong role in initiating youths into warfare. Densmore's vague reference to singing, dancing, and recitation of war deeds suggests that the ogichidaag held the ceremony for the young boys to begin the process of initiating new members. Until they had actually won war honors, the ogichidaag would not accept individuals as full members. After the opening events, warriors brought the untried youths forward and seated them on the ground in a circle. In the center of the circle one of the warriors killed a dog, removed its liver, cut the bloody organ into small pieces, and put the pieces on the ends of long sticks, one for each boy. If a youth chewed and swallowed the morsel without reaction, the warriors considered him brave enough to join the next war excursion. All those assembled to observe the ceremony jeered those who flinched or pulled back from the proffered meat.[42] Ruth Landes recorded a similar test of bravery, but she linked flinching from the test with false claims to spiritual power.[43]

Not only was manidoo power necessary to exhibit simple bravery, but the warriors wanted to be certain not to include anyone in the war party who did not bring such assistance with him. Like dreams, tests of bravery weeded out those who lacked spiritual support.

Once the war party left the village the trials did not end for youths eager to prove themselves for the first time. Seasoned warriors placed a number of restrictions on the new recruits. Joseph Nicollet stated that they had to continue to blacken their faces for the duration of the war expedition, were forbidden to wear any sacred items on their person, and further had to hide their faces beneath their blankets as they left home.[44] Landes added that they had to camp at a distance to the rear of the main party in little shelters of boughs with two recruits in each, and they joined the rest of the camp only when about to engage the Dakota. The older warriors had plenty of food and even meat, while the boys received only parched wild rice or wild rice partially cooked with a little maple sugar. The veterans also required the rookies to put mittens on both hands when they left the village and to wear these until they engaged the Dakota.

Additional restrictions, which paralleled those among girls observed during their first menstrual retreat, suggest that a young man's first war expeditions were a crucial transitional time on their road to adulthood. The youths wore a small stick hung from the wrist for use in scratching the head or body, much as did young girls during their first menstrual retreat. Older warriors warned the young men that breaking this taboo would result in nasty and uncomfortable consequences once the group returned home. This could include breaking out in boils all over one's body. The recruits were at risk during their initiatory phase because they lacked protective medicines carried by the warriors.[45] Georg Kohl additionally reported that the boys were required "to have, like the women, a cloth or species of cap on the head and usually walk with drooping head, speak little or not at all." Further, he noted, the youths were "not allowed to join in the dead or war songs."[46] Veterans also cautioned the young men not to step over any article belonging to another, particularly weapons, as such an action rendered them useless. Maajii-giizhig (Ma'djigï'jig, Great Sky), one of Densmore's informants, reported that a youth who stepped over another man's gun was chased and severely punished by the weapon's owner.[47] Again this resembles women's menstrual restrictions prohibiting them from stepping over others' belongings. Finally, Bishop Frederick Baraga states that these boys had to walk exactly in the footsteps of one of the veteran warriors and that these restrictions continued for the first three war parties in which a youth participated.[48]

Such restrictions for adolescents of both sexes implies a concern that both men and women, in their transition from youth to adulthood, needed to acquire and learn to use spiritual power. Such power the Anishinaabeg perceived as necessary for successful life as an adult, and it had to be handled carefully and respectfully as misuse could lead to loss or the power or worse— illness and possible death for oneself or members of one's family. Although restrictions lessened after the transitional moment of puberty, gendered rules requiring certain practices continued throughout adult life to ensure proper relationships between the human and manidoog communities.

Adult warriors also took care to invoke manidoog aid when they planned war parties. Good dreams were of paramount importance for the success of the war party, and indeed, a mayosewinini often began contemplating a war party because of a dream. The war leader then began to gather support for the excursion among both human beings and the manidoog. Sometimes the planning began in the winter months for an expedition the following summer. Unless conflicts over Dakota and Ojibwe hunting areas erupted, the two rarely conducted war when snow was on the ground due to the difficulty of traveling safely and surprising the enemy under such conditions. Warriors also focused in these winter months on hunting for family subsistence and on stocking up on foods and materials that might be needed either for the war party or by their families in their absence.

Once the mayosewinini made the decision to begin war preparations, he withdrew from his family to a separate lodge. He then began singing songs to bring additional dreams and strengthen his connections with the manidoog that promised him aid in battle. In his dreams his slain relatives visited him to harden his resolve, and his manidoog provided him with useful information, such as where to procure food along the way to Dakota country, how to find the enemy camp, and how to ensure a surprise attack. Manidoog might also reveal how many of the enemy a man would kill.[49] A clear dream assured the mayosewinini that he and the war party would go and return safely. A vague dream warned that he would lose some men.[50]

After a mayosewinini spent a few days singing, drumming, and dreaming in his separate abode, other men in the community noticed his seclusion, and they then dropped by the lodge in ones and twos to ascertain the reasons for the grief that caused such behavior. The potential war leader then related the deaths that his family had suffered at the hands of the Dakota and also told a portion of the dreams he had received guaranteeing victory and indicating how to achieve it. However, as the ethnographer and traveler Kohl emphasized, the mayosewinini told "only 'a portion,' for he generally keeps the main point to himself. It is his secret, like a general's war plans."[51] If a visitor agreed with his course of action and found inspiration in his own dreams, he joined the mayosewinini in his seclusion and song. The mayosewinini, if he had confidence in the visitor and the visitor's dreams appeared to strengthen the cause, appointed this man his associate or "adjutant," and both became leaders of the upcoming excursion. Kohl added that the Ojibwe "always consider it better that there should be two leaders, in order that, if 'the dreams of one have not strength enough,' the other may help him out."[52] The respect for manidoog power, then, reinforced fluid and polycephalitic leadership.

For the rest of the winter these two men sang and drummed each evening and smoked many pipes as they sought to improve the strength of manidoog assistance for their campaign. They also developed a plan of operations and sent out tobacco or a war pipe stem to men of various villages, inviting them to take part in the campaign.[53] If enough men accepted the tobacco to join the war party and the mayosewininiwag agreed on all parts of the plan, they set a date for departure.[54] Such advance warning was necessary so that the participating warriors could begin preparing themselves spiritually by fasting, dreaming, and refraining from sexual intercourse. They occasionally dropped in on the mayosewinini to have him evaluate their dreams. One of Landes's informants explained, "The leader could not take [just] anyone at all. He had to know their power."[55] If the mayosewinini rejected the vision a warrior brought to him, the leader sent him back to try again.[56]

All leaders, whether war or civil, had an oshkaabewis who assisted them as pipe bearer, messenger, and aide de camp. Ojibwe dictionaries translate the term not only as "helper" but also as "assistant" and "adjutant," the very words that Kohl used in his description of the second man to join the war leader's expedition. In her account of Ojibwe war traditions, Densmore elaborated on the role of oshkaabewis. She stated that a warrior who wished to lead a war party sent an oshkaabewis with tobacco to invite warriors in neighboring villages to join together in an attack on the Dakota. The oshkaabewis invited the men to a council in their respective villages, where he explained why he sought to undertake the expedition and then, while singing a song, offered a pipe to the assembled men one at a time. All who were willing to join the expedition smoked the pipe, though warriors had no obligation to accept a given invitation to war. After the council the oshkaabewis returned to the individual who had initiated the war party and delivered news of his recruitment success in a song.[57]

When the time agreed upon arrived, the warriors who had accepted tobacco to join the war party encamped near the mayosewinini's lodge.[58] This signaled their decision to join the war party. The assemblage of a sufficient number of warriors to ensure success was a form of community sanction for the enterprise.[59] The mayosewinini held a feast during which he expanded on the reasons for the proposed expedition and asked for a final pledge from the warriors, who by now had painted themselves black. The mayosewinini appointed four men to act as his aides during the expedition. Like the earlier tobacco messenger, they were called oshkaabewisag. One carried the mayosewinini's pipe and another the war drum, and all four organized the war dances, the provisioning, and the camps each night en route to the enemy. The mayosewinini himself bore the war banner, eagle feathers sewed onto a four-foot strip of cloth fastened lengthwise to a pole. Densmore's main informant, Odjibwe, told her that a man named Gagagiwigwan (Raven Feather) kept the banner during peacetime but loaned it to any war party that requested it since the banner was the common property of all the warriors.[60]

At the feast given by the mayosewinini, those who agreed to accompany the expedition joined the mayosewininiwag in a war dance at the cemetery where the relatives and friends whom they hoped to avenge were interred.[61] At these dances, held every night until the warriors departed, the leading warriors related past accomplishments, enacted former exploits, and sang their personal war songs and songs honoring past victories over the Dakota.[62] One song even told about a man who stayed home to shame those who failed to join the warriors without an appropriate excuse.[63] The war drum that accompanied these dances was different from the water drum used for Midewiwin ceremonies. It had two heads, measured about twenty inches in diameter, and was four inches thick. When the mayosewinini finished drumming, he passed tobacco to the assembled warriors, who began to smoke it. The mayosewinini then gave a speech on the honor of going to war. He revealed his manidoog power in some way, such as lifting a large stone as though it weighed very little to demonstrate his great strength. Finally, the mayosewinini petitioned the manidoog for the safety of those who accompanied him into battle.[64]

The female relatives of the warriors played important roles in the preparations for the expedition. They observed the dances, painted black like the men and with their hair disheveled and strewn with duck down to symbolize mourning. They also had experienced personal loss, and they sought to lend their generative power to the war effort. Certainly the political support of the women's council for the war party was also important. This participation paralleled the fasts that wives, children, and other relations observed to improve a hunter's chances of locating game. A war dance similar to that performed publicly took place in the lodges of all the warriors who intended to take part. Kohl relates that a woman known as the woman of sacrifice was important to major war expeditions.[65] In most cases this woman was the wife of the mayosewinini, another indication that the wives of leaders often played parallel roles within the community.[66] The Dakota, Blackfeet, and other plains tribes also brought a woman dressed in white with them into war. Her white dress probably symbolized White Buffalo Calf Woman, who brought the pipe to the Plains tribes, and she carried a large medicine bag with a decorated pipe.[67] In the periodic peace negotiations initiated by the tribes (and not arranged by whites), women always walked in advance of the male negotiators as the two parties approached one another. The presence of the woman of sacrifice, therefore, likely permitted the Dakota and Ojibwe to change plans, give gifts to cover the dead, and negotiate a peace when they met the enemy.

Other sources support Kohl's description. Densmore concurred that usually only one woman accompanied an Ojibwe war party.[68] In a diary entry Edmund Ely referred to a substantial war party that went out from Fond du Lac in 1842, consisting of thirty-eight men and one old woman. Ely indicated that this left perhaps five or six able-bodied men in the community.[69] As the presence of women was not mentioned in connection with the more common smaller war parties, they may have been present only when the conflict involved the entire community. Women may also have played a role in encouraging the warriors. Odjibwe told Francis Densmore that Omiskwawegijigokwe (Woman of the Red Sky), the wife of a war leader who accompanied him into battle, composed and sang a song on the battle field, dancing as well to urge him on.[70]

When the time came for the war party to depart, the war leader held a dog feast exclusively for the warriors, at which they ate the head of the animal. Through participation in this feast, the warriors made their final commitment to the expedition.[71] Untried youths venturing forth for the first time probably attended, but they already had passed muster at the earlier dog feast by eating the liver without flinching or protesting. The mayosewininiwag spoke to the women who would remain behind and established a time for their return from the expedition.[72] The warriors in full war paint then took their places in their canoes and sang their death songs as they paddled away from the village.[73] The village women boarded their canoes and paddled back and forth in front of the war party for a short distance.[74] If the war party traveled on foot, the women, who had whitened their faces with clay, walked to and fro in front of them for a short distance while singing a farewell song. Eventually the women separated and stood in two lines between which the men walked. Still singing, the women returned to the village.[75]

Both of these practices by the women mirror the role of women in establishing lasting peace between two Native nations. If two nations agreed to negotiate peace, both brought their families and camped near one another while they completed preparations for the necessary ceremony. The warriors dressed in their finest attire and each camp sang and issued war cries as their delegations approached each other. Leading each delegation was an oshkaabewis holding a pipe, followed by four women. Next came the mayosewininiwag and behind them the warriors. The women walked to and fro in front of the warriors. Their presence prevented violence between the warriors of the two delegations because to shoot at each other would endanger the lives of the women, which they considered an ignominious act. As these delegations advanced, each sang praising the valor of the other. The warriors fired their guns into the air, did not reload, and disarmed. The women who walked before them singing strongly also received praise for their bravery. The tribe that had asked for peace sent forward its oshkaabewis, who offered the pipe stem in turn to each of the opposing leaders. The other side sent its pipe bearer forward for the same purpose. During this exchange of pipes, both sides sang more songs. After completing the ceremonies that established peace, the two tribes camped near each other for some time, engaged in social dances and encouraging intermarriage, which further established alliances by creating kin ties. At these dances a woman sometimes beckoned to an attractive warrior, threw her blanket over his head, and took some of his finery as they danced together.[76]

The warriors carried little with them on a war expedition, as encumbrances slowed them down and impeded their ability to surprise the enemy. Usually they brought only their weapons, pipes, moccasin repair kits, and personal medicine bags, plus the war drum and war banner. Medicine bags were of critical importance, and the warriors prepared them with particular care.[77] Kohl observed that "these they inspect before starting as carefully as our soldiers do their cartridge-boxes & place in them all their best and most powerful medicines, and all their relics, magic spells, pieces of paper etc. in order that the aid of all the guardian spirits may be ensured them."[78]

Warriors carried a number of medicines specific to warfare. In particular, *bizhikiiwaak* (cattle herb medicine), *minisinoowaak* (island herb medicine), and *waabanoowaak* (eastern herb medicine) counteracted the effects of medicines the enemy carried. A blend of various herbs comprised each of these medicines, the precise measurements of which warriors obtained from Midewiwin practitioners. Gechi-midewijig knew the proper proportions of the herbs and knew the four songs that ensured their efficacy. Bizhikiiwaak was especially strong. War dances included songs in praise of this medicine. According to Densmore's informants, in earlier times the warriors chewed the bizhikiiwaak and spat it onto their bodies and equipment to make themselves strong. On one occasion Densmore's informant Odjibwe went into a fight without his medicine. The warriors had barely commenced to fight when Odjibwe froze as if paralyzed. His friend Naaskigwan immediately ran to him, sang a song, and gave him medicine from his own bag mixed with water and also sprayed the medicine on Odjibwe's feet and limbs. This revived him and soon he was fully able to participate with the others.[79] As late as 1911 when Densmore conducted her fieldwork, she stated that bizhikiiwaak was still in use as a stimulant and a coagulant to minimize the flow of blood from wounds. For the Anishinaabeg, medicine was too important to leave behind because it connected the warrior with manidoog power and thereby ensured success.

Even if the warriors traveled part of the journey by canoe, portages required them to carry all supplies over land at times. They sometimes did not take food with them since they fasted on the road.[80] Mayosewininiwag, however, were no fools; all Ojibwe had experience with fasting and knew it led to physical weakness if carried on for too long. Densmore's informant Odjibwe reported eating while traveling with a war party, and likely this was the norm. When they brought food, they might not have enough for the entire journey, and when allied Ojibwe villages lay between the war party and their targets, warriors expected communities to resupply them, particularly if the call for the war party had originated there. If the war party ran out of provisions outside Ojibwe territory, the mayosewinini, like the headmen of the hunting camps, chose a place to camp and conducted a ceremony to locate game.

After a war party departed from Ojibwe territory the warriors observed a number of restrictions to ensure the continued favor of the manidoog. Kohl reported that "they will never sit down in the shade of a tree, or scratch their heads, at least not with their fingers. The warriors, however, were permitted to scratch themselves with a piece of wood, or a comb."[81] Indeed, as the danger increased, the ties of the war party to the manidoog needed constant attention, and the occasions for calling upon their aid multiplied dramatically. During the entire journey to Dakota territory, dreams and discussions of dreams continued. If one of the warriors had a dream with bad portents, he went home lest he endanger the rest of the group.[82] Sweat lodges and pipe ceremonies sought to maintain manidoog guidance for the group. Kohl elaborated on some of the reasons for continued manidoog consultation:

They now have all sorts of information to acquire, to divine, to guess, and beg from the spirits. At one moment a doubtful trail of the foe is discovered, and it is necessary to know where he is hidden. At another moment they desire a little rain or fog to secure themselves from detection; and this must be produced by incantation. The leaders of the band then take up the decorated war pipe, which is always carried before them, and one offers it to the other, that he may try his strength; but through modesty or want of confidence, no one is particularly desirous of taking it. At times the pipe will go around twice or three times before anyone will accept it. At length a great clairvoyant or "jongleur" will step forward—generally the commander in chief—seize the pipe, and prophesy that by the time he has smoked it so deep, or when he has smoked it out twice or thrice, the hoped-for fog or rain will arrive and with it the time for attacking.[83]

As Kohl's remarks suggest, the warriors particularly valued the ability to predict or alter weather conditions. Frances Densmore's research into Ojibwe war songs bears this out. Her informant Maajii-giizhig related that during the preparations for an attack on a Dakota village that took place during his first war expedition, "the leader then called for the wind and the wind came. The Dakota heard the wind singing through the tipi poles, and the flapping of the tipi canvas, but did not hear the soft tread of the Chippewa as the latter entered the camp."[84] And "before attacking a Dakota village, the leader of a war party frequently 'called on the thunderbird to send rain' in order that the Dakota would remain at home, not changing their camp or wandering in the vicinity, where they might detect the approach of the Chippewa."[85]

Densmore's informants related a number of instances during a war expedition in which the leader needed to call upon his manidoog for assistance. According to Odjibwe, the following ceremony took place each evening when they encamped. The warriors seated themselves in a row facing Dakota country; the four oshkaabewisag sat immediately in front of them, and the mayosewinini with his war drum sat in front of them all. On these occasions, the mayosewinini placed two crotched sticks in the ground with a crossbar between them, on which he leaned the stem of his lighted pipe while the bowl rested on the ground. Then the mayosewinini sang alone with no accompaniment or punctuation from the war party while gazing in the direction of the enemy's country to divine their location.[86]

Success nearly always depended upon maintaining the element of surprise, and surprise could be aided or impeded by weather conditions. A mayosewinini who could direct these natural forces to the aid of the Ojibwe war party significantly increased the probability of success. Fur trader George Nelson in his journals for 1802–4 further suggested that the warriors "think that their chief can assume at least the track or footmark of any animal if not its shape, by which means he can go in any direction he pleases, without the risk of being discovered, except by those 'qui sont aussi pas de medicine qu'eux meme' or who have as much power as themselves, who immediately distinguish the difference."[87] Because each individual had relationships with different manidoog who provided unique gifts, various mayosewininiwag over time demonstrated a variety of skills, all of which contributed to the success of their expeditions.

In addition the warriors made preparations to care for the wounded when expecting a large engagement with the Dakota. Each side attempted to take their dead with them rather than leave them to be scalped. The enemy often pursued a war party that carried away its wounded in an attempt to capture the wounded. Densmore related that an older man accompanied every war party, carrying extra medicine and water in readiness to attend to those in need of assistance.[88] Indeed, Ely commented that many "fathers followed their sons" on the war party he witnessed leaving Fond du Lac in June of 1842.[89]

Because these encounters provided opportunities for young men to demonstrate their bravery, there were various war honors and a number of ways to achieve them. Eagle feathers were the most important, but they were not the only war honors. Warriors earned the right to wear certain types of pelts or colors of war paint as a result of demonstrating various kinds of bravery during combat. Warriors marked their arrows, ensuring that the correct man received the recognition. As guns replaced arrows, warriors called their shots and awarded honors on this basis.[90]

There were means to gain war honors other than through combat. One man carried the war banner, or eagle staff, of the community from which the war party originated and guarded it with his life. During battle, he ran back and forth with it, making himself a target to distract attention from his companions. Another warrior drummed and sang during the battle to inspire the men and ensure continued contact with the manidoog assisting them. According to Odjibwe, the Ojibwe always sang, if possible, before making an attack. If they intended to surprise a Dakota community early in the morning, the mayosewinini led them in singing and beating the drum very quietly until the attack commenced.

Even touching the enemy was worth honoring. Densmore's informant Odjibwe, after shooting a Dakota, ran forward and dragged him toward a clump of bushes where the man later died. For catching the wounded Dakota by the arm, Odjibwe earned the right to wear a skunk-skin badge on his right arm. On another occasion, Odjibwe wore his brightest finery during battle, making himself a target to demonstrate his bravery.[91] Such finery, including any eagle feathers that warriors had earned the right to wear, made them more conspicuous during a fight. Furthermore, a warrior demonstrated bravery and inspired others in an open fight by throwing aside clothing and weapons and rushing to engage the enemy with his bare hands. If the Dakota missed him on the first shot, the warrior could then retreat and gather his weapon.[92]

After the battle, victory dances honored those who had distinguished themselves. Members of a war party who did not distinguish themselves received no acclaim for their mere presence with the expedition, an encouragement perhaps to attempt acts of bravery.[93] Warriors gained honor not only by taking a scalp but also by losing their own. Alexander Henry reported a major conflict in which the Dakota killed thirty-five Ojibwe in the spring of 1766. The survivors complained to Henry that the Dakota had retreated without even "doing the honors of war to the slain" by scalping them: "We consider it an honor to have the scalps of our countrymen exhibited in the villages of our enemies in testimony of our valor."[94]

Warfare between the Ojibwe and the Dakota in the late eighteenth and early nineteenth centuries continued to serve as a vehicle to turn Ojibwe hunters into warriors and improve their standing in society.[95] Warfare also concerned territorial issues, of course, but the Ojibwe conceptually linked revenge for departed family members and revenge for trespass on resources that supported living family members, who would die if deprived of resources.

But warfare itself and the acquisition of status it engendered created reciprocal needs to be met: if they were victorious, warriors had further responsibilities to the manidoog who had pitied and helped them. They hung deerskins and other items, especially clothing and tobacco, in the trees on the field of battle as offerings for the manidoog. Then they collected their dead and took scalps and other items from their enemies to bring home to their communities.[96]

On the journey home a victorious war party composed songs to sing at the upcoming victory dance.[97] They sent runners ahead to inform the community, which could then prepare for the arrival of the main party. The night before entering the village the war party practiced their victory songs and dressed in their war regalia. The next morning the warriors fired guns to signal their approach, and the women came out of the village to meet them. Just as they had when the warriors departed, the women moved back and forth in front of them in canoes or on foot.[98] The warriors turned their scalps over to the lead woman of the welcome party, who dressed them and fastened them inside a hoop hung from a pole. The missionary William T. Boutwell described one such scalp. The flesh side was tanned and painted with vermillion and then "a piece of wood is turned in the form of a horse-shoe, into which the scalp is sewed the threads passing round the wood which keeps it tight. Narrow pieces of clothe and ribbons of various colors, attached to the bow, were ornamented with beads and feathers. A small stick, which serves for a handle to shake it in the air when they dance was attached to the top of the bow by a string."[99] Frequently a man gave the Dakota scalp he had taken to his wife.[100] At Leech Lake the war party gave one to a woman whose husband had been killed on the expedition.[101] As they entered the village the women took the warriors' blankets, beadwork, tobacco bags, even their guns. Then they led the procession dancing into the village with the scalp bearers in front waving the scalps and singing.[102]

While the entrance ceremonies were being performed, other community members had been busy cooking and preparing a place for the fete. In a tradition known as "feasting the Dakota," Ojibwes placed dried meat, wild rice, maple sugar, and other dishes on the ground next to the scalp poles. After the feast those in charge of the event seated the victors in a row. Friends and relatives of the warriors then brought gifts and laid them before the warriors. During this time the community sang a song to the warriors. Then the warriors rose, danced, and sang the songs they had recently composed describing their martial deeds. Members of each warrior's clan distributed gifts in the warrior's honor to all the people in the community. In addition to the newly composed songs of the victorious warriors, family members composed songs to honor them, and bereaved women "danced the scalps" to fulfill their personal and familial obligations.[103]

These celebrations were open to the full community, and little boys and girls as young as six watched with intense interest and imitated the actions of their mothers and fathers.[104] The victory dance continued until daylight, and at its conclusion, the Ojibwe carefully wrapped the scalps for the next dance. Often the village would dance the scalps for several nights in succession before sending them to another village for additional dancing.[105] When Schoolcraft's expedition to Lake Itaska traveled through Cass Lake, Boutwell reported that the community there engaged in the scalp dance for at least five consecutive nights.[106] Next the same oshkaabewis who had invited warriors from neighboring villages to join the war party carried the scalps to their villages, in each of which the same ceremonies were observed. He also bore with him tobacco and the songs warriors composed concerning how they took the scalps.[107] After the scalps had completed the circuit of all villages that had participated in the war party, the Ojibwe planted the poles bearing the scalps in the grave of an individual killed by the Dakota.[108]

In order to ensure success, both war leadership and the process of conducting war itself required the assistance of the manidoog. Indeed, Kohl observed in the 1850s that hunters and warriors were steeped in "the superstitions and incantations" of their society.[109] All skill and luck came not from the individual but from manidoog intervention. Those who demonstrated consistent success as mayosewininiwag gathered increasingly large war parties. As their success continued, their reputation and influence increased and crossed village lines. Their leadership, although temporary, somewhat restricted, and not hereditary, therefore qualifies as a form of charismatic authority. Communities certainly perceived these men as set apart through their especially strong ties with the manidoog beings whose aid was so central a feature of human existence that people depended upon them for food, health, safety, and success in warfare. The route to this authority was open to any who could acquire it without hereditary or class distinctions.

Densmore's informant Odjibwe related that his first expedition as a mayosewinini consisted of himself and his cousin Niibinikamig when both were about twenty years old. They disguised their intentions, telling others that they were going on a hunting expedition so that their elders would not restrain them and also as a precaution against failure. Odjibwe sang every night that they encamped. On the fourth morning they came upon one Dakota traveling alone and killed and scalped him. When they returned home with the scalp, their village held a great feast and dance in their honor, celebrating both the victory and the connection to the manidoog that made victory possible.[110]

The charismatic authority of unusually successful mayosewininiwag caused individuals to seek out their opinions on other topics of importance to the community as well. If also oratorically gifted, mayosewininiwag could approach the authority commanded by hereditary leaders within the community. However, nothing precluded hereditary leaders from asserting themselves in the sphere of war. Throughout the historical record various hereditary leaders also recounted occasions on which they led war parties. During peace, whites referred to some of them as "war chiefs," presumably because of their previous active participation in war leadership. Such participation in warfare potentially allowed ogimaag to demonstrate that they had manidoog aid crossing into many spheres of life. Moreover, because mayosewininiwag recruited warriors across village boundaries, they gained respect and influence outside their communities— clearly a concern for hereditary leaders, and perhaps a reason why so many chose to pursue this path during their youth. Those leaders chosen as giigidowininiwag or representatives of several communities at treaty proceedings with the federal government earned this recognition in most cases by succeeding in the dual roles of ogimaa and mayosewinini. Thus, although ogimaag leaders had a kind of charisma of office, they could add to it personal charisma and respect outside their home community by organizing successful war parties.

4

Gechi-Midewijig

MIDEWIWIN LEADERS

*The mide doctor will never refuse you if you go to him with
cooking . . . put it in front of him . . . fill his pipe . . . and tell him
"I want to be mide because I am so lonesome and I want to have
my spirit strengthened."*—**Ruth Landes**

*The men who were heads of families had, a few days previous
to their arrival here, attended a medicine dance and feast, at
which were about thirty-five men, who after much consultation
and delivering speeches on the subject of our coming among
them, agreed together that they would not send their children to
school, or listen to God's book; they would retain their customs
and habits.*—**Frederick Ayer**

Religious leadership, like war leadership, provided another
charismatic avenue to diffuse and consolidate power in Anishinaabeg communities. The Midewiwin, or Grand Medicine Society, the traditional religious organization of the Anishinaabeg to
which most healers and other religious practitioners belonged,
offered another opportunity to demonstrate expanded connections with manidoog assistance that helped the community to
survive. As in the case of mayosewininiwag, gechi-midewijig
demonstrated enhanced access to manidoog assistance through
public ritual performances that included feasts, tobacco, dance,
and songs. Anyone could have a dream or vision that led the
individual to seek initiation into this organization, resulting in
a leadership that included a broad cross section of the village

community.[1] This alternative avenue to leadership served in part to democratize access to respect and authority within the community. However, for ogimaag, recognition as a religious leader offered an additional opportunity to expand their influence through charismatic means.

The mingled respect and fear accorded those who had advanced to high levels of initiation within the Midewiwin society also impacted the degree to which others both from within and without their communities felt willing or constrained to look to their views for guidance. Some scholars have suggested that Midewiwin leadership subverted traditional political leadership in the early nineteenth century. However, the antiquity of Ojibwe Midewiwin practice combined with the long history of Midewiwin participation in many chiefly families suggests a more ancient connection between religious and political authority.

Like war parties, Midewiwin membership was open to anyone who had had the proper dream, and initiation ceremonies often incorporated individuals from other villages, allowing an opportunity for those from other communities to observe and evaluate the abilities of their neighbors. But unlike for mayosewininiwag, Midewiwin initiation made one a *medewid* (plural *medewijig*) for life, and one's prowess in connecting with the spirit world generally improved rather than declined with age. As a result, membership in the society could either bring ambitious ogimaag more authority or give authority to those outside the traditional leadership lineage. These power relationships are more thoroughly examined after an assessment of the age of the society and a description of its meaning to the Ojibwe people.

A number of scholars, such as Harold Hickerson in his early works, Charles Bishop, John A. Grim, Victor Barnouw, and Karl Schlesier, have tried to argue a post-contact date of origin for the Midewiwin Society. They base their claims largely on the absence of specific descriptions of the ceremony in seventeenth-century European records. However, four factors point to a more distant origin for this tradition.[2] First is the assertion within Midewiwin oral tradition that the society derives from ancient times.[3] The oral traditions of other Native American revitalization traditions to which some scholars have compared the Midewiwin, such as the Ghost Shirt Dance of the plains and the Handsome Lake religion of the Iroquois, do not claim ancient origins predating the historically documented lives of the prophets who brought the ceremonies to their communities. Not only do these movements make no claims to pre-date contact with European visitors, but they deliberately and clearly incorporated the results of colonialism in their underlying theologies. Second, Midewiwin songs and stories preserve archaic words and idioms that had already passed out of common usage by the mid-nineteenth century, according to William W. Warren, the Métis son of La Pointe fur trader Lyman Warren.[4] Musicologist Frances Densmore confirmed this in her early twentieth-century study of Midewiwin songs, stating that many of the songs contained words "unknown in the conversational Chippewa of the present time."[5] Third, Densmore further concluded that "the antiquity of these songs is shown by the fact that many of them are widely known among scattered peoples who came originally from the same locality."[6]

A final form of verification comes from the technology of radiocarbon dating. Recent radiocarbon dating places a Midewiwin birch bark scroll in the protohistoric, or pre-contact, period, and there is evidence from excavations at Whitefish Island near Sault Ste. Marie, Ontario, that the local community conducted Midewiwin ceremonies there around 1560 CE—nearly one hundred years before Anishinaabeg peoples in the area are believed to have had contact with Europeans.[7] Particularly in light of these new archeological discoveries, recent scholarly reassessments of Midewiwin origin arguments by Laura Peers and Michael Angel as well as Harold Hickerson's own retraction of his earlier post-contact theory tend to support Anishinaabeg assertions of its great age.[8] Regardless of its actual antiquity, the Midewiwin society was of sufficient age by the early nineteenth century that it was deeply intertwined with all aspects of Anishinaabeg life from birth to death. Because of its importance, the Midewiwin provided another significant path to charismatic authority and community leadership.

Although most American observers came to refer to the Midewiwin as the "Grand Medicine Society" due to the medicinal knowledge that was (and still is) passed on to society members, this is not an actual translation of the term. Ojibwe scholar and fluent speaker Basil Johnston suggests that the term may mean a variety of things in the original Ojibwe. It could mean either "the good-hearted ones" (from *mino*, "good," and *dewewin*, "hearted") or "the resonance" (from the term *midewe*, "the sound"), this second meaning referring to the importance of songs, drums, and shakers to society rituals.[9] Other authorities, Native and non-native, provide similar meanings. The Ziibiwing Cultural Society of Michigan provides a meaning similar to the first of Johnston's translations, suggesting that Midewiwin means "from the heart way of life."[10] Religious studies scholar John Grim relates a meaning similar to the second of Johnston's, suggesting that the correct translation is "drum doings" (from *mide*, meaning "sound of the drum," and *wiwin*, meaning "doings."[11] Scholar Nicholas Deleary also presents a translation tied in with the sound of the ceremony, suggesting that *Mideway* means "sounding voice" and *wiwin* means "good all over, " so that the term could mean "sounding good all over."[12] That there are variations in the exact translation is not surprising given the dialectical differences across Ojibwe country. The difficulty may also stem from the fact that the word *Midewiwin* itself is archaic and therefore not easily translatable; another indication of the great age of the tradition.

However, definitions alone do not provide an understanding of the society, its meaning for the Anishinaabeg people, or its role in Ojibwe life. Like the Ojibwe language, the Midewiwin has local variations that have developed over time, which is why scholars may occasionally collect conflicting information. Generally stated, the teachings of the society are devised to help the individual to achieve the Anishinaabeg goal of *mino-bimaadiziwin*, a good life in the fullest sense. A good life was a long life free of disease, hunger, and misfortune. Right living, according to the philosophies of the Midewiwin society, as well as the use of the songs and natural plant remedies that the manidoog gave to the Anishinaabeg, would bring these gifts. The society built upon the relationships with manidoog that an individual had already established through dreams and fasting and provided avenues for additional manidoog assistance, had the relationships established at puberty not brought mino-bimaadiziwin.[13] As historian Laura Peers noted, the Midewiwin was (and is) understood to be literally "a life-giving ceremony . . . performed to cure serious illnesses, and its teachings helped the people to live properly so as to obtain success and health in life."[14] Scholar Theresa Smith further suggests that as the Anishinaabeg perceive life as more than simply continued physical existence, mino-bimaadiziwin necessarily "involves commitment to relations with the other persons in the cosmos, for only under their tutelage can one find the strength one needs to live well."[15]

The Midewiwin society teaches a social code of conduct that members are encouraged to follow. Frances Densmore's informant told her that elders enjoined the men to respect the women, and they instructed women to be moderate in speech, quiet in manner, and prudent in decision making. After receiving this teaching, Densmore noted the patience and courtesy of the Midewiwin elders with whom she worked.[16] Basil Johnston spoke further of the morality espoused by the Midewiwin society, stating that members believed a good character necessary to receive or confer long life. In the pursuit of this, they followed certain precepts:

Thank Kitche Manitou for all his gifts
Honor the aged; in honoring them, you honor life and
wisdom.
Honor life in all its forms; your own will be sustained.
Honor women; in honoring women, you honor the gift of
life and love.
Honor promises; by keeping your word, you will be true.
Honor kindness; by sharing the gifts you will be kind.
Be peaceful; through peace, all will find the Great Peace.
Be courageous; through courage, all will grow in strength.
Be moderate in all things; watch, listen and consider; your
deeds will be prudent.[17]

In keeping with Ojibwe regional variability and overall cultural flexibility, Three Fires gechi-midewid Edward Benton-Banai presents these ideas somewhat differently, identifying the core teachings given to the people from the manidoog in the following manner:

To Cherish knowledge is to know Wisdom
To know Love is to know peace
To honor all of the Creation is to have Respect
Bravery is to face the foe with integrity
Honesty in facing a situation is to be brave
Humility is to know yourself as a sacred part of the creation
Truth is to know all of these things.[18]

In its various forms Midewiwin theology incorporated the basic guidelines for living in communities in a responsible manner—something characteristic of all major world religions. Although such codes of conduct of course always represent the ideal that human societies hope to achieve in the midst of a complicated and sometimes corrupt world, having an idea of what a community looked for in its best and brightest members provides an important insight into why certain individuals were looked up to and respected more than others.

On the other hand, while Midewiwin theology did not encompass the concept of hell or a similar place of eternal suffering for wicked deeds, practitioners did believe that evil actions had consequences. Power in and of itself was understood to be good or bad only in its uses. Some manidoog had reputations for often conferring gifts that the individual could use to harm others, but these were always balanced by powerful gifts of healing as well. In essence, healing and harm were seen as two sides of the same coin—to be able to accomplish one implied the ability to accomplish the other.[19] When individuals used their powers to harm others or for personal gain at the expense of others, they might achieve a short-term end, but eventually that power would rebound on the users. Results included the illness or untimely death of the practitioner or members of the person's immediate family.[20] As such, gechi-midewijig who were advanced in years and had suffered no unusual family tragedies were looked upon with reverence as almost saintly. Their teachings and advice were sought on a variety of topics. And if such an individual was also an ogimaa, his influence was very wide indeed.

Anishinaabeg communities held formal Midewiwin ceremonies annually in the spring and fall of the year. Generally these gatherings coincided with important events in the seasonal subsistence cycle, though the actual subsistence activity around which they were organized varied by region. For example, in Manitoba these ceremonies were held around the time of spring and fall fishing camps.[21] In Wisconsin, where the climate better supported an annual wild rice crop, fall ceremonies were held in conjunction with the wild rice harvest as it was believed that this helped to mature the rice.[22] Although fur trade records frequently mentioned when Native people gathered to hold ceremonies, they were quite vague concerning what ceremonies were being performed. Missionaries, however, whose business was

The Midewiwin ceremony calendar at three Ojibwe villages

Year	La Pointe	Fond du Lac	Yellow Lake/Snake River/ Pokegoma
1830		NA*	Jan. 16
1831	Sept. 17	NA	
1832	Sept. 15, Oct. 10	NA	
1833	Jan. 30, Sept. 9	Aug. 29	Nov.
1834	June 3	June 13	April
1835		June 3	
1836		May 25	Sept.
1837	Oct.	Spring	
1838	Sept. 12	Jan. 19, Sept. 15	Spring

*The Fond du Lac mission was not opened until 1833.

Sources: Archives, Minnesota Historical Society, St. Paul: Frederick Ayer, letters to David Greene, December 1, 1833, and October 8, 1838, American Board of Commissioners for Foreign Missions, Correspondence, 1827–1878; William T. Boutwell, Journal Kept While at Leech Lake, William T. Boutwell Papers, 1832–1881, 72–73, 77–78, 106–8, 139, 169, 194–95; Jedediah D. Stevens, Diaries 1829–1830, Jedediah D. Stevens Papers, 1827–1876, 65.

Archives, Superior Public Library, Superior: Sherman Hall, Miscellaneous Letters of Sherman Hall and His Sisters 1831–1875, in Early Protestant Missionaries in the Lake Superior Country, 3: 2, 42.

Archives, Wisconsin Historical Society, Madison: Edmund F. Ely, Diaries, Edmund F. Ely Papers 1833–1904, no. 1, July–September 1833, 22; no. 4, 4 May 1834–22 June 1834, 20; no. 8 (6), 11 March–30 August 1835, 14–15; no. 10, January–February 1836, 57–58, 79; nos. 11–20, 1836–1854, 119, 148, 153, 166–67; Florantha Sproat, letter to Mother, September 12, 1838, Florantha Sproat, Letters, 1838–1845.

Missionary Herald: "Letter of Mr Hall dated Sept. 17, 1831," Missionary Herald 28 (1832): 50; "Extracts from a Communication of Mr. Ayer, Yellow Lake, May 15, 1834," Missionary Herald 31 (1835): 116.

religion, tended to keep more specific records that either identified ceremonies as Midewiwin, Grand Medicine, or gave sufficiently detailed descriptions of the proceedings for the ceremony to be identified as Midewiwin. Sampling the diaries and letters of the missionaries affiliated with the American Board of Commissioners for Foreign Missions to three Ojibwe communities in northern Wisconsin is instructive. Over the course of the years between 1830 and 1838 the records demonstrate the frequency of Midewiwin practices in the spring and fall of these years (see the ceremony calendar on p. 154).[23] In addition to the seasonal gatherings of the society, the Midewiwin held ceremonies to end periods of mourning, to heal the sick, and to provide proper burial for the dead.

At the seasonal gatherings, formal initiations admitted new members, both men and women, to each of the eight ranks, or degrees, in the society.[24] According to Ojibwe missionary George Copway, the gechi-midewijig had discretionary authority to determine who joined the society, and occasionally even young children were extended an invitation. Generally initiates were expected to have had a dream or vision directing them to join the society, or in the case of children, a relative may have received the vision on behalf of the child. The ceremony is also prescribed to the very ill for its healing properties "as it is thought in this way they will receive the favor of the Great Spirit and get better."[25] For the sick, the seriousness of their condition allowed them to bypass the one or two years of instruction other individuals received prior to initiation. However, lacking the instruction of a conventionally initiated member, they were subsequently barred from becoming ritual officers or healers regardless of the degree they held.[26] William Warren related the following account of what initiates did to prepare to become medewijig:

The person wishing to become an initiate into the secrets of this religion . . . prepares himself during the whole winter for the approaching ceremony. He collects and dries choice meats, with the choicest pelts he procures of the traders' articles for sacrifice, and when spring arrives, having chosen his four initiators from the wise old men of his village, he places these articles with tobacco, at their disposal, and the ceremonies commence. For four nights, the medicine drums of the initiators resound throughout the village, and their songs and prayers are addressed to the master of life. The day that the ceremony is performed is one of jubilee to the inhabitants of the village. Each one dons the best clothing he or she possesses, and they vie with one another in the paints and ornaments with which they adorn their persons to appear to the best advantage within the sacred lodge.[27]

During the year-long initiation process, individuals learned from a senior member of the society the theology, songs, and ceremonies appropriate to the degree sought. Final initiation ceremonies did not commence the first time the medewijig and initiates entered the lodge in their finest clothes. Rather many accounts attest that several days of preparations including sweat lodge ceremonies were key to preparing both the gechi-midewijig and the new initiates prior to the initiation.[28] Explorer and geologist Joseph Nicollet recorded an excellent description of such a sweat lodge from his travels to Leech Lake in 1836–37:

However many people are supposed to enter into the vapor lodge, its vault cannot have more than four or eight arched supports. Mark on the ground a square or octahedron. Plant a flexible branch from a young tree at each angle and fold these branches toward the center of the lodge making them converge at the pole of the base of the polygon. Tie the arcs together at their converging point so as to form a vault not exceeding a height of three or four feet. Form a noose halfway up the vault from thongs encircling the arched supports and tighten it to consolidate the whole frame. Cover with woolen blankets, leaving room for an entrance through which one can slip in and out, and the lodge is completed. A bed of sand is laid out at its center on which are placed some round stones, four or eight of them, according to the number of arched buttresses forming the lodge. These stones are heated outside and then brought in where their surface is sprinkled with water, which vaporizes and fills the lodge with steam. Branches are laid out to serve as seats for the mide, or bathers. Add a vessel containing water and two sticks tipped by sprinkling brushes for dipping and spraying water and you have a complete madodiswon [sweat lodge], built and ready to serve.[29]

Once the sweat lodge and preparations for the initiation ceremony had been completed, the medewijig put on their finest clothes and entered the lodge. Missionary Edmund Ely provides a vivid description of one such ceremony in the 1830s:

At an appointed time the eight and the applicant proceed to some private place where he is instructed in the part he is to act in the mituei [Midewiwin]. This is accomplished within eight days and every night the eight leaders drum and sing for a while. On the eighth day a lodge is prepared by the women who are called to a feast and certain of them designated to the business. On the ninth day at an early hour the pieces [gifts] are hung up. The eight men enter the lodge and commence singing. After four songs the applicant and all the people enter attired in their best. The pieces are spread for the applicant to sit upon, who takes his seat with his back against the post. Four songs are then sung. The seven of them rise, each taking in his hand an otter skin medicine sack, the head of which is medicated with what they may severally esteem most potent, take their stand in a row at the end of the lodge back of the applicant while the leader stands behind him and holds him by the shoulders. The first moves round the lodge till he comes in front of the applicant when he thrusts his sack at him and proceeds in his orbit and takes his stand at the foot of the row while the applicant is quivering under the potent shock. The second then does the same and so the seven. The first performer being again at the head of the row takes from his sack a sea shell and as he approaches the person again blows into it and puts it into the mouth of the applicant. He stops before him shaking his sack a moment. The shell falls from the mouth of the subject. The performer picks it up and places it a little distance from him and proceeds to his place and so the seven. The shells being placed in the order of their performance. The seven then take their stations on the path in the middle of the lodge while in the center stand three or four with drum and kettle who sing while the applicant, accompanied by the leader who held him by the shoulders makes four circuits of the lodge with sack in hand (which had been previously given to him). When he approaches the first of the row and thrusts his sack at him who falls prostrate sometimes in contortions under the shock at every successive circuit another is brought down until all the seven lie on the ground. They then slowly rise in a sitting position. The then initiated and indoctrinated member lays before each of them one of the pieces. Then everyone of the initiated present drum and sing for a moment men women and children for the children are sometimes initiated at an early age and if they are not able to perform their part the parent does it for them. This occupies a long time if many are present. Then every one uses his sack on whomsoever they meet of the initiated and a ludicrous scene follows. Then follows a general dance moving round the lodge, which concluded, they retire and part.[30]

Although the spring and fall initiation ceremonies such as the one Ely describes constitute the most commonly documented activity of the Midewiwin society, once initiated, members could officiate at a variety of other types of ceremonies based upon their degree in the society, which indicated their knowledge and experience. The most widely recorded activity of the society is to provide healing, which the members did either through small family rituals or through the powerful process of initiation into the society itself. All members had knowledge of and could practice healing on a basic level. As Baraga stated, "Every old Indian, man or woman, is the instructor of youth, more or less, according to his capacity and disposition. And so their children hear and learn from infancy all the oral tales and traditions, and the whole stock of moral and other knowledge, which is conserved by the tribe."[31] In particular, the Midewiwin society was believed to hold a great deal of knowledge on the use of plants to treat illnesses, although most of this knowledge was circulated only among the higher degrees within the society. In 1962 anthropologist Edward Rogers identified a number of healing specializations among the Round Lake Ojibwe of Ontario, including the *mide-mashkikiwinini* (herbal specialist), *midenaabe* (spirit man), and *madwe'ikewinini* (drum man). Significantly, the name of each healing specialist appears to be linguistically tied to the Midewiwin.[32]

Nicollet identified the most common form of healing ceremony as the *nanaandawii'iwewin*, where a medewid is given gifts and food to heal someone who is sick. The medewid comes to the lodge of the sick, sings, and speaks to the manidoog for the herbal medicine he is about to administer while walking around the lodge. Then the medicine is given to the patient, after which the healer accepts his presents on behalf of the spirits and makes his way around the lodge while singing and showing the gifts to the spirits. After this the medewid continues treating the patient daily, but without repeating the ceremony, although the family is still expected to give him a little gift or a little food for his time.[33] Should the medewid's efforts prove ineffective, Ely reported, the doctor took the presents he had been given and set them before another medewid, who then tried his medicines on behalf of the patient.[34]

While nanaandawii'iwewin appears to have been performed primarily by men, women also had important healing roles.

Medewid women were brought in to hold ceremonies at particularly difficult births to ensure the health of mother and child.[35] Medewid women also gathered the morning after the birth for a feast at which only maple sugar was served and the women prayed for the child.[36] Their expertise in midwifery was also accompanied by knowledge of plants that would augment their skills.[37]

Less well publicized but no less important was the role medewid played in calling the game for hunters during times of scarcity. If the village was hungry, someone would bring food and tobacco to a medewid member of the hunting group to request the ceremony. Noodinens gave Frances Densmore the following account of this ceremony:

My father was a Mide, and one day, when the provisions were almost gone, a young man entered our wigwam with a kettle of rice, some dried berries, and some tobacco. He placed this before my father, saying: "Our friend, we are in danger of starving; help us." This man was the ockabewis who managed and directed things in the camp, and his arms were painted with vermilion. My father called his Mide friends together and they sang almost all night. The men sang mide songs and shook their rattles. No woman was allowed to go in that direction. The children were put to bed early and told that they must not even look up. My mother sat up and kept the fire burning. My father came in late and sang a Mide song, and a voice was heard outside the wigwam joining in the song. It was a woman's voice, and my mother heard it plainly. This was considered a good omen. The next morning my father directed that a fire be made at some distance from the camp. The ockabewis made the fire, and the Mide went there and sang. They put sweet grass and medicine on the fire, and let the smoke cover their bodies, their clothing, and their guns. When this was finished, my father covered his head with red paint and applied it to the shoulders of the men. They took their guns and started to hunt, feeling sure they would succeed. No woman was allowed to pass in front of the hunters when they were starting. The ockabewis killed a bear that day and every man got some game.[38]

Joseph Nicollet also documented this practice at Leech Lake in the 1830s and asserted that it must be a medewid who performs the ceremony to call the game.[39] Nicollet further elaborated that calling the game in this manner was known as *manidookaazowin*, a practice the ABCFM missionary Edmund Ely mentioned as occurring often at Fond du Lac, where the prominent community member Maangozid, a third degree medewid, often officiated.[40] Fur trader George Nelson reported in his diary for 1823 similar ceremonies in Canada and likewise affirmed that these ceremonies were usually successful.[41] Further, although the account given by Noodinens suggests that only men could be present at game-summoning ceremonies, John Tanner's captivity narrative states that his adopted mother Netnokwe, a prominent medewid, often dreamed the location of game and received community recognition for her abilities in this regard. After her death Tanner often found himself the one asked to perform manidookaazowin.[42] Indeed, his excellent skills as a hunter combined with his ability to manidookaazowin led him to be counted among the gichi-anishinaabeg in his community.

The medewijig then, were not only responsible for the initiations of new members into their society. Their role included ensuring the general health of the community, ensuring their continued well-being through the ability to hunt during periods of scarcity, and ensuring the growth of agricultural crops. Clearly the Midewiwin was a tradition deeply embedded in the way that early nineteenth-century Anishinaabeg understood and interacted with their world. And yet it did more—it provided the Anishinaabeg with a means to communicate in writing.

Since full initiation ceremonies were sometimes held only once or twice a year, the Anishinaabeg developed a pictographic writing system to record on birch bark the vast array of songs, stories, and rituals associated with the Midewiwin. These birch bark scrolls held mnemonically recorded elite knowledge, which elders used to instruct those seeking to become society members, leaders, and healers.[43] The use of these scrolls also demonstrates the continuity of the theological traditions of the lodge over the years. As noted earlier, the scrolls have even been used by archeologists to demonstrate the pre-contact origin of Midewiwin ceremonies. George Copway, a nineteenth-century Ojibwe who became a Methodist minister, comments that there were three central repositories for these scrolls near Lake Superior. Each of these repositories was guarded by ten gechi-midewijig, who examined the scrolls every fifteen years and at that time replaced those that had decayed. The decayed scrolls were distributed equally among the guardians, who considered these remnants very sacred and used them for a variety of purposes.[44]

Copway further observed that the pictographic writing used on these scrolls comprised more than two hundred figures. Reinforcing Densmore's observation, he stated that scrolls could be read accurately by persons from distant villages who had been educated in reading pictographs.[45] As these scrolls record not only songs and rituals but also the story of the Anishinaabeg migration from the East Coast to the western Great Lakes region, some can even be regarded as stylized geographic maps.[46] Those that described rituals also included clan symbols to indicate where persons of certain clans needed to locate themselves. As noted earlier, these clan symbols were central to personal identity. The Ojibwe drew the mark of their doodem whenever they drew a scroll, made sacred art, or signed a binding agreement with another human.[47]

In addition to providing members with a means to communicate over time and distance, the Midewiwin society also gave them another means of extending their kinship ties. As Kohl observed in the 1850s, "The members of the order regard each other as related, and call themselves in their conversation uncle, aunt, &c."[48] Although not all Ojibwes chose to become members of the Midewiwin society, for those who did, as religious scholar Christopher Vecsey has observed, the Midewiwin provided "a central event, a common heritage, and an organized leadership" as well as a common mythic past that bound people together across band and lineage lines.[49] Indeed during the eighteenth century, if not earlier, the Midewiwin society became such an integrative force that it spread beyond the "Three Fires" of the allied Ojibwe, Odawa, and Potawatomi peoples and was embraced by most of the Native peoples of the western Great Lakes.[50] Historian Richard White noted Midewiwin practice among the Miami nation of Indiana and Michigan, autobiographer Mountain Wolf Woman described her participation in Midewiwin ceremonies among the Ho-Chunk of Wisconsin, and nineteenth-century Indian agent Lawrence Taliaferro commented several times on its practice among the Dakota living near Fort Snelling.[51] Many of these tribes encouraged intermarriage with one another; shared a similar language base, world view, and beliefs about the origin and treatment of disease; and had stories centered around the culture hero Wenabozho. Hence it is not surprising that they would also find much of value in the Midewiwin tradition.[52] Midewiwin teachings may have spread even further. Scholar Nicholas Deleary has identified several Algonquian-speaking tribes living outside the Great Lakes area whose terms for their religious leaders suggest that they also practiced Midewiwin traditions, albeit with local variations:

Anishinabe (Ojibwe)	Midewinni
Penobscot	Mede'olinu
Abenaki	Meda'ulinu
Delaware	Mete.'innu
Maliseet	Mete'welen[53]

This is not to suggest that all of these nations gathered together in one central location for the performance of Midewiwin ceremonies. Most villages held their own initiation ceremonies, although they often shared the members of the highest degrees across villages for those levels of initiation. But it did mean that Midewiwin members traveling to other villages could participate in local ceremonies and be received there as kin. Further, Nicollet states that "when a Midewiwin is to be celebrated in a village, one can be sure all the other villages of the same tribe will send their delegations."[54] Thus regardless of whether or not the ceremony fostered intertribal unity in the ways earlier scholars have theorized, it did create kinship ties and mutual obligations between villages. For those of advanced degrees, Midewiwin membership provided an avenue for charismatic leadership that would be recognized across several communities.

Practices of gift exchange and food sharing among society members further cemented the fictive kinship relationships created by lodge membership along familiar traditional lines. All initiates brought gifts to the lodge to be distributed among those who assisted with the initiation process. Thus the society also created bonds among its members through gift exchange that helped families expand networks of obligation beyond village and community.[55] Once initiated, members had to attend Midewiwin ceremonies at least once a year to renew the connections to manidoog that had been established during initiation.[56] As a result the Anishinaabeg annually renewed social connections with other Midewiwin members among their own villages and with neighboring communities and tribes.

Food sharing also strengthened and renewed the fictive kinship ties created through initiation. Boutwell described the culinary requirements for a Midewiwin ceremony held in May of 1835. Two people prepared ten large kettles of food that consisted of potatoes, squashes, rice, corn, meat, duck, and fish. The hosts for the feast gradually called the assembled medewijig to partake of the feast according to rank, starting with "the chief." Since Boutwell had arrived on the scene with his interpreter looking for Eshkibagikoonzh, the first ogimaa of the Leech Lake community and a fourth degree medewid, Boutwell's reference to "the chief" probably indicates that Eshkibagikoonzh had been asked to eat first at this feast.[57] Eshkibagikoonzh expanded his considerable influence by becoming a gechi-midewid.

Feasting not only provided another means to share resources but also had long been an important connective ritual between humans and manidoog. At such feasts participants ate for their spiritual relatives, ancestors, and manidoog, whom they invited to the feast, and thanked for its bounty.[58] The extended kinship relationships with manidoog embedded in the Anishinaabeg cosmos, as discussed in the first chapter, continue to be of importance in Midewiwin practice. The dancers and singers who receive the initiation gifts are understood to receive these on behalf of the spirits who worked through them during the ceremony. As an avenue to charismatic leadership, the Midewiwin society gave young men and women initiated into the society an opportunity gradually to join the ranks of community leadership as they advanced within the society. Because knowledge and skill were enhanced with each successive degree attained, prestige and authority took a significant commitment in time and gifts to achieve. Each individual initiation added to the spiritual support of the community, contributing to the well-being of the community as a whole. And in turn, the community endowed those seeking advanced degrees, and the elite knowledge and manidoog relationships that accompanied them, with sociopolitical power due their enhanced ability to help the people.[59]

Despite this, the Midewiwin society did not have a fixed leadership in the sense of a hierarchical priesthood, hereditary or otherwise. While there were eight levels or degrees of initiation in the society, these referred more to specific areas of knowledge and skills held by each rank. There were no limits on the number of people who could achieve each degree or level of initiation—theoretically everyone in the community could choose to attain all eight levels of initiation. Yet it is likely that only those with a strong commitment to and interest in theology sought all eight degrees. Each level of initiation required careful study and preparation, including the accumulation of gifts to give away, which increased in number with each successive degree. As a result, while some ritual positions could be held only by persons of a particular rank, the leaders who officiated at gatherings of the society, especially those called to conduct initiations, were men "chosen for the office at each meeting of the society."[60] And the choosing did not start with the highest in rank but with the lowest. Today at the Round Lake Midewiwin lodge a person seeking initiation into the Midewiwin starts the string of invitations by offering tobacco to an individual to officiate at the ceremonies—generally a high degree mide who had officiated on another occasion. This leader would then pass tobacco to the other leaders who would assist, and those leaders in turn would each pass tobacco to an oshkaabewis to assist through the entire ceremony.[61] Missionary William T. Boutwell observed a Midewiwin feast organized in a similar fashion in 1835:

> the person/persons who gave the feast, never themselves partake of it. They prepare what they wish to give, and then call the chief or any other one to whom they please, to give it, and it is for them to invite as many or few, as they choose. In the feast above, the Chief was first called. He then called in 3 or 4. After they had ea[ch] taken their turn in beating the drum, and shaking the rattle, and pronouncing the benediction upon the persons who gave it, others were then called. And so it proceeded, suite after suite were called, until all the old medicine men were collected. Next the young men indiscriminately, were called. . . . Next the women were called, and all fed to the full.[62]

While it is difficult to say whether these examples mirror the process related to Densmore by her elderly informants at the turn of the century, they certainly do reflect a similar fluidity in Midewiwin leadership. Moreover the process of invitations via tobacco to bring together those needed to complete the ceremony reflects the process followed in forming war parties. In both cases charismatic leadership was temporary.

These leaders directed the order in which tasks took place and determined the selection of songs sung at various points during the initiation ceremony.[63] Yet historian Michael Angel suggests that given the importance of kinship among the Ojibwe, it is likely that a midewijig given tobacco to conduct Midewiwin ceremonies requested the assistance of gechi-midewijig with whom they had lineage ties.[64] An individual likely knew the abilities of kinfolk better than those of others in the community, contributing to this pattern. In fact, despite assertions of the nonhereditary nature of Midewiwin leadership, anthropologist Ruth Landes insinuated that Midewiwin offices often ran in bilateral family lines.[65] Reasons for this included the fact that the families of gechi-midewijig had increased access to goods via the gifts received from those seeking initiation, and the ability of the midewijig to have visions advising the initiation of their relatives. This may account for the consistent Midewiwin prominence in successive generations of some families among the hereditary ogimaag.

Gechi-midewijig also had important roles outside formal Midewiwin gatherings. According to Christopher Vecsey, "they maintained curing, upheld morality and combated Christianity while conserving aspects of traditional religion."[66] Furthermore, Vecsey has argued that "the Midewiwin provided the structure through which religious specialists could join together to make group decisions."[67] On at least one occasion the medewijig at Yellow Lake joined together in an attempt to prevent ABCFM missionaries from settling in their community. Frederick Ayer reported that in early December 1833, "the men who were heads of families had a few days previous to their arrival here, attended a medicine dance and feast, at which were about thirty-five men, who after much consultation and delivering speeches on the subject of our coming among them, agreed together that they would not send their children to school, or listen to God's book; they would retain their customs and habits."[68] Assuming that the medicine dance mentioned here was a Midewiwin gathering, it demonstrates that leaders did not restrict themselves to discussing esoteric theology at such ceremonies but also addressed issues of moral concern to the community as a whole. Further, these leaders, like the ABCFM missionaries, understood the offer of an American education to involve Christian conversion. On this occasion the gechi-midewijig acted much as the council of gichi-anishinaabeg. They met, discussed an issue of religious concern to the whole community, reached a consensus decision, and then chose a giigidowinini to deliver the decision.

The presence of Christian missionaries certainly came within the purview of their leadership as gechi-midewijig. Missionaries and their planned schools challenged the traditional teachings and values of the community. Moreover, since previous formal education had primarily operated within the context of Midewiwin society initiations, the missionaries and their school challenged Midewiwin leadership on a variety of levels. The Yellow Lake leaders went on to clarify their position to Ayer as follows: "If the Great Spirit had designed they should be instructed, they said, he would have had this word communicated to them before. The Great Spirit designed they should have a different religion and different customs from the whites."[69] Here the medewijig asserted to Ayer that as the religious leaders of the community, they would have received any new religious truths intended for the people of Yellow Lake and provided instruction in them. However, in keeping with Indigenous religious pluralism, they did not deny Ayer's beliefs but rather stated that Christianity was not what God intended for their people. Yet it is telling that they did not overtly ask the missionary to leave the community. It was the ogimaa, the civil authority, together with the gichi-anishinaabeg, who determined who could share community resources.

The topics of education and missionization might seem to fall logically under the purview of the gechi-midewijig, but other sources demonstrate how expansive their influence and interests might become. The following story recorded by Indian agent Henry Rowe Schoolcraft concerns how the Ojibwe first met Europeans. Through the power of his dream a medewid gained community approval for a trip that changed the economic and military future of his people:

A principal man of the Medawewin named Masewapega, dreamed a dream, in which he beheld spirits in the shape of men, but having white skins, and their heads were covered. They approached him with a smile on the face, and the hands extended. This dream he told to the principal men of his tribe in a council, and over a feast to his dream-spirit. He informed them that the spirits he had seen in his dream resided in the east, and that he would go and find them. For one year Masewapega prepared for his journey. . . . He saw another log hut, from the chimney of which arose a smoke. It was occupied by the white spirits of his dream, who came out and cordially welcomed him with a shake of the hand. When he returned to his people, he brought the presents he had received of an axe, a knife, beads, and some scarlet cloth, which he had carefully secured in his medicine-bag, and brought safely to Moningwanakauning. Collecting his people to council, he showed them the sacred presents of the white spirits. The next season, numbers followed Masewapega on his second visit to the whites. They carried with them many beaver skins, and returned with the fire-arms that from this time made them the terror of their enemies. From this time the dispersion of the tribe from Lapointe can be dated. The Indians say eight generations or "string of lives" ago, which, estimating an Indian generation by thirty-five years, would make 280 years ago.[70]

This story demonstrates a gechi-midewid seeking the consent and support of the community before embarking on the journey to fulfill his vision and, upon his return, sharing with the people in council the benefits his vision. While visions were usually personal, this one had impacts for the whole community and therefore required the consent of the gichi-anishinaabeg before it could be acted on. Likewise, there are a few examples in the historical record of individuals who sought community sanction for their visions.

John Tanner described two separate occasions when his village was summoned to listen to someone's vision that had ramifications for the entire community. Tanner's account contains few dates, but his narrative written in middle age was first published in 1830, so these events, which he witnessed as an adult with a family, likely took place in the 1810s or 1820s. In the first instance he recounts how a man named Manidoo-giizhig disappeared for a year and, when he returned, claimed to have visited the abode of the Gichi-Manidoo, who gave him instructions to share with the community. Manidoo-giizhig must previously have obtained the backing of the ogimaa and gichi-anishinaabeg for his visions, as the chiefs "built a great lodge and called all the men together to receive some information concerning the newly revealed will of the Great Spirit." The ogimaa Little Clam led the meeting, explaining why he had called it, singing, praying, and explaining the vision Manidoo-giizhig had received. In this example the ogimaa and gichi-anishinaabeg play a very clear role in sanctioning new religious ideas brought to the community, and the ogimaa himself, rather than the prophet, is the one who explains the vision. We know a little about what this vision entailed for the community as Tanner stated that the injunctions communicated to them were "of a kind to be permanently and valuably useful to them," including refraining from theft, fraud, and alcohol. Likely these were social concerns the ogimaa and gichi-anishinaabeg wished to see observed in any case, which quickly brought them to support Manidoo-giizhig. Tanner related that this vision resulted in "more orderly conduct" and "somewhat amended condition" of his village over the next two or three years.[71]

The second occasion Tanner related concerned a man called Ais-kaw-ba-wis, whom Tanner described as a poor hunter and whose children began to suffer from hunger following the death of his wife. Ais-kaw-ba-wis also called the gichi-anishinaabeg together, by which time Tanner was apparently counted among them as one of the most successful hunters in the village and gichi-anishinaabe of his own extended family household. Tanner related that Ais-kaw-ba-wis announced to the gichi-anishinaabeg that he had been favored by a new revelation from Gichi-Manidoo. He showed them a round ball of earth, about four or five inches in diameter, rolled smooth and smeared with red paint. This ball, he said, he received from Gichi-Manidoo, who took pity on him while he cried and sang and prayed in his lodge. Gichi-Manidoo told him: "I give you this ball, and as you see it is clean and new, I give it to you for your business to make the whole earth like it, even as it was when Nanabush first made it. All old things must be destroyed and done away; everything must be made anew and to your hands, Ais-kaw-ba-wis, I commit this great work." In the usual private conversations following the meeting, Tanner expressed that he did not believe these visions, although it seems apparent that many of the other gichi-anishinaabeg accepted the vision and followed the influence of Ais-kaw-ba-wis for some time. Tanner stated that he "hesitated not to ridicule his pretentions wherever I went" and subsequently suggested that Ais-kaw-ba-wis used his position to call frequent feasts to compensate for his poor abilities as a hunter. Nevertheless, Ais-kaw-ba-wis "gained a powerful ascendancy over the minds of the Indians," and Tanner found that all his "efforts in opposition to him were in vain." In fact, Ais-kaw-ba-wis eventually even turned Tanner's in-laws against him by accusing him of sorcery, and he forced Tanner to leave the community for some time.[72]

The mythical story of Masewapega as well as the historical accounts of Manidoo-giizhig and Ais-kaw-ba-wis all demonstrate that an individual who received a vision pertaining to the entire community could, after seeking the validation of the gichi-anishinaabeg, wield significant local influence. While Masewapega is identified as a "principal man of the Medawiwin," and therefore likely had some sway before meeting with the gichi-anishinaabeg, Tanner specifically notes that both Manidoo-giizhig and Ais-kaw-ba-wis were men who did not hold prominence in their communities until after they received religious authority. For these men—being poor hunters, not noted as warriors, and lacking descent from an important lineage—religion opened up the door to community distinction. If such men gained so much respect and influence from their religious authority, ogimaag must have become truly formidable when they bolstered their political position with the support of the manidoog.

Masewapega's acts as a gechi-midewid can be seen as the flipside of the coin to the actions of Eshkibagikoonzh fourth degree medewid and the ogimaa of Leech Lake. During his visit to Leech Lake in 1836–37, explorer and geologist Joseph Nicollet had the opportunity to observe an array of political actions as his presence inspired a new hope of a returned French "Father" to the political landscape. At one point Nicollet observed that the *madoodiswan,* or sweat lodge, used to cleanse, purify, and heal, is sometimes "practiced by a chief who has something to ask of his nation but who, deprived of some authority or power as chief, seeks the sponsorship of the medicinal rites to impose his views."[73] Hickerson concurred, expressing that "a chief who has something to ask of his nation and [has] no right to ask or demand it as chief, shelters himself under the rights of medicine to accomplish his object."[74] These observations suggest that ogimaag had a tradition of seeking Midewiwin support through such ceremonies. Nicollet elaborated on this point: "First of all he [the ogimaa] invites four mide for a steam bath. He expresses his views to them, and they in turn, guided by the chief's recommendations invite scores of others. They dispatch the oshkabewis all over the land, bearing small sticks, a foot long, painted in different colors. One is delivered to each person invited and a date is set."[75] Interestingly, the sticks intended for individuals who must decline the invitation but who consent to the sender's actions are returned to the sender; they are brought out during the ceremony and stuck in the ground, both to "bear witness to the fact that the absent ones were invited" and to signify the "consent of those for whom they had been intended."[76] Those able to attend came, listened to the proposal of the ogimaa in a sweat lodge, and then deliberated upon the proposition among themselves. On this occasion Eshkibagikoonzh must have received a positive answer to his request, as he left following a week of such ceremonies to go to the English trading posts in Canada in hope of getting ammunition and other aid.[77] It should not be assumed, however, that just because an ogimaa sought the support of the gechi-midewijig, he always obtained it.

Where Eshkibagikoonzh displayed his Midewiwin credentials to encourage the senior members of the society to support a political decision to seek British aid, Masewapega sought the sanction of the gichi-anishinaabeg before pursuing a spiritual act, his vision. For the Ojibwe, distinction between these two kinds of actions may at times be very small. We do not know what Eshkibagikoonzh said to the assembled medewijig, but it is possible that like Masewapega, Ais-kaw-ba-wis, and Manidoo-giizhig, he announced that the course of action he proposed had come to him in a dream, in order to give it more validity. While the impetus to go and meet Europeans came to Masewapega in a dream, taking action on that dream clearly had political consequences. Sociopolitical authority and religious authority in Ojibwe society had overlapping borders, blended, and became inseparable.

As with war leadership, hereditary ogimaag also could serve as Midewiwin leaders, but such a dual role was not expected of them. James Smith noted that while ogimaag were normally members of the Midewiwin, they were "not necessarily the senior members of the society nor the organizers of the seasonal rituals."[78] Midewiwin leaders seldom appear in the written records generated by non-natives because Midewiwin leaders were concerned primarily with internal affairs that did not draw the attention of fur traders or government officials.[79] However, the few references we have are telling. Baraga stated that those medewijig considered "more or less skillful" in the ceremonies of the people were not considered chiefs and did not exercise any of the chief's functions in councils, particularly those councils concerned with land cessions.[80]

This statement does not take into account, however, the large number of individuals who were lower degree medewijig. This would have included many if not all gichi-anishinaabeg and ogimaag, given the necessity that they be able to perform the ceremonies to call the game. These individuals, while perhaps active in the Midewiwin, would have been less noticeable to European observers, who likely perceived only those officiating in the rituals as religious leaders. This, combined with the Western bias assuming a distinction between political and religious leaders, masked from European eyes the dual roles many influential Anishinaabeg men held. Since many European observers were only temporary visitors to Ojibwe communities, unless they arrived at the appropriate time of year to witness Midewiwin ceremonies, they assumed that those with whom they negotiated political concerns did not also hold religious responsibilities. Even missionaries such as Baraga missed this important link between religious and political power. Yet when discussing the Midewiwin directly, Baraga does admit that as the Midewiwin is the religion of the Ojibwe people, all community members are connected to it.[81]

However, the ogimaag and gichi-anishinaabeg, expected to ensure the well-being of their families and community, were particularly responsible for mino-bimaadiziwin. Humans needed strong connections with the manidoog to make successful decisions, an issue even more important to leaders making decisions for the whole village. In fact, if we look again at the definition of *gichi-anishinaabeg*, this term can be variously interpreted as "great man" or "old man."[82] Anthropologist John A. Grim related that at least in Minnesota and Ontario, "to say 'old man' was synonymous with saying 'great shaman of Midewiwin.'"[83] Certainly the expectation that one needed spiritual power to achieve long life implied that all those who reached advanced age must be powerful. Further, the chances that someone who reached advanced age had been initiated into at minimum the first degree of the society for healing purposes would be quite high.

European and Anglo American officials separated the topics of discussion they brought to Ojibwe communities. Political affairs, especially involving land, dominated their meetings with community leadership. Land and its resources were the responsibility of the hereditary ogimaa in consultation with the gichi-anishinaabeg and young men and the women of the community, and as a result the ogimaag dominated discussions with these outsiders. This situation likely made many observers less attuned to those issues in which the religious leadership was consulted more formally. Councils called within Ojibwe communities for their own purposes likely addressed multiple issues before the community, which might vacillate between what Westerners would define as sacred and secular concerns. Indeed, Giacomo Beltrami, an Italian visitor to northern Minnesota in the mid-1820s, related that a gathering of "all the principal men of the tribe" constituted a "grand conclave or council of Medicine."[84] Therefore the weight of medewijig input in a variety of councils within the community has likely been underrepresented in previous scholarship. At the very least, the medewijig had an important role as they ritually purified the meeting place at the beginning of all councils to keep negative forces out of the deliberations.[85] Councils always opened in a sacred manner as they began with smoking the pipe, an act Europeans saw more as a custom than as a religious ritual ensuring a good outcome.

Anglo American misinterpretation of the importance of the pipe to all councils is part of a larger problem with their observations. Contemporary European and American observers, particularly those not fluent in the Ojibwe language, did not always identify accurately the kinds of councils they saw. Government officials were more interested in trying to co-opt a generalized leadership through bestowing medals on individuals with whom they negotiated than in trying to understand the actual modus operandi of the Anishinaabeg system. Similarly, missionaries took no pains to learn the structures of Anishinaabeg religious leadership. Both government officials and missionaries expected an eventual if not rapid assimilation of Anishinaabeg people into American society, which would involve eliminating both traditional Anishinaabeg leadership and religious practices.

Another reason that Western observers may have misinterpreted what kind of council gathering they observed was that many of the structures supporting ogimaag, gechi-midewijig, and mayosewininiwag were virtually indistinguishable. This complicates further the context of community decisions recorded in historical sources. All of these leaders could designate an oshkaabewis, whose duties included inviting other leaders to council, generally by passing out invitation sticks and, once the guests assembled, assisting with the opening tobacco and pipe ceremonies required to ensure manidoog guidance for their decision making. Most formal meetings, including those that involved dances and feasts (which outsiders dismissed as "entertainment") had purposes other than social interaction. Mayosewininiwag, ogimaag, and gechi-midewijig all issued "invitations to smoke" before turning to address whatever pressing issue brought the council together.[86] Such gatherings discussed issues of war and peace, recruited supporters for a particular plan, celebrated a naming feast or funeral banquet, or obtained the assistance of a great jaasakiid or *jiisakiiwinini*, a ritual specialist who held the distinctive shaking tent ceremonies that brought manidoog to the community to answer specific questions.[87]

A number of leaders whose reputation and influence extended beyond their local bands were known Midewiwin members. In some cases they possessed particularly strong spiritual powers or were even specialist practitioners in certain methods of healing. General statements of such power are numerous in the literature. One was made to William Johnston at Leech Lake in 1833. Ojibwes assured the young fur trader that despite the stormy character of Leech Lake, "our head chiefs, when they wish to cross it, find it always smooth."[88] Similarly, the Berens River ogimaa Yellow Legs, who died around 1830, was said to be able to walk on water when going to an island in Lake Winnipeg to procure medicines.[89] There are also many examples of war leaders calling on manidoog aid for their war parties, as discussed in the previous chapter, including acts of divination, calling of fog, wind, or rain, and effects that would render the war party silent.[90]

The records of the period contain many specific examples of ogimaag who also held important religious offices and possessed remarkable spiritual powers. For example, Broken Tooth, ogimaa of the Sandy Lake band, was also a jiisakiiwinini.[91] While his Midewiwin status is not clear in the available records, jiisakiiwininiwag were often though not always Midewiwin members. Broken Tooth was said to have revived his wife from a near death condition with his breath.[92] This is an act similar to part of the Midewiwin initiation ritual in which initiates "die" and then receive new life.[93]

Contemporaries at Fond du Lac, where Broken Tooth's son Loon's Foot married the daughter of the Fond du Lac ogimaa Zhingob (Balsam), also described Loon's Foot as a senior practitioner of the Midewiwin society and a jiisakiiwinini.[94] Pierre Cotte, the fur trader at Fond du Lac, related that he had witnessed a Midewiwin ceremony where Maangozid shot with a musket another gechi-midewid, who was then revived by the power of the lodge rituals without exhibiting any sign of a wound.[95] Even after Loon's Foot converted to Christianity, due to his extensive Midewiwin knowledge he was still entreated by the Midewiwin members at Fond du Lac to provide instruction to the men who would lead upcoming Midewiwin ceremonies, much to the ire of the local missionary.[96] Loon's Foot's grandfather, the hereditary ogimaa Biauswah II of Sandy Lake, also performed the duties of a jiisakiiwinini. That the grandfather, father, and son all performed jiisakiiwinini ceremonies is strong evidence that such specialized knowledge and power often passed within families from generation to generation.[97]

Other influential families also demonstrate this pattern. Yellow Hair of Leech Lake, his son Flat Mouth or Eshkibagikoonzh, and grandson Flat Mouth II or Niigaani-binesi also served multiple roles as hereditary ogimaag, mayosewininiwag, and high degree Midewiwin.[98] Yellow Hair may have been first of their family to hold the role of ogimaa as sources suggest that he used his reputation as a man with "supreme knowledge of medicine, especially such as destroyed life" to launch himself into political ascendancy.[99] Apparently his enemies conveniently died of no known cause when they got in his way.[100] Eshkibagikoonzh was known for his Midewiwin skills, not to mention some reforms he brought to the initiation process, requiring the initiate to have two sponsors instead of just one.[101] Such reforms could not have been accomplished were he not a high-ranking individual in the Midewiwin society. His position within the Midewiwin may also have brought him to the notice of the Leech Lake ogimaag Daybashah, who adopted Eshkibagikoonzh as his heir.[102] Niigaani-binesi eventually attained the fourth degree in the Midewiwin society.[103] Nicollet witnessed an initiation of his sister Ruth, although he does not note to what degree.[104]

At La Pointe, Waabojiig was Buffalo's uncle, and both served their communities as mayosewininiwag, ogimaag, and gechimidewijig, demonstrating that the ogimaag authority could also pass from uncle to nephew within the patrilineal line. Buffalo is mentioned several times in missionary papers as presiding at funerals in addition to his prominent political role.[105] He also led a Midewiwin initiation for a sick girl reported by missionary William Boutwell in 1832. After describing the dress, dancing, and medicine sacs of the participants, Boutwell noted that "the old chief Bizhiki [Buffalo] made a sort of address, invoking as I suppose the spirit in behalf of a sick child."[106]

Kohl and Schoolcraft both described Zhingwaakoons, or Little Pine, of Sault Ste. Marie as a hereditary ogimaa, gechi-midewid, jiisakiiwinini, mayosewinini, and orator.[107] Kohl elaborated on the religious abilities of Zhingwaakoons, remarking that he had had strong dreams in his tenth year, leading him to become "a great medicine-man," and that "he also had a number of birch-bark written songs and traditions," a hallmark of gechimidewijig.[108]

While it is difficult to determine what rank various ogimaag held in the Midewiwin, what the documents do make clear is that communities recognized persons with special connections to manidoog power, whether through the Midewiwin society or as specialist practitioners like the jiisakiiwinini, as persons with a distinctive authority. As anthropologist John Grim has observed, the special status Ojibwe communities accorded to religious practitioners stemmed from "personal experience of the highest value in the Ojibway world, namely, contact with the numinous regions."[109] Such connections with manidoog power were very valuable possessions, and the stronger such connections were, the more they were worth, and the more esteem they were accorded. The active pursuit of those avenues of communication that transmitted manidoog power, open to any member of the community, provided an important charismatic avenue to social position and power. As Grim described it, "The aggressive pursuit of spirit power may bring the shaman some financial success and political influence, but even more important is the social status given to one who communes with the manitou."[110]

Despite the inherent temptations and dangers of seeking enhanced connections to manidoog power, many chose this route to improve social status and authority. The Ojibwe not only encouraged but also expected such ambitions on a moderate level, since no one could survive without manidoog help to make crops grow, to call game, to protect oneself from enemies, and to heal the sick. Indeed fasting to secure such assistance was a basic passage into adulthood. Even if the Midewiwin did not offer a consistently successful route to political leadership, it did expand the influence of hereditary ogimaag, both those who attained high degrees in the society and those whose membership was less prominently displayed.[111]

The interband integrative functions of the Midewiwin also increased political cooperation among bands and enhanced the reputation of those leaders who officiated at these interband events.[112] Just as opportunities to lead war parties democratized access to prestige and authority, so the Midewiwin also set up a procedure by which power, otherwise attainable only through heredity or physical prowess, could be redistributed throughout the community. This important source of charismatic authority offered opportunity on a broad democratic basis to all within Ojibwe society. It was also a means hereditary leaders consistently accessed to expand their influence or at least hold their own against religious practitioners within their communities who tested the bounds of their authority.

That many hereditary ogimaag chose to bolster their authority through the pursuit of additional connections to manidoog power also deepens our understanding of the nature of chiefly conversion to Christianity. Creating alliances with other sources of religious power helped to stabilize and expand an individual's authority. Therefore, as the new religious tradition of Christianity expanded into Anishinaabeg communities, some Anishinaabeg leaders sought to join the church and use its authority in a similar manner. As Zeisberger, a Moravian missionary, wrote concerning the Delawares, "Indeed many of the headmen and chiefs had tried to join the church seeking to become masters of it."[113]

Ogimaag, who had their hereditary authority to fall back on ultimately, felt less threatened by Christianity since it did not initially challenge the primary foundation of their power. Rather their concern was for the United States to continue to recognize their status as hereditary leaders, which conversion could facilitate. Those leaders whose sociopolitical rank depended entirely upon their prestige as religious leaders of Indigenous traditions resisted Christian influence much more strongly and attempted to prevent fellow community members from joining the Christian faction and leaving their own.[114] As Laura Peers has noted, "Midewiwin leaders were the most vocal opponents of conversion, and they took the brunt of missionary attacks on 'heathenism.'"[115]

This divergent meaning of religious conflict and conversion within Ojibwe communities meant that the choice between

Midewiwin and Christianity opened up a new field for the contestation of chiefly authority as it came under increasing stress in the face of American expansion and the failure of the fur trade. The expansion of foundations for claims to religious authority allowed potential successors to the hereditary ogimaag at Fond du Lac to argue their case for authority more persuasively before the community. A number of leading men shifted back and forth between Midewiwin and Christian practice, testing the new Christian manidoog and whether their ties to this new power translated into community authority. Yet the introduction of Christianity at the time when pressures increased to cease warfare and Indigenous traditions made this new tradition appear more attractive to ogimaag seeking to expand their influence or at least to maintain it in the face of increasing American pressures to assimilate. If the community joined them in the new religious rites, their authority could continue into a new era.

5

The Contest for Chiefly
Authority at Fond du Lac

A person who is an expert hunter, one who knows the communications between lakes and rivers, can make long harangues, is a conjurer and has a family of his own; such a man will not fail of being followed by several Indians.—**Andrew Graham**

Anishinaabeg ogimaag did not claim coercive power, but they held important roles in mediating conflicts over the use of community resources, including fisheries, hunting grounds, maple sugar stands, and garden plots. European American fur traders and military officials had learned that when they wished to build in Native communities, they should make formal requests to the chief and council and present appropriate gifts on an annual basis. Although the traders and military officials seem not to have made the connection, these gifts created and maintained fictive kinship ties necessary for neighbors to coexist peacefully. Native people also considered these gifts to be compensation for the resources given up for the location of buildings and the support of the foreigners who inhabited them. When these or other outsiders refused to seek permission, present gifts, or share their food in times of need, the Anishinaabeg considered it a grave insult. Missionaries in particular often neglected to participate in appropriate gift exchange, largely because their cultural context and sense of mission discouraged an understanding of Anishinaabeg cultural norms.

The first mission society to have a long-term presence in the western Great Lakes after the departure of the Jesuits in 1763

o

Records Commerce

Mountains

Elm
Birch
Maple &c

□ stable   Ely's   School H.
□ mission □ House

A.F.T
fort
□ □ □
□ □ □ □
□ □ □

δ o

△△△△△△ △△ △
Ind. Vill.

N

Ind. Gardens

Prairie

Mission Prairie

Hills

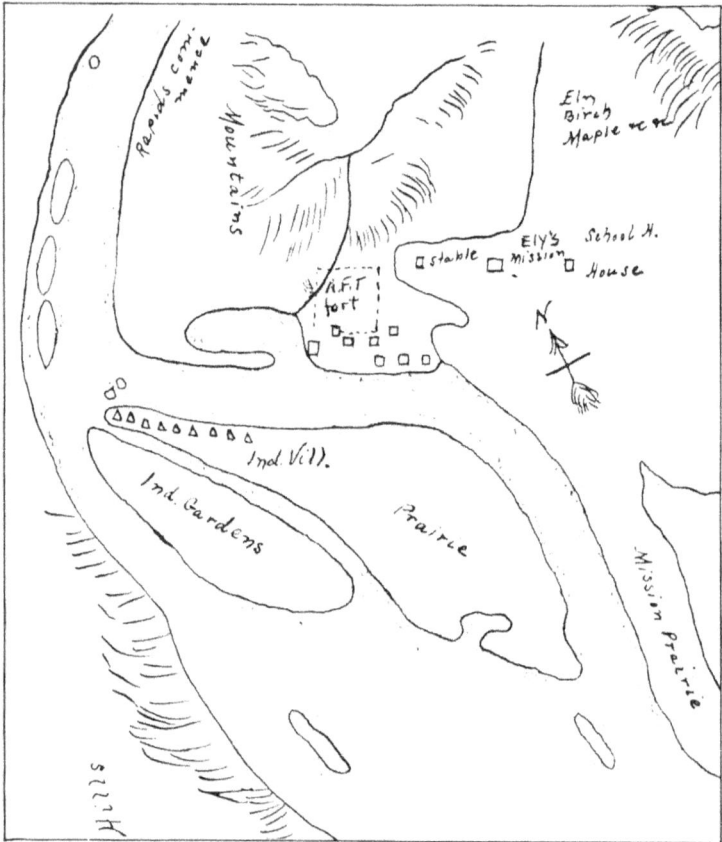

Fond du Lac Indian community, 1837. Used by permission of the Northeast Minnesota Historical Center, Duluth MN, s3045b3f4 Edmund F. Ely Papers.

was the American Board of Commissioners for Foreign Missions (ABCFM). Founded in 1810, the ABCFM incorporated two years later. Based on the benevolent and charitable societies appearing on the East Coast in the wake of the Second Great Awakening and inspired by the thrilling stories of British missionary work in India, the American Board "represented a new phase of organizing activity" as it "sought to join clergy and public in a religious crusade of global proportions." The founders believed that involvement in mission activities, whether as actual missionaries or through donations, promised to revitalize Christian religion and spread it to those who lived in ignorance of Christianity. The actual birth of the ABCFM took place at the Andover Theological Seminary, where a group of zealous young student evangelicals formed a secret society called the Society of Inquiry on the Subject of Foreign Missions. They carefully screened prospective initiates, took meeting notes in code, and laid surreptitious plans for promoting missions to the "heathen." After news of their association leaked out in the pages of the *Panoplist*, an evangelical periodical, the group publicly organized, and the *Panoplist*, later the *Missionary Herald*, tantalized its readers with missionary exploits in an effort to encourage other young people to join the cause or donate resources for its support.[1]

While scholars William McLoughlin and Clara Sue Kidwell have examined the ABCFM's missionary work among southeastern tribes, historians have paid less attention to their work among Ojibwe peoples, perhaps because the *Panoplist* had little to celebrate in relation to these ABCFM efforts.[2] Many Ojibwe communities forced ABCFM personnel out after only a brief stay. For example, the station at Sandy Lake, Minnesota, operated for only two years (1833–34), and that at Yellow Lake, Wisconsin, for three (1833–36).[3] On the other hand, the mission at La Point and Bad River, Wisconsin, had a longer life.[4] Founded in 1833, mission operations remained open until 1870.[5] These missions ran schools that were coeducational, with roughly equal numbers of male and female students, and provided instruction in the Ojibwe language.[6] Furthermore, the ABCFM put a great deal of effort into these missions, as indicated by their publication of no less than fourteen texts in the Ojibwe language between 1835 and 1847.[7]

In her path-breaking work *To Be the Main Leaders of Our*

People, Rebecca Kugel described the utter failure of ABCFM personnel to attain their objectives among the Minnesota Ojibwe in the early nineteenth century. Unlike the Episcopalians who came after them, the missionaries of the ABCFM refused to respect the basic patterns of reciprocity that the Anishinaabeg regarded as essential to establishing social, political, and economic alliance between neighbors. Despite their desire to attain technological aid and basic education from the missionaries, the Ojibwe leaders, frustrated with the perceived greedy and antisocial behavior of the churchmen, which included applying corporal punishments to unruly school children, drove the ABCFM personnel from their communities. They had tolerated these rude outsiders long past point of politeness solely out of fear of their spiritual power and the "bad medicine" they could therefore inflict.[8] In contrast, the Minnesota Ojibwe communities generally accepted the Episcopalian missionaries, who complied with the rules of reciprocity largely through the guidance of Enami'egaabaw, a Canadian-born Ojibwe minister. According to Kugel, the Ojibwe civil chiefs considered the Episcopalian missionaries to be potent political allies against their traditional opponents, the war chiefs, whom fur trade factors backed. Furthermore, the Episcopal Church assisted the Ojibwe in pressing the federal government for overdue supplies and treaty payments.[9] Episcopal Bishop Henry Benjamin Whipple, a staunch advocate of assimilation, himself on occasion lobbied in the halls of Congress on behalf of Ojibwe leaders.[10]

Kugel's dichotomy, however, may not be universally applicable in Ojibwe country. Because her primary interest is the power and agency that political factionalism created among the Minnesota Ojibwe, she addressed only the ABCFM missions in Minnesota, neglecting the successful missions at La Pointe and Bad River, Wisconsin, which endured for decades. Moreover, the animosity between fur traders and missionaries that she described does not account for support from American Fur Company trade factors who requested ABCFM missions and schools in Ojibwe country. Indeed, missionary William T. Boutwell was on such friendly terms with the factors of the American Fur Company that he married Hester Crooks, metis daughter of Ramsay Crooks, president of the AFC, and named one of his sons Lyman Warren Boutwell after the La Pointe factor who first petitioned the ABCFM to send missionaries to the Lake Superior region.[11]

By the early nineteenth century the personnel of the fur trade were separated into two groups based on class, ethnicity, and religion. The American Fur Company formed in 1821 sent Anglo American supervisors to manage a fur trade that had largely remained intact at the ground level since its inception in the seventeenth century. Its organizational and managerial control had shifted in the recent past, passing from the French to the British in the 1760s and then from the British to the Americans in the early nineteenth century. After the Americans obtained possession of the western Great Lakes region in the decade following the War of 1812, New England Protestants, some of whom were affected by the Second Great Awakening, came to manage a business operated at the local level largely by persons of Catholic, French, and often Indian descent.

ABCFM missionaries provided the children of American Fur Company management with the education necessary to enter the upper echelons of the trade and with a moral value system meant to be identical to the one their parents had imbibed in New England. As for the Ojibwe, the missionaries came not to trade with them and fit into their society but to change them. Missionaries, therefore, presented a new kind of challenge to local hereditary and charismatic authority in Ojibwe communities. Regardless of their understanding or ignorance of Anishinaabeg customs, missionaries refused to respect or abide by social obligations that derived from the cultural practices they sought to change. As a result their actions often became lightning rods for factional conflicts pertaining to Ojibwe relations with the American government. On one occasion that occurred in 1836 and 1837, mission actions became the locus of a contest between Nindipens and Maangozid for succession of hereditary ogimaag authority in the Ojibwe community at Fond du Lac. On one level, the dispute centered on the failure of ABCFM minister Edmund F. Ely to obtain community permission for building a house at Fond du Lac. On another level, however, the conflict reflected tensions between hereditary and charismatic authority that the increased American presence in the region exacerbated.

Both Nindipens and Maangozid legitimately claimed authority as ogimaag. The most fundamental grounds for Ojibwe chieftainship in nearly all cases was patrilineal descent from a chiefly lineage. Maangozid descended from an ancient line of chiefs going back over a century and regarded as one of his prized possessions a birch bark scroll that recorded his august family tree.[12] His family also demonstrated charismatic authority through specialized contact with the manidoog, which they likewise passed down through the family. Maangozid, like his forefathers and brothers, not only participated as a member and leader in the Midewiwin society but also received the spiritual power and training of a jaasakiid.[13] His lineage, however, had not supplied the chiefs of the Fond du Lac community. Although his father was the influential ogimaa and jaasakiid Broken Tooth, he led the Ojibwe village at Sandy Lake and had no claims to Fond du Lac. Unfortunately, Maangozid had several brothers whose claims on offices at Sandy Lake took precedence over his own.[14] But marriage ties also linked the most influential families of the various Anishinaabeg communities to one another, strengthening the alliances and mutual obligations of ogimaag. Seeking another avenue for his ambitions, Maangozid made such a marriage with Wemitigoozhiikwe, the daughter of Zhingob, ogimaa of Fond du Lac, and his only child at the time.[15]

Following marriage, an Ojibwe husband customarily lived

with his wife's family for a year, during which time all of the products of his labor, primarily hunting, went to his wife's family.[16] In cases where a father had no male heirs and approved of his son-in-law, he gave the son-in-law lavish gifts at the end of the year and asked the younger man to stay with the family to provide for him and his wife in old age. The father-in-law also often offered the young man additional daughters in marriage and the inheritance of his hunting territories.[17] Maangozid probably received such an offer when he contracted his marriage to Wemitigoozhiikwe. Zhingob exercised unquestioned leadership of the village, and Maangozid's marriage to his daughter brought the young man political privileges. United States expeditions in the 1820s and 1830s mentioned Maangozid as a prominent member of the Fond du Lac community, and in 1820 Governor Lewis Cass awarded him medals, a symbol of United States approval of him.[18] He often seemed to function as a lesser chief of the tribe, and some evidence suggests that Zhingob designated Maangozid as his giigidowinini.[19] In this role Maangozid had little authority to make or mediate decisions, but he announced the final decisions of the ogimaa and council to other interested parties and spoke for the ogimaa in council as directed. Even more important, Maangozid was a gechi-midewid, a position that gave him a special claim on power in a society such as the Ojibwe that did not distinguish between temporal and spiritual, political and religious.

By lineage, spiritual authority, marriage, and office, Maangozid confidently expected to succeed Zhingob as the community's ogimaag upon his father-in-law's death. However, late in life, Zhingob exercised his chiefly privilege to take a second wife, and she gave birth to a son, Nindipens. At the time of Zhingob's death in 1835, Nindipens had only barely reached adulthood and apparently had not yet served in any official capacity.[20] Observers mentioned Nindipens only as kindly tending his father during Zhingob's final illness. The conflict with Reverend Edmund

Ely six months after his father's death marked Nindipens's entry into public life.[21] Maangozid had assumed that his heredity, marriage, experience, and age entitled him to the position of ogimaa at Fond du Lac, and as will become evident, at least a portion of the Fond du Lac community supported his claim.

The rival claims of two brothers-in-law set the stage for conflict, which erupted over Rev. Ely's building project. While personal ambitions, conceptions of legitimate authority, and other issues precipitated the conflict, the broader historical context raised the stakes. The conflict took place amid mounting United States pressure for land cessions that culminated in the July 1837 treaty conference at St. Peters, where the Ojibwe succumbed to American pressure and made a major land cession. News of the impending conference was circulating in 1836 when Ely began his unauthorized building project, and the news heightened Ojibwe anxiety over land and land use. Maangozid, who received his first U.S. chief's medal from territorial governor Lewis Cass in 1820, had a long history of friendly relations with American officials, but in the 1830s many Anishinaabeg began to raise questions about American reliability as allies. Criticism of the United States left Maangozid vulnerable as community opinion shifted away from this alliance. Despite his youth and inexperience, Nindipens astutely chose the right issue at the right time to stake his claim.

Edmund F. Ely had opened his mission station at Fond du Lac in 1834. Although at first Ely intended to return to the station he had operated the previous year at Yellow Lake, circumstances altered his plans. When he arrived at Fond du Lac, a letter awaited him from his patron William Aitkin, regional manager of the American Fur Company, warning him not to continue into the interior that year. High waters had created a severe shortage of wild rice, on which traders and missionaries as well as Native people were dependent for winter food.[22] Aitkin advised Ely to remain at Fond du Lac on the shore of Lake Superior, where access to fish offset the scarcity of rice. Adjusting to the sudden change in plans, Ely made arrangements to set up a mission station at Fond du Lac. He took bed and board with the family of William Aitkin's son Alfred, while the post manager, Pierre Cotte, offered to build him a one-room schoolhouse.[23] The generosity of these intermediaries meant that Ely did not initially have to negotiate directly with the Ojibwe for food, shelter, or land for the mission. These circumstances also left Ely oblivious to the protocol of securing such privileges, since the seasoned fur traders had conducted negotiations with and presented gifts to the Native community on his behalf. Soon he moved out of Alfred Aitkin's household and began to sleep as well as teach in his schoolhouse.

The following summer of 1835, Edmund Ely married Catharine (Goulais) Bissell, a Métis graduate of the ABCFM boarding school on Mackinaw Island at La Pointe. For a time the newlyweds continued their residence in the schoolhouse. In anticipation of having children, Ely decided to build separate living quarters so that they could move out of the schoolhouse. In December 1835 Ely wrote to David Greene, who oversaw the missionary activities of the ABCFM:

About two hours since I received letters from Boutwell [ABCFM missionary at Leech Lake], I had written him concerning building. He advises me to put up a log building large enough for our convenience and use our present building for a schoolroom. . . . We cannot contract with the [American Fur] company to build for want of men. I think therefore of going to Le Pointe, after the Sabbath, to see Hall [ABCFM missionary at Le Pointe] and if possible to get a man for the year and proceed directly to getting out and hauling timber for the house, while the snow is yet on the ground. If we get a man I think we can get a building ready in the month of April. Shall calculate to leave my school in the hands of Peter and Mrs. Ely.[24]

Ely carefully considered a site for his house on land that the Native community did not use for gardening or sugar bush, and he consulted with Aitkin, who also planned an expansion that forced Ely to settle for his second choice of locations.[25]

Ely's building plans, therefore, were neither casual nor careless: he conferred both with his fellow missionaries and with his fur trade patron, and he selected land that to his eyes was not in use. Despite all these considerations, however, it never occurred to Ely to consult the local Indian community concerning his building project. After all, he received his funding from the ABCFM, and he thought he resided at Fond du Lac at the pleasure of the American Fur Company. Furthermore, he no doubt subscribed to one of the central tenets of United States Indian policy: that Native peoples had only the right of occupancy and not absolute ownership of the land. Nevertheless, the local Native community claimed sovereignty over undeveloped as well as improved land, a right that the rival ogimaag asserted vigorously in the following months.

In some situations Ely's omission might have drawn less criticism. However Ely consistently violated community norms. His stinginess with gifts was already notorious. Ely felt that giving gifts to members of the community ran counter to the civilizing project he had embarked upon because, so he believed, it encouraged laziness and profligacy rather than industry and thrift. Most egregiously, however, he married outside the village and failed to forge a genuine kinship bond that would have brought him into the exchange network of the local village and enmeshed him within its various reciprocal relationships. Instead he lived alongside the local village, used its resources, and taught their children impractical skills when they could have been contributing to their families' subsistence.

Up to this point, despite Ely's selfishness, the community had largely left him alone. Zhingob's illness and Nindipens's youth at the time of Ely's arrival certainly contributed to this oversight.

However, people also needed time to assess Ely's relationship to the other social, political, and economic elements of the community. Indian agent Henry Rowe Schoolcraft had introduced one of the first ABCFM missionaries, William T. Boutwell, to Ojibwe communities, during his diplomatic tour in the summer of 1832.[26] Schoolcraft had specifically asked the ogimaag to allow the missionaries to visit and reside in their villages. Consequently, the Fond du Lac community told Ely on at least one occasion that they understood the missionaries to be subagents of the government and beholden to the Indian agent. Nindipens visited Ely with Eninabondo, who often served as mayosewinini, and a second man, Badabi, and Ely reported that they asked him, among other things, "if we were not entrusted with some secret of the President, which we were to keep from the Indians."[27] The visiting Ojibwes told Ely, "If we staid among them, we must help them—advise and council with them."[28] Yet the fur traders also supported the missionaries, and for a time the missionaries lived in their homes. Also, like the fur traders, the missionaries hired members of the local community to labor for them and traded goods for food with community members. As a result the missionaries also seemed to have alliances with the fur traders. Finally, the missionaries claimed spiritual authority like the Catholic missionaries of old, but these new men of God were both stingier and marriageable.

The relationships among the foreigners had never been firm. French missionaries of previous eras had promoted French political goals, and both French and English officials sometimes claimed or demonstrated supernatural authority. Traders acted, at times, in political, religious, and economic spheres. For example, at Fond du Lac William Aitkin appointed Pierre Cotte, a devout French Catholic, as local manager of the post. In the absence of Catholic missionaries and later, when the single itinerant Catholic missionary for the region was elsewhere, Cotte and his wife officiated at funerals, baptisms, and other ceremonies for the Catholic, or nominally Catholic, portion of the Fond du Lac community. The very permeability of social, political, and religious boundaries meant that new arrivals received careful and meticulous assessment, especially those overtly claiming the spiritual authority so necessary for survival.

If Ely's marriage and general selfishness troubled the community, his arbitrary decision to build wherever he liked using not only the community's land but also its timber and other resources caused far greater concern. In February 1836, Ely instructed Brabant, a man he had hired at La Pointe, to commence cutting and hauling timber for the house.[29] While Brabant had worked for Ely since their return from La Pointe several months earlier, up to this time he had conducted repairs on Ely's existing building.[30]

The day after Brabant began work on the new house, Nindipens visited the building site and asked Brabant about his latest project. Brabant replied that he was building a house for Ely. Nindipens then addressed Ely, reprimanding the missionary for failure to discuss the new building with him. Nindipens based his assertion of authority over the community's timber and land resources on Zhingob's deathbed pronouncement that anyone who wanted to build at Fond du Lac needed Nindipens's permission.[31] Rather than admit that he had committed a serious offense and seek permission of the village for the building, Ely could barely hold in check his anger at what he regarded as "this show of authority." But instead of scolding the headman as he wished to do, he permitted Peter, his first convert in the community, to speak on his behalf. Peter informed Nindipens that he "ought to hold his peace about this—that in other lands people had their children instructed at great expense, but we had come here to instruct the people w/out charge, & they ought to feel thankful." Peter's words no doubt reflected Ely's feelings, but the missionary did not understand the nature of Ojibwe political society or that his own position in the community was very tenuous.

Ely's obliviousness to his situation precipitated a debate among the Ojibwe at Fond du Lac that had far-reaching ramifications. Many people focused on the fact that Ely was not kin: he had neither married into the community nor offered gifts sufficient to be accepted as fictive kin. The community had little need for Ely's gifts of salvation and civilization because they did not fill empty bellies or protect people from their enemies. Worst of all, Ely and his wife pushed these "gifts" on the villagers in a coercive style abhorrent to the community. At the same time, other community members had no particular objections to the missionary, and they were reluctant to follow the lead of someone as young and inexperienced as Nindipens. The far more experienced Maangozid had always supported United States personnel in the Fond du Lac region, and from the first he approved of the missionary's residence at Fond du Lac. Soon after Ely's arrival in 1834, Maangozid had sent two of his sons to attend Ely's fledgling school.[32]

The day after Nindipens's visit, Gandanonib—Maangozid's son and Nindipens's nephew—invited Ely and Brabant to his lodge. He told them not to listen to Nindipens: "For my part I am very glad you are building. If he says anything more to you, I myself will go to his lodge and speak to him on the subject— he does not own this land more than we. We are many and he is alone and if he says anything there will be more who hear us than him."[33] Gandanonib thereby asserted his family's chiefly claim to grant land use privileges within the community. With the death of Zhingob, Gandanonib asserted that his father Maangozid was the only "medal chief" in the community. Medal chiefs were those prominent men who had received a medal from an allied colonial power, in this case the United States. As such they often represented attempts by these external nations to appoint leaders within various communities. Further, although he did not reveal this to Ely, Gandanonib's mother was Nindipens's sister. Gandanonib could lay a claim to the resources of the local community equal to that of Nindipens—perhaps more so, for he descended from chiefly lineages on both sides. But if Gandanonib expected the community to uphold his family's chiefly claims over those of Nindipens, his meeting with Nindipens and the other headmen was disappointing.

On February 26, 1836, Nindipens, Gandanonib, Inini, and Miskwaa-giizhig came to visit Ely.[34] Ely called Isabella, Cotte's daughter-in-law, to interpret. She had been educated at the ABCFM boarding school in Sault Ste. Marie, so she was not only bilingual but also was a full member of Ely's church.[35] Nindipens addressed the assembled group: "I came in to hear what you had to say—Perhaps if I should speak, the Indians would not hear me. . . . I know my heart is bad and perhaps I shall say something wrong. . . I felt bad when I heard that you laughed at me—when I came the other day."[36] Nindipens was acknowledging that he had committed a faux pas: he had not called a meeting with the headmen of the village to discuss what should be done about Ely's transgression before he directly challenged the missionary over the issue. Nindipens freely admitted to his anger, a flaw that impeded his ability to press for his chiefly rights. But he was unwilling to surrender the point:

> You ought to have asked permission of me before you began to build. This land is mine. All the land which you see around here, & all which my father has trod is mine. He gave it to me before he died. All the trees are mine also. . . . The traders have always asked permission of me, even when my father was alive & have given me something for it. . . . It is true I am not the Chief. The governor did not make me so. I have not a medal—as you see—but my Father was a chief—& I own this land. I know of no one who owned this land, but my Grandfather—& my father gave it to me.[37]

This was the heart of Nindipens's argument. Not only did he base his claims on the hereditary rights of ogimaag, but his claims also revealed important aspects of the Ojibwe perception of the relationship between fur traders and ogimaag. Nindipens strongly asserted his claim to the land and all that grew upon it. He received this hereditary right through his father and his grandfather. Furthermore, the fur traders had always recognized this chiefly jurisdiction by asking the men of his lineage for permission to use the land and by giving gifts to compensate the community for the resources they used. Nindipens insisted that while his father lived, those wishing to use the land had sought his opinion and had given him gifts in recognition of Zhingob's status. Further, he stressed his father's intent to pass on stewardship of the land to him. The other members of the community, including Maangozid, regarded Nindipens's claims as legitimate even though Maangozid tried to assert a preeminent authority as a more mature and seasoned statesman.[38]

Nindipens, however, lacked one important token of authority: a representative of the United States government had never awarded him a chief's medal. In contrast, Lewis Cass had presented a medal to Maangozid in 1820 for rendering assistance to Cass's expedition. Furthermore, Nindipens could not combat Maangozid's claims without community consent. Since neither the community nor the American government had extended official recognition to him as ogimaa, he was, perhaps, unsure the community would support his position on the matter. Therefore he issued a challenge to the headmen to dispute his claims: "If I do not own this land, let these Indians who sit here—speak." He also tried to clarify his relationship to Maangozid and their relative power. He did not question the importance of the older man, but he did assert limits to his brother-in-law's power: "Maozit the chief does not own this land. I say it before his Son— (who was also present). He is chief but when I speak—it is as I say—& Ma-ozit interprets it."[39] Maangozid had been Zhingob's giigidowinini, and he had received his medal from Cass while serving in this capacity. No doubt the community realized that

European and American officials commonly made the mistake of giving medals to giigidowininiwag rather than to the chiefs themselves.[40] Yet because communities recognized the role of giigidowinini as a high office and their ogimaag generally also received medals, they did not challenge this practice. For giigidowininiwag, receipt of an American or European medal often gave the individual the additional distinction of speaking on behalf of the power who bestowed the medal.[41] Maangozid attempted to use the fact that he had received a chief's medal to claim the prerogatives of ogimaa of the community. Certainly from the perspective of European and American powers, this creation of authority for medal recipients had long been the intention behind the custom of bestowing them. While Nindipens conceded that bearing a medal conferred some standing, he did not recognize that it gave Maangozid authority beyond the community-recognized position he had held prior to Zhingob's death. As a result, Ely reported, "[G]andanonib became offended at this talk and left the room."[42]

Believing he had won round one, Nindipens dropped by Ely's residence the next evening just in time for supper. Apparently he had decided that the reason Ely had not asked him for permission to build at Fond du Lac was because of Ely's ignorance concerning Fond du Lac's political structure. Nindipens asked Ely who he thought was ogimaa of Fond du Lac. Ely replied that he believed Maangozid was the ogimaa. Nindipens seemed to expect this answer, and he proceeded to instruct Ely on the validity of Maangozid's chiefly claims: "I will tell you well what Ma-osit is. His father was chief of Sandy Lake. He (Maosit) does not live here." In other words, Nindipens recognized Maangozid's claims to chiefly ancestry, but he disputed Maangozid's contention that this august lineage from a different community entitled him to leadership at Fond du Lac. Because Maangozid's lineage lay with another village, Nindipens denied the validity of Maangozid's membership in the Fond du Lac community although for years he had lived there as the husband of Nindip-ens's sister and had participated in political affairs. Nindipens continued: "When the governor came here, he [i]nquired who was interpreter here. He was told Maosit. Therefore he gave him a medal. Now Maosit does not care for them. He no longer interprets for them."[43]

Nindipens presented a "middle ground" interpretation of the medals that foreign powers bestowed upon prominent community members. The young leader recognized that medals gave the wearer a certain status, but he insisted as many a middle ground negotiator had before him that this was a status vis-á-vis the United States rather than within the Fond du Lac community. Moreover, Nindipens suggested that Maangozid no longer acted even in this capacity. Nindipens then once again asserted his own claims: "When you call the Indians together, they will tell you it is I who owns this land."[44] This time, however, he added a barely veiled threat: "You will not build—unless I permit you. I have a few soldiers who will listen to me. Will you proceed to cut my timber?"[45] Nindipens encouraged Ely to do the right thing and treat with him for building rights.[46] Failure to negotiate identified Ely an enemy subject to the policing of the community's warriors. At same time, Ely's request for permission to build at Fond du Lac and the presentation of appropriate gifts promised to reinforce Nindipens's claim to represent community interests as their leader.

Non-native sources such as Ely's diary provide only tantalizing glimpses of the internal process by which the headmen at Fond du Lac tried to resolve the leadership crisis. One who probably played a prominent role in the process was Naagaanab, the brother of the deceased ogimaa Zhingob and an uncle to Nindipens and to Maangozid's wife.[47] While his familial relationship with the deceased ogimaa could have made him another contender, he instead seems to have been interested in promoting Nindipens's claim. Nearly a week after Nindipens's visit, Naagaanab called on Ely. The purpose of the visit was to inquire politely about the construction project, but Naagaanab also used the visit to instruct Ely gently and indirectly on Ojibwe customs concerning land use. He reportedly asked Ely what he thought about the "Indians, their gardens, sugar camps, etc."[48] Perhaps Naagaanab quizzed Ely to determine how well he understood Anishinaabeg land usage as well as to determine the degree of Ely's culpability for failing to ask for permission to build or to offer gifts for the privilege. By now Ely recognized that he needed a better understanding of these things. Following Nindipens's suggestion that he ask other members of the community about property rights, he queried Naagaanab about who owned the land on which another well-respected member of the community, Jiimaanens, cultivated his gardens. Naagaanab replied, "He who made it owns it."[49]

This response evokes a number of interpretations. If Naagaanab understood Ely's definition of land ownership, his response reflected Anishinaabeg religious and cultural ideas about land—that only the creator owned the creation he brought into being. On the other hand, if Naagaanab referred to usage rights, his statement indicated that the individual who planted the garden had rights to its produce; in the case in point, the garden land belonged to Jamins. He might have intended to convey both meanings. As Zhingob's brother, Naagaanab had a long history of diplomatic experience, and he probably perceived a political edge to Ely's question and gave a purposefully ambiguous answer. In the end, however, the important distinction between the rights of Jamins and those of Ely entailed community membership. Jamins was a full member of the Ojibwe community, while Ely was not. Therefore Ely's use of the land fell into a completely different category. But it appears this point was so self-evident to Naagaanab that he did not overtly make it to an oblivious Ely.

Naagaanab also told Ely that an unnamed member of the

community had brought tobacco to him on Ely's behalf because he thought that Ely's school and his aid to the sick benefited the community. Thus evidently some people did value what Ely brought to the community, while others did not. After listening to the unnamed person who defended Ely, Naagaanab had paid a visit to Nindipens. His nephew once again emphasized his hereditary right to determine land use and accused Ely of trying to cheat the community. Naagaanab perhaps represented a segment of the community that had not made up its mind on the subject. Families continued to come in from their winter hunting grounds during the weeks when the debate reached its greatest intensity, and so the entire community only gradually became aware of the building project and the chiefly power struggle it had sparked.[50] Ultimately Nindipens's paternal uncle Naagaanab supported the claims of their common lineage. Before he left Ely, he related the "genealogy of their five Grandfathers—chiefs," thereby establishing his family's right to adjudicate issues of land usage.[51]

The following evening several headmen held a rather bizarre staged conversation in Ely's presence. Nindipens, Naagaanab, and Ozaanaamikoons arrived at Ely's home and discussed Ely's building project among themselves in front of Ely and without his participation in the conversation. Although Ely failed to record all their remarks verbatim or even to present arguments besides those offered by Naagaanab, what he did report is revealing. If he did not already know it, Ely learned that he was not the only individual who wanted to undertake a building project in the Fond du Lac community. Pierre Cotte, the local fur trade post manager, sought to construct a house for his son and daughter-in-law. Unlike Ely, Cotte had behaved appropriately and consulted with community leaders before beginning construction. He had argued that as a trader who brought essential goods into the community, he should not have to pay for the privilege of building. Furthermore, although Cotte insisted that he should be exempt from providing gifts, he had asserted that Ely should not be. This argument seemed suspect, at least to Naagaanab. He suggested that Ely also should not be expected to give gifts for two very telling reasons. First, no matter what gifts Ely offered, some in the community would claim that they were insufficient, creating an unnecessary quarrel within the community itself. Second, if the community refused gifts from Ely, the missionary would later have no grounds to claim that he had purchased the land. As Naagaanab said, "If he does not pay, the land will still be ours, and he can stay on it as long as he pleases."[52] Naagaanab, evidently familiar with such land controversies in other communities, took the long view of the issue. On the other hand, Nindipens, who needed the gifts from the land transaction to begin building networks of obligation that would reinforce his chiefly position, still wished to press for at least some goods.

Ely's stream of visitors continued. Two weeks after Nindipens initially challenged the building project, a variety of community members still visited Ely several times a day. Ely's land use remained a subject of intense interest in the community for a number of reasons. First, Ely persisted in cutting local timber while the community debated the subject. The missionary was oblivious to the fact that Fond du Lac timber was as much at issue as the construction of the house itself. Second, in keeping with Anishinaabeg political structures, private caucusing constituted an important part of community consensus building. This meant constant debate among various gichi-anishinaabeg until they achieved an agreement. Visiting Ely allowed various council members to gather their own firsthand information concerning his side of the controversy as they sorted out both the land use and leadership issues. These visits also demonstrated their abhorrence of coercive measures. Some headmen held conversations in his presence in order to influence him to behave appropriately, but they did not directly order him to do what they believed was right. Finally, since he had precipitated the crisis, the community expected Ely to honor and acknowledge the time these leaders spent discussing the situation with him by providing meals to the deliberators.

If Ely had recognized how important the distribution of usage rights to land and resources was for validating chiefly leadership, he could have exerted significant influence in this situation. Had he recognized the formal claims of either Maangozid or Nindipens with a request to use community resources and a presentation of appropriate gifts, Ely might have shaped the outcome. Perhaps many of the discussions concerning chiefly rights took place in his presence in order to give him an opportunity to make his case in culturally appropriate ways. On the morning of March 8, for instance, Maangozid, Nindipens, and Inini arrived, and each presented his position about Ely's project: "Ma-o-sit was in favor of giving permission to erect my house forthwith, but N. [Nindipens] objected."[53] Seeing Ely hauling timber for his home that afternoon, Nindipens returned and told Ely that Maangozid had lied, once again repeating his contention that Maangozid lacked the authority to grant such permission. Inini then offered to intercede on Ely's behalf with Nindipens if Ely provided the meal that evening, thus prompting Ely to make the culturally appropriate gift of food acknowledging Inini's assistance and the time the gichi-anishinaabeg would spend discussing the matter. Again and again the community attempted to instruct Ely on proper community behavior, community political processes, and the ways to influence them. Not only did they take pains to provide this education; they repeatedly offered Ely opportunities to put these lessons into practice. However the missionary again and again proved to be an usually stubborn, recalcitrant, and unruly pupil.

Another lesson Ely failed to learn was that political conversations involving an ogimaa in an Ojibwe community were never perceived as private. When Inini and Nindipens next arrived, they pursued their own fact-finding mission instead of negotiating. They asked Ely what Maangozid had said to him. Although Ely willingly repeated what he remembered of Maangozid's words that afternoon, he refused to tell them anything Maangozid said to him in private.[54] From an Anishinaabeg cultural standpoint, Maangozid's words did not constitute a private matter. Any discussion between a gichi-anishinaabe and an outsider constituted a diplomatic negotiation that affected the entire community, particularly if that discussion involved land use. Anishinaabeg property was not private in either a personal or a political sense, and neither were conversations concerning it.

Nindipens must have interpreted Ely's refusal to discuss his conversation with Maangozid as an indication that Ely sought to make a separate arrangement with the medal chief. To prevent such a coup, Nindipens granted Ely his long-awaited permission the next day. Perhaps made aware that many of the gichi-anishinaabeg still deferred to Maangozid's experience over his own youth, Nindipens delivered the decision very formally following chiefly protocol. Rather than inviting Ely to his lodge, he called Peter, Ely's convert, as the missionary's representative. Peter was also a student in Ely's school and a member of his church. Ely had given Peter his Christian name when the church admitted him to communion, so the community probably considered this as an adoption, making Peter the closest thing to "family" that Ely had at Fond du Lac. In addition, Peter had been politicking among the headmen of the community on Ely's behalf throughout the course of the controversy. In any case, Peter, member of both the community and the church, was in an excellent position to interpret Nindipens's words for Ely in a manner that Ely would understand. Summoning Peter rather than Ely also emphasized Ely's status as a foreigner.

At the meeting Nindipens's message consisted of "a long preamble about his title," probably the genealogy with which ogimaag usually started formal council meetings. Then, still speaking to Peter, Nindipens informed him that Ely could go ahead and build his house, although he issued a caveat. There was still one more local man Nindipens wished to speak with when the man returned to the community. After that final consultation, Nindipens told Peter, he intended to call the community together, tell them that Ely desired to build, mark the bounds of his field, and mark the trees Ely could cut for firewood. Nindipens then indicated that as he understood it, there were "three ways in which [Ely's] Mercy to the Indians might be manifested." He might teach community members "to read and write," he might preach "the word of God," and he might give "provisions to the Indians."[55] With this speech Nindipens signaled that he accepted the position of those members of the community who believed that Ely's program of education and missionization constituted a positive contribution. At the same time he also made clear that Ely had certain material obligations to the community in which he had chosen to live, in particular the redistribution of available provisions. In order to connect himself to the community by the fictive kin ties that were essential to his residency, Ely was expected to continue to participate in the network of obligations that bound village members to one another.

Ely, however, interpreted much of Nindipens's speech within his own cultural framework. As translator, Peter probably used the term *mercy* to express the same idea as *pity*, which in Anishinaabeg culture described an obligation to give what one has to those who are in need. Of course, Ely interpreted this term within his own cultural framework. To him, mercy expressed a special and more limited gift bestowed on those who demonstrated through behavior and actions a worthiness to receive. His appraisal of need and the Anishinaabeg assessment of need constituted very different definitions. Ely had no problem with the first two of the obligations Nindipens enumerated for him. He had come to the community expressly to teach and preach.

But the third stipulation was the sticking point. Since he had moved to the community, Ely had developed a reputation as stingy with gifts in general and with gifts of food in particular. The only exceptions were his donations to the very ill and his relief efforts during the widespread famine over the winter of 1834–35, his first at Fond du Lac. From the community's perspective, sharing food with others was the most fundamental way to show group membership, community spirit, and leadership. But Ely's cultural orientation defined such gifts as "charity" and defined narrowly those who qualified. That Nindipens and the Fond du Lac community perceived Ely as a rich man, while by his own cultural criteria Ely considered himself poor only exacerbated this issue. Nindipens, still speaking to Peter, related that Ely "never thought of giving the Indians, at least some families, an occasional kettle to cook although there is a Store here from which I [Ely] could purchase and I [Ely] am well able to do it."[56] This selfishness, Nindipens said, "tried his feelings."[57] While Nindipens admitted that he had heard Ely did feed some, he had never witnessed this generosity himself. Of course Ely, as he recorded in his diary, interpreted Nindipens's remarks as an inappropriate personal request for presents of flour and pork. How ironic that at the close of the meeting each man believed the other to be guilty of greed.[58]

The next day Ely, fed up with the situation, asked Nindipens to visit his home. His frustration is evident in his diary, where he could not bring himself to identify Nindipens by name: he wrote that he "Called the Indian in." During this meeting Ely demanded to know exactly which trees, grass, and other resources Nindipens intended to give him and declared that if Nindipens sought to limit him to those trees marked with an axe, then Nindipens could keep his land or negotiate with someone else for its use.[59] Nindipens's reply reflected his pleasure at Ely's acknowledgment of his authority as well as his concern that the inexperienced woodsman might cut down materials for which continued growth was valuable to the Ojibwe community: "You say right, I have been waiting for you to say this. I do not wish any one to freeze on my land. I do not want to mark all the trees. I want you to ask me when you want timber. If I am not here and you want wood, or hay, well, take it. And when I come here, tell me. Now you say well. Heretofore you have not cared anything about me. It will be just so, you may cut what wood and hay you want. I will tell you where to get it."

At last Nindipens was able to assert the authority for which he had struggled. He now became the benevolent "father" sharing his resources in return for simple respect. Moreover, because asking for resources, even after the fact, meant offering appropriate gifts according to Anishinaabeg cultural rules, Nindipens expected the majority of Ely's goods to filter through him. Access to these goods would then increase Nindipens's ability to expand his own authority through redistribution. Finally, performing the appropriate role in this drama, Ely called in other members of the community to witness Nindipens's statements.[60]

Having won this round of the struggle for leadership, Nindipens settled into the position as ogimaa. On March 12, Nindipens stopped at Ely's home to inform the missionary that he could claim the timber he had already cut, adding that if any community members objected to the site where he had chosen to build, he could build in the area just behind his present house.[61] A week later, wishing to remind Ely of his status as ogimaa, Nindipens visited again. He showed the missionary two bundles of cedar sticks representing each member of the community, which he used to call the people together for important councils.[62] One bundle represented the gichi-anishinaabeg (headmen) and the other men of his own age (likely warriors). Neither of these bundles expressed any rank among the men they described. The only stick that indicated any rank identified Nindipens himself. It was larger than the rest and had a head carved on it, indicating his position as hereditary ogimaa.[63]

In the wake of his victory Nindipens also took upon himself the leadership role of mediator, not only of social and political issues but also of religious concerns. About ten days after presumably settling the question of Ely's building project, Ely and the Métis fur trader Pierre Cotte got into a heated theological dispute over Sunday's Bible reading. Cotte was a devout Catholic and the leader of Fond du Lac's Catholic community in the absence of a priest. Ely claimed that the Catholic prayer book did not include the second commandment relating to idolatry, which he then related to the Catholic tradition of venerating saints.[64] Cotte fired back, accusing Ely of making things up and claiming that they were not written in the Bible. Ely, who likely used a few heated words himself, described Cotte as speaking in "a violent strain of anger and abuse."[65] After hearing of the heated exchange, Nindipens dropped in on Ely, who explained to the ogimaa why Presbyterians disapproved of praying to saints. Not surprisingly Nindipens, who espoused at least a nominal Catholicism, took Cotte's part.[66] He gave it a decidedly Ojibwe twist though, by suggesting to Ely that addressing Christ through his mother expressed greater respect than addressing Christ directly. Although Ely failed to record the outcome, Nindipens's attempt demonstrates that he sought to assume a broader mediating role between two important religious leaders in keeping with his new authority as ogimaa.

Although interest in Ely's building project had waned during April as the community dispersed to harvest maple sugar, it reemerged in mid-May as the community reassembled. The continuing debate over the position of ogimaa also returned alongside it. On May 15, Eninabondo, one of the headmen of Fond du Lac who exercised additional authority as a mayosewinini, called on Ely.[67] While they discussed several topics, Eninabondo's primary interest was the hereditary chieftainship. He argued against Maangozid's claim, and he informed Ely that when the headmen met to discuss his building project, as Nindipens intended, he would ask permission to speak before the council on the subject of who should be recognized as ogimaa.[68] Eninabondo, a medewid, rejected offers of teaching or missionizing from both Ely and Cotte, but he still did not support Maangozid, a fellow gechi-midewid, as a candidate for leadership. Eninabondo may have opposed Maangozid because he lacked the appropriate qualifications and perhaps because the jaasakiid, despite his Midewiwin affiliation, supported Ely's presence in the community.[69]

By mid-May Ely had cut all the timber he needed for his building. Behaving judiciously, he formally called on Nindipens and Eninabondo on Friday, May 20, gave them tobacco, and asked them to call a council of community leaders so that he could ask them for a building spot. At the very least the community had succeeded in using social pressure to force Ely to participate in the proper forms of diplomacy. The headmen delayed their final decision on a building site since many people had not yet returned from their sugar camps. The council did take the opportunity, however, to inform Ely that his current project was not the first transgression with which he was associated. Cotte, acting on head trader William Aitkin's orders, had built the schoolhouse in which Ely now lived without proper permission. The community had let that building project slide for a time but now, in the face of a second infraction of protocol, wished to assert their rights. They informed Ely they would allow him to stay for the present but made no promises for the future.[70]

Larger political issues also concerned the community. Over the winter they had heard that "the Americans wished to do with them as they had done with other Indian nations. They would get possession of a little land, then claim much and finally drive the Indians away entirely."[71] As a result one of the gichi-anishinaabeg, Manidoons, asked Ely, "We wonder to what end [you] came here & why so anxious to stay. You are not like the traders. We want you to tell us well why you came. We believe you to be a forerunner of the Americans. We do not hate you—We hate those who sent you here."[72] With a treaty conference approaching at which Anishinaabeg knew the United States sought to acquire land, the significance of Ely's building project increased not merely as an internal issue of land usage within a single community but also as a diplomatic issue with the United States as a whole.[73]

The Anishinaabeg people seem to have perceived ABCFM missionaries stationed among them as representatives of the United States government, seeing the missionaries' actions as representing American interests as a whole. As earlier noted, this perception perhaps began when Henry Rowe Schoolcraft, United States agent to the Ojibwe, had asked his charges during a tour through Wisconsin and Minnesota in 1832 to accept ABCFM missionaries into their communities. The Ojibwe therefore categorized the missionaries not with fur traders but rather as United States subagents. The looming treaty conference made knowledge of their purpose and intentions crucial. Even Ely recognized the shift in community sentiment: "It is apparent that there is a strong prejudice against the American Government—and it is increasing rather than diminishing."[74] Furthermore, other villages besides Fond du Lac were responding to the ABCFM missionaries in their communities in a similar fashion. They charged that missionaries were agents of the American government who took land without properly obtaining permission.[75]

Yet Schoolcraft's introduction was not the only reason that Ojibwes associated the ABCFM missionaries with political leadership. They also interpreted missionaries in light of their own understanding of political and religious authority. Missionaries claimed charismatic religious authority and actively sought to encourage members of Anishinaabeg communities to share their beliefs. To the Anishinaabeg their attempts to convert members of the community constituted a political act, particularly since missionaries tended to concentrate their efforts on headmen, whom they expected to influence their lineages to follow suit. This approach paralleled that of Indigenous prophets, who occasionally appeared within their communities and who expected to be treated as important men. The various conversations Ely documented between himself and various gichi-anishinaabeg confirm this. Nearly every discussion between Ely and his guests covered three topics that the Fond du Lac leaders apparently viewed as linked—the issue of legitimate succession to the hereditary chieftainship, Ely's request for land, and whether Ely's proselytizing harmed or benefited the community.

While the Ojibwe also understood the regional Catholic missionary, Frederick Baraga, according to their cultural interpretations of religion and power, the Fond du Lac community did not appear to construe the Catholic missionary as a United States official. Catholicism had initially been introduced to Anishinaabeg communities by the French, and this faith had made some inroads into their communities despite the absence of official missionaries between 1763 when the French politically withdrew from North America and Baraga's arrival in 1835. Further, Frederick Baraga was an Austrian whom the Slovenian Brotherhood in Europe had sent, and so the Anishinaabeg perceived him, like Joseph Nicollet, as a visitor from a people distinct from the United States.

Baraga visited Fond du Lac for fourteen days in May as anxiety mounted over the treaty, the ABCFM missionaries, and the choice of ogimaa; if residents revealed the tension in the community to him, he chose not to include this in his letters. At the very least, Baraga encountered none of the hostility with which ABCFM missionaries were contending. However, it does appear that Nindipens attempted to draw the bishop into the local political conflict. Baraga commented that "the chief and several men came to me and begged me not to leave them, but to remain with them always. . . . They showed me the place where they wished to have the mission church and the home of the missionary."[76] While Baraga does not identify Nindipens as the chief who approached him with this request, this is a likely assumption, given that Nindipens appeared to practice at least the form of Catholicism that fur trader Pierre Cotte and his wife promoted at Fond du Lac. As a French Catholic and a fur trader, Cotte also remained largely free of accusation despite holding Catholic meetings in his home. But then, Cotte, as a Métis, had a much stronger understanding of the cultural norms of the community and, as a fur trader, was already involved in distributing annual gifts to community leaders. The concerns the local community had about Ely and his mission obviously did not apply to the Catholic priest.

Baraga not only lacked direct ties with the United States government but also understood the gift exchange requirements of Anishinaabeg communities and regularly contributed to them, in strong contrast to the actions of the ABCFM personnel. His letters home to his sister in Austria consistently request items useful to give as gifts to Indian people.[77] Ely, in contrast, rarely shared his goods with the community, and once disrupted Midewiwin ceremonies to take back ribbons he saw some participants wearing that he claimed were stolen from his house.[78]

As a result the ABCFM missionaries occupied a more suspicious place in the Anishinaabeg political landscape. Manidoons, a medewid, probably expressed the suspicions of many concerning Ely's preaching when he announced: "The English and French had been among them of old, & it was very strange that they should but just now, hear these things [the ABCFM message] and that from an American."[79] On another occasion Manidoons contended that the ABCFM missionaries were "instructed by the Americans and were trying to deceive the Indians" so that they could make slaves of them.[80] Manidoons further accused Ely of withholding important diplomatic information, since Ely had resided at Fond du Lac for two years and had never mentioned to the community the intentions of the United States government to acquire more land from the Indian nations.[81] Ely's insistence on the preeminence of his own spiritual authority constituted an attack on the religious authority and sociopolitical standing of charismatic leaders in the community, especially those of the Midewiwin, like Manidoons. Moreover, in the Anishinaabeg view, which linked spiritual and political power, Ely's religious claims confirmed rather than undermined a general belief in his political role on behalf of the United States.

In the days following May 23 a number of different headmen visited Ely to ask about his school and his intentions. Eninabondo came to ask for tobacco so that he could call a council for the next day to provide Ely with a final answer regarding his building. Ely gave Eninabondo the tobacco as well as a pan of flour "to feed them while in council."[82] Perhaps the Indians' recent hostility encouraged him to act according to community norms, but whatever lessons he had learned were superficial. Ely increasingly criticized the Midewiwin in such a way that even the non-Christians he counted as friends began to resent the missionary deeply. As Gaashkibaaz angrily told him, only half the things Ely said of Gichi-Manidoo were true: "The miteui [Midewiwin] was made for the Indians and our religion for us. The books also for the white men. He did not want me to say anything about the miteui, they loved God."[83] To Ely's undoubted chagrin, a Midewiwin celebration delayed the expected council.[84]

A week later on May 31 the council summoned Ely to attend their meeting and hear its decision. Ely, who was entertaining Baraga and Cotte at his home at the time of the summons, had not realized that the council intended to meet that day.[85] Cotte, who acted as interpreter in the council's dealings with Ely, had probably persuaded Nindipens to postpone the council until Baraga arrived. The Catholic trader might have hoped that Baraga would influence the outcome, but on the other hand, Baraga's presence also tempered Cotte's usual ire toward Ely.

Baraga had already declined to change his residence to Fond du Lac, and throughout his ministry the priest demonstrated a tolerance and respect for his fellow missionaries regardless of faith, even attending baptisms and funerals of ABCFM personnel at La Pointe.[86]

At the council itself Nindipens presided. First he addressed Cotte, asking the trader's opinion concerning Ely's presence at Fond du Lac. Cotte replied that Ely benefited the community by teaching the children. Nindipens then pointed out that Ely knew about Cotte's resistance to Ely's building project, but Cotte denied ever saying any such thing. Nindipens then denied ever receiving advice from Cotte to halt Ely's building project.[87] This exchange formally established Nindipens's impartiality in the dispute and served as a further demonstration of his skill in his new role of ogimaa.

The council continued, as usual expressing the minority opinion first. An old man said that the Indians in the Folle Avoine disliked the building plans of Ely's associate Frederick Ayer at Pokegoma and feared that the Americans would come there to live: "We do not hate you, we hate what we've heard of the treatment of the Americans towards other Indian Nations."[88] Two or three others voiced similar concerns, and all ended their statements by stating they would accept Nindipens's decision on the matter. Then Maangozid, in his old role as giigidowinini, described Nindipens's chiefly descent, once again demonstrating to the community and to Ely why Nindipens had authority over the issue. Now it was Nindipens's turn to speak. Expressing humility, he said that although he rightfully owned the land, he was not the ogimaa. Therefore he refused to sell the land on the bluff that Ely desired, but he would lend the missionary another tract up the creek for a period of four years. He also told Ely to plant in the same field as the fur trader William Aitkin, probably in recognition of Aitkin's patronage of the mission.[89] Nindipens instructed Ely to show mercy to the Indians, once again a reference to redistributing his resources so as to become a contributing member of the community. Finally, Nindipens stated that if any of Ely's associates came and also wanted to build at Fond du Lac, they also had to ask the council for permission.[90]

At the end of the council Ely invited Nindipens and Eninabondo to his home, where he wrote a contract for use of the land for four years, which Nindipens and Eninabondo signed.[91] Nindipens immediately redistributed among the members of the community the flour and tobacco he had received from Ely per the terms of the lease. A week later Eninabondo called on Ely and told him that the "*Ogimaa* Nindipens was much pleased to have me live here."[92] This was the first time that either Ely or Eninabondo had referred to Nindipens by this title. Ely's surprise plus the novelty of it caused him to underline the title in his diary. Ely's gifts to Nindipens had allowed the latter to demonstrate conclusively his ability to control outsiders and to provide for community needs. From this point on, no one in the community expressed any doubt as to Nindipens's position as ogimaa of Fond du Lac. Maangozid had lost, though he would reassert claims at various points in the future.

Nindipens had demonstrated his right to the office of ogimaa. He had steered Ely into compliance with Native customs and demands by persuasion rather than force, as an ogimaa should. However, Nindipens's position remained delicate, and other issues loomed as serious challenges. The resistance of the non-Christian faction of the community to Ely or any other American acquiring claims on community land represented one such significant challenge to this authority. To meet this challenge Nindipens needed to demonstrate that he could keep Ely in line. Unfortunately but predictably, Ely almost immediately failed him. Ely decreased the quantity of goods he gave Nindipens for his "loan" of the land, using as an excuse that the proposed purchase had become only a lease.[93] Next Ely refused to provide food to three visiting Indians whom Nindipens brought to see him.[94] Ely clearly realized what Nindipens expected, since after the visitors left, he asked if Nindipens had expected him to feed them. When Nindipens replied affirmatively, Ely added insult to injury by pointing out that the river was full of fish and they could get their own food if they put out their nets. Ely interpreted Nindipens's demand for hospitality in terms of Anglo American values of individual self-sufficiency, ignoring Nindipens's still fragile status within the community. Nindipens did not reply to this insult, but he immediately left Ely's home.[95] Ely's diary entry reveals that his treatment of the ogimaa was intentional rather than accidental. He wrote about the encounter in condescending language and made sarcastic use of Nindipens's title: "It is probable the Ogima is a little wounded. If he is, let the ogima take care in the future, not to take too much upon himself."[96] Ely failed to see the larger political currents that eddied around him. His personal frustration over the land dispute both clouded his judgment and impaired his mission.

Ely's misunderstanding cost him. By undermining Nindipens's authority through his refusal of gifts of food, he forced Nindipens to reassess his decision to grant Ely access to community resources. As a result the community began to sanction thefts and vandalism of Ely's property. On Sunday June 12 two men stole Ely's canoe.[97] This event gave Maangozid the opportunity to step in and attempt to demonstrate that he was the more skillful negotiator. He called on Ely on June 16 and asked for tobacco and a kettle of food with which he could call a council and ask the community to refrain from violence against the missionary.[98] Nindipens and Eninabondo soon appeared and agreed to sell the land to Ely outright if he offered them additional goods, as he had initially had agreed. Ely conceded. He gave them an additional barrel of flour and fifty plugs of tobacco, bringing the total for the purchase to two barrels of flour and ninety plugs of tobacco, a total of about twenty-five dollars' worth of goods.[99] In this transaction Maangozid had again functioned as medal chief for the Americans, brokering a settlement between the community and the missionaries. This would not be his last attempt to bolster his authority.

In mid-August word reached Ely that Maangozid, who was at La Pointe, had decided to reject the Midewiwin and become a Christian, even going so far as to turn over his *mitigwaakik* (water drum), medicine sac and rattle to the missionaries.[100] Maangozid had been one of the leading Midewiwin leaders at Fond du Lac, a position that granted him a great deal of charismatic influence, so this choice warrants further examination. Significantly, the previous year three Methodist ministers had wintered at La Pointe. The ministers were not white men but Ojibwes from Canada. These men, one of whom was the famous George Copway, commanded the respect of the ABCFM missionaries, were regularly invited to dine with local white elites, preached in the ABCFM church at La Pointe, and even assisted with their efforts to translate the Bible into the Ojibwe language. Like Midewiwin leaders, the Ojibwe ministers had access to spiritual authority and functioned as charismatic leaders within the Ojibwe community. At the same time, because of their Western-style dress, manners, education, and Methodist faith, they also garnered the respect and cooperation of Anglo community leaders closely connected with the Indian agent.

Maangozid sought to obtain comparable respect to improve his political position within the Fond du Lac community. He had left Fond du Lac under the pall of political defeat. Historian Rebecca Kugel described him as "deeply mortified and distressed. He had been humiliated before the whole of the Fond du Lac community."[101] Nindipens's Catholicism had earned him a close working relationship with the fur trader Pierre Cotte. Maangozid expected his conversion to Protestantism to gain him similar allies, and at Fond du Lac this meant Edmund Ely. Furthermore, as a former gechi-midewid, Maangozid sought to advance to a higher position of authority through teaching and preaching within Ely's church, as he had within the Midewiwin society.

Maangozid returned to the Fond du Lac community on August 24 and began to spend a considerable amount of time with the Ely family, both working for them and worshiping with them.[102] His background as a Midewiwin leader made him comfortable with the idea that a religious leader needed to spend a certain amount of time learning theology and ritual before attaining a position of authority. However, Maangozid would accept a miishinoo relationship with the Elys for only so long before expecting a share of their religious authority. Already on September 8, Ely noted that Maangozid "was our officiating priest at the family altar this evening. A little before we were ready for family worship his wife came in and said they were alone, their son gone, and they should be glad to come in and worship with us every morning and evening. After reading the 23 Psalm with some other passages from David, the old man prayed at unusual length, and as I thought with unusual fervor."[103] Maangozid obviously relished this opportunity to act as religious leader within the Ely family and hoped for the same respect he had seen ABCFM personnel accord Copway at La Pointe.

However, despite his preference for Maangozid's chiefly claims over those of Nindipens, Ely consistently questioned the sincerity and quality of Maangozid's conversion. Ely later asked his wife Catherine, a Métis who had received a Western education at the ABCFM school at Mackinac, to give him an account of what Maangozid had said in his long and fervent prayer. Catherine replied that "after making several petitions," Maangozid repeated "them as though God were speaking to him by way of promise."[104] Although a convert eagerly seeking to learn Christian theology, he still structured prayer with expectations formed by his Midewiwin experience.

Yet Maangozid's recorded discussions with Ely reveal genuine religious feelings achieved through Christian practice. For example, on one occasion he told Ely that "when he began to pray, he did not know what he was going to say, but as he proceeded, he was taught to say a great deal—that he seemed to forget himself and not to know where he was or what he was doing, only that his mind went upward, he seemed to see God and was talking to him."[105] Maangozid's statement expressed real religiosity but not of the sort Ely approved. Furthermore, Maangozid "dreams of religion and dreamed last night that the Spirit talked to him and told him that he was very poor."[106] While Maangozid found this fulfilling, Ely expressed concern that Maangozid "sees faintly in consequence of his strange blind pagan notions which are as second nature to him."[107] Ely struggled to disabuse Maangozid of the notion that he could talk directly to God. More critically, Ely did not know how to impress the headman with the sense of original and indwelling sin that was necessary for full Presbyterian conversion yet was a concept completely alien to Ojibwe religious expression. Maangozid "insisted on his love of God and the purity of his heart."[108] But much to Ely's frustration, he "does not seem to know anything of humbling for Sin—or mourning on account of imperfection—nor does he seem to discern it in himself."[109] No matter what biblical parable or passage Edmund and Catherine enlisted to their cause, they could not get the point across. Still, Maangozid continued to worship daily with the Ely family and to seek further theological education whenever both were in residence at Fond du Lac.

By October other community headmen began to express an interest in Maangozid's conversion. Gandanonib informed Ely that he had spoken to Maangozid's brother, who told him that Maangozid "would not love God long."[110] Furthermore, he warned Ely that Maangozid "would pray so long as we would feed him."[111] By embracing Presbyterian Christianity, Maangozid obtained gifts from Ely that the missionary denied Nindipens and other members of the Fond du Lac community. Still, Maangozid showed no signs of backsliding when Ely traveled to the fishing grounds to pray with him and his family on Sunday October 16.[112] Three days later Ely and his family moved into their new house, the source of so much community agitation.[113]

The community's pressures on Maangozid to abandon Ely remained ineffective until December, when Catharine Ely caught Maangozid's wife sewing and criticized her noncompliance with Sabbath rules. By way of defense Maangozid told the Elys that "Inini's people had been calling her a fool for doing as the *whites* did."[114] Worse, Maangozid had received death threats from at least two members of the community, who told him "if he continued to pray next spring, they would kill him."[115] He suggested to the missionaries that the reason his wife broke the Sabbath was out of fear for their lives.[116] Still, he insisted that he and his family remained steadfast Christians.

By February Maangozid's Christian faith began to wane. On the eighth he engaged Ely in conversation over breakfast concerning the Mishibizhii, who lived in Lake Superior and had a copper tail. This manidoog figured prominently in many stories and Midewiwin teachings as a powerful and malevolent being. Maangozid related to Ely that he owned a piece of the creature's copper tail, which he could not discard or he would dream the creature bit him and he would become sick.[117] On February 13 the Elys caught Maangozid in a sweat lodge with Gandononib, Inini, and Uejanimaso.[118] The next day the Elys went to Maangozid's lodge to inquire about his activities. He claimed that he had gone to visit Inini, and the other men who were there asked him to assist them in holding a Midewiwin ceremony. He declined and suggested that they wait until more Indians came in from their hunts. Then they began to sing and asked Maangozid to help them with some songs he knew better than they did.

These men appealed to Maangozid as a learned teacher and

earnestly sought his instruction—an expression of deference and respect that Maangozid had recently sought but not received through Christian channels. The men talked to Maangozid about his new vocation, saying that they pitied his poverty as a Christian. They suggested to him that when others converted to Christianity, the missionaries clothed them, fed them, and housed them. Maangozid did not even sleep in Ely's house.[119] The Elys pointed out that they had given Maangozid old clothes and invited him to dinner often but did not think it fair to invite him to live with them when they could not offer the same opportunity to all. Maangozid suggested that if he lived with the Elys, his friends would have less opportunity to persuade him to return to the Midewiwin lodge.[120] In the face of his friends' flattery, pity, and persuasion, Maangozid increasingly questioned his new faith. While he attempted to convince the Elys that he remained a good Christian, Gandanonib's son William informed the missionaries the next day that Maangozid intended to assist in holding the spring Midewiwin ceremonies, a charge that Maangozid promptly denied.[121]

The close relationship between the Elys and Maangozid's family chilled after this confrontation. Although the demands of the seasonal round of sugarbush and fishing camp work could explain his family's absence from Fond du Lac over the next few months, some of Ely's converts visited him in the intervening period. The Elys did not see Maangozid again until May, when they traveled to his camp at the foot of the rapids. When they arrived they heard the water drum and shaker, and singing filled the air. Gaashkibaaz and Maangozid were preparing for a Midewiwin ceremony at which they planned to officiate.[122] A few weeks later Maangozid explained to the Elys that he had embraced the Christian religion following Nindipens's succession as ogimaa because he thought that the "Indians did not care anything about him—but now he finds they do care for him."[123]

On the previous Sabbath Maangozid had just gotten ready

to visit the Elys when one of his people entered his lodge and begged him not to go to Elys' home. The visitor argued that when others visited Ely, they received nothing from him, and the visitor then adorned Maangozid with beads and metal armbands and painted his face.[124] By accepting the gifts Maangozid agreed to not visit the Elys. Certainly the Elys had not showered him with gifts in this manner for his political support and adherence to their faith. Maangozid had felt that the community had rejected him and his leadership the previous summer when they had settled on Nindipens as their leader. He sought to obtain a new leadership position and perhaps join a new community by converting to Christianity.

However, Maangozid had not received gifts or respect from the Elys, at least not on a level appropriate to his status as a gichi-anishinaabe and giigidowinini. His community now expressed respect for and deference to him and asked him to lead Midewiwin ceremonies, reminding him of his superior knowledge by pointing out that they did not know all the proper songs without him. As a result they drew him and his support away from Ely. On May 26 he called on Ely to tell him that after much contemplation he had determined to practice neither Christianity nor Midewiwin, following the Ojibwe traditions only as necessary for warfare. Yet he still loved God and intended to come on Sundays to hear Ely's sermons.[125] Ely told him that he greatly dishonored God and treated him with contempt and mockery but said Maangozid would always be welcome at Christian instruction should he choose to keep all of God's commandments, a condemnation of Maangozid's willingness to participate in Ojibwe traditions of warfare.[126]

Despite Maangozid's religious decision, Ely still supported him politically. While Ely was speaking with Nindipens on June 5, Eninabondo stopped in and suggested Ely should call the community together and ask permission before setting his nets for the spring sturgeon run. When Eninabondo asked for flour to call the council together, Ely said he could not supply it on the Sabbath—but then later confided to his diary that he questioned "whether it will be expedient to give it to him. Maosit is the government organ of communication with the [village] and it is right for us to respect him as such. It will also shut out others from calling for food and tobacco to call councils."[127] Ely certainly failed to understand the connections between gifting, religion and politics in Anishinaabeg society. Earlier the same day Ely had denied tobacco to a group gathered at Enimaso's lodge, who had offered to listen to his religious teachings if he provided them with tobacco to listen to him speak. Ely, who failed to realize that any gathering or teaching session involved tobacco, replied, "God never hires men to listen to what He says. If they hear and obey, they shall be saved and if they will not hear and obey they must go to Hell."[128]

Maangozid trod a thin line between Christian and Midewiwin religious worlds, implying to Ely that he might still become a Christian to maintain Ely's political support. Ely did not realize that Maangozid's backing of his mission strengthened the missionary's position in the community far more than anything he might have done to augment his authority. On June 9 the Elys jeopardized their entire endeavor by alienating Maangozid in no uncertain terms. Catherine Ely told Maangozid that the Midewiwin society members could not make her fall down with their medicines. Maangozid began to reply with stories of disbelievers who had fallen to the society's medicine. Edmund Ely then told Maangozid that he would give him a kettle of food for the ceremony so that Maangozid could demonstrate his medicines on him.[129] The Elys not only mocked Maangozid's beliefs and his position within the society; they also specifically asked him to do what in Ojibwe society might be the only thing that might qualify as sinful behavior—they asked him to use his medicine to harm rather than to help.

This must have been very confusing to Maangozid. After this

couple had shared their table and teachings with him on many occasions and exhorted him to avoid sin, they now demanded that he commit what was in Ojibwe terms an extraordinarily evil act that would eventually rebound in sickness or death within his own family. How could friends and allies make such a demand? Maangozid, visibly shaken, told Ely not to trifle with medicine and informed him that it would be "a very bad act" to comply with Ely's request, as he would surely die.[130] Further, in his agitation Maangozid revealed the behind-the-scenes politicking he had done on Ely's behalf. He informed Ely that Gandanonib had recently called the Indians together and encouraged them to eject Ely from the community because he spoke against the Midewiwin. The people said among themselves that "they had permitted me [Ely] to build my house, and they could pull it down again."[131] When they consulted Maangozid, however, he had told them that "he loved me [Ely] very much and they must do nothing to me."[132] All he had to do was say the word, and the community would pillage Ely's house. Ely replied that he did not believe in the power of the Midewiwin and would neither take back anything he had said about it nor remain silent about his beliefs: "I came here to preach against sin. The Miteui [Midewiwin] and all other sorcery was condemned in the Scriptures. . . . Your insisting on the Virtues of the Miteui belies God's word."[133] That was too much for Maangozid. No matter what benefits he thought an alliance with Ely as a representative for the United States brought, he had reached an impasse. He replied that he had thrown away everything in pursuit of Christianity: "Now he did not want it—he did not care—he was willing to die and risk all."[134]

Maangozid avoided Ely until late August. In July most of the village leaders left to attend the treaty gathering at St. Peters, from which they trickled home in mid-August. On Thursday, August 24, a group of about a dozen men including Maangozid came to Ely and asked him to write a letter for them to the Indian agent at Le Pointe. In it they complained of Nindipens's leadership and asked the agent not to recognize him but instead to bestow a medal "on some other more worthy."[135] Ely agreed but informed them that he did not agree with their sentiments and would also write letters for Nindipens if asked.[136] Maangozid wished to remain the only medal chief at Fond du Lac, and he had significant community support in this endeavor. However, the United States government had chosen to recognize Nindipens as a Fond du Lac chief at the 1837 treaty gathering, and Maangozid never obtained enough clout to challenge Nindipens's authority.

While Nindipens and Maangozid continued to use Ely in various ways to jockey for position, Ely's continued disavowal of community norms and his identification with the United States government ultimately doomed his mission. As community dissatisfaction with his presence and with United States policy generally increased, Ely gradually got the message that he and his family should move on. The final straw was the unauthorized butchering of one of Ely's oxen, which was quickly cut up and distributed among the community. Since Ely refused to share resources that he developed on village lands, the community forced him to do so. Ely understood the message, even if he could not fathom the cause, and in 1839 he moved his family to the more Anglicized community at La Pointe.

Ely, Nindipens, and Maangozid never really understood one another's cultures, but the conflict over land usage rights at Fond du Lac reveals a great deal about leadership among Anishinaabeg communities. While charismatic leadership positions provided some individuals in the community with a chance for advancement, authority, and prestige, charismatic credentials alone could not trump the credentials of local ogimaag. Only ogimaag from hereditary lineages had the authority to designate land usage rights in the village community, to mediate disputes, and to use social pressure to force compliance with community norms governing the redistribution of resources. Age, spiritual authority, and chiefly medals all played important roles, but they were not determining factors. Still, before the community would fully regard an individual as an ogimaa, a demonstration of ability was required, such as Nindipens achieved through his protracted negotiation with and eventual lease of land to Ely. The judicious management and distribution of community lands and the extension of ties of mutual obligation were central to chiefly authority and identity. Ely never learned either of these lessons, and Nindipens's inability to instruct him in proper behavior in the end undermined his authority in the community and led to Ely's expulsion.

Conclusion

The Anishinaabeg of the late eighteenth and early nineteenth centuries lived in a universe suffused with powerful manidoog that positively or negatively affected their daily lives at all levels, from subsistence to warfare to courting to politics. These manidoog became incorporated into Anishinaabeg lives through webs of reciprocal social relationships that extended the notion of kin far beyond biological relatives. They brought needed gifts or blessings to help Anishinaabeg people survive and reinforced the close relationship between the Anishinaabeg and the natural world around them that provided more than simple subsistence. These basic components of Ojibwe world view are fundamental to understanding where Anishinaabeg believed power lay and the nature of the leadership structures these sources of power supported. Although all members of society formed relationships with manidoog that helped their families, exceptionally strong connections enhanced an individual's influence and personal standing within the community. Access to manidoog assistance, while it seldom allowed gifted individuals to usurp the positions of ogimaag, augmented hereditary authority and sometimes even allowed ogimaag to expand their influence beyond the borders of their home communities.

Anishinaabeg peoples felt a constant need for communication with and assistance from manidoog in everyday life expressed through song, dance, tobacco, feasting, fasting, and dreams. Societal expectations demonstrated this from birth when the parents of a newborn selected someone from among the elders of the community to learn the name of the child. Nicollet reported that the individual chosen for this task was the one who had the most power—emphasizing that this was the actual expression his informants used. This procedure was vital, extending to the newborn child not only the influence and protection of the namer but also those of the manidoog that assisted the namer. Intrigued by these remarks, Nicollet inquired what defined those with the most power, and was told those "whose power is considered to be equal to that of the spirits in the arts of warfare, hunting, and healing."[1] These were the very strengths Anishinaabeg expected from their leaders. Political leaders had to demonstrate a strong connection to the manidoog who would give them guidance and assistance for the people because political and economic decisions were always made with the larger community of humans, manidoog, and their reciprocal obligations to one another in mind.

Gifts made these relationships possible. The gifts and blessings that passed between family members, between leaders, between humans and manidoog, between all "persons" in the Anishinaabeg universe wove the fabric of society together. They defined relative power among the parties, established reciprocal obligation, protected against times of adversity or scarcity, and made sure that individuals, even when relatively isolated, never believed that they faced the odds alone. The basic needs of society structured the kinds of decisions required of leaders, while their connections with manidoog and other social groups impacted the success of their actions and decisions.

This interest in constantly expanding circles of kin and mutual obligation refutes the assumptions of those scholars who have characterized Ojibwe society as "atomistic." Internally, leadership in Ojibwe communities addressed the allocation of sugarbush, wild rice beds, fisheries, and garden plots. Households seldom functioned as discrete autonomous political units, as atomists claim, but depended on participation in a village unit for all claims to resource use. Externally, the same ogimaag who dealt with such day-to-day issues also negotiated with other Anishinaabeg villages, with leaders of other Native nations, and with agents of colonial governments. When necessary, a leader skilled in war solicited or was asked to lead war parties made up of members of the village against their enemies. The village also served as the primary unit for the celebration of full Midewiwin rights, led by a community member with particularly strong ties to the manidoog, as demonstrated through multiple levels of Midewiwin initiation and through other services, such as healing the sick. The village community, through its various types of leaders, made the primary economic, political, and religious decisions for its members. Marriage, gift exchange, defensive needs and religious ceremonies in turn made villages socially and politically dependent on one another.

Individuals and communities constantly sought contact and counsel with others as often as possible, rather than shunning such interaction. Although political disputes could cause a village to fission into two separate groups, such disputes could not sunder the familial ties of their respective members and the reciprocal obligations these entailed for the cross-community actions of war parties and religious ties of the Midewiwin society. Such fission led not to increased confusion but to expansion of influence into new territories. New villages generally retained for a time close political ties with the parent village from which they splintered but gradually became more independent. New villages continued to emerge and separate from parent villages even when territorial expansion was not possible.[2] Many of these new villages, even after becoming politically independent, still retained political and religious affiliation with the parent village.[3] Individuals moved between villages, villages reallocated resources, and political alliances shifted. Fluidity rather than atomism characterized Anishinaabeg society, and this flexibility shaped the nature of Ojibwe leadership.

The fluidity of Ojibwe social organization was highly appropriate to conditions of economic and physical survival that on occasion necessitated wide dispersion into smaller groups.[4] Anthropologist Fred Eggan described the Ojibwe situation: "The conditions of . . . life demanded a local group small enough to subsist by hunting and gathering but large enough to furnish protection against hostile war parties and raids. The extended family was adequate for the first condition, but was at the mercy of any war party; the tribe, on the other hand, was too unwieldy to act as an economic unit for very long."[5] The village then became the ideal compromise between the two, in which most activities of life were conducted. A polycephalic system of many potential leaders who organized and regulated village life is not only aboriginal in origin but also provided stability and security to Anishinaabeg communities.[6] Fluid, decentralized systems of social organization provided Anishinaabeg communities with an adaptive strength as flexible and powerful as water itself.

Village ogimaag demonstrated their power by expanding the "social capital" of the community through gift exchange and intermarriage.[7] The vagaries of the natural world meant that there was no guarantee of a steady food supply. Sharing food among several families mitigated the unevenness of production and balanced the needs of the community. Taking up the mantle of mayosewininiwag or gechi-midewijig extended gifting relationships with other influential families across village boundaries, resulting in a network of obligation that could quickly respond to economic and political changes. Such networks, like life in general, were not static. They were constantly shifting and constantly in motion like currents in a stream. Yet this fluidity securely bound the components of larger alliance systems together. Atomists have pointed to this fluidity as a weakness, seeing the small family unit as the only stable building block of social structures. However this interpretation omits two important things. First, fluidity might indicate strength rather than weakness, and second, a major social goal might be to affirm, expand, and renegotiate relationships rather than simply maintain a static social space. Diffuse systems of leadership allowed a flexibility in which those with the most experience and demonstrated success supervised specific tasks.[8]

Ojibwe social structures and world view intricately linked ogimaag to their villages and identified their obligations to these communities. The right to lead, to negotiate with outside groups, and to manage village lands and material resources within the community through redistribution and allocation descended to these hereditary ogimaag through patrilineal lineages. The ogimaag led by building consensus among various constituencies—the gichi-anishinaabeg, the warriors, and the women—through persuasion and skillful oratory. The degree of their influence, particularly outside their own communities, was based on reputation and ability. Anishinaabeg leaders held power not through coercive decrees but by earning respect. Respect came from being born to a chiefly lineage, from making decisions that benefited the people, and from skillfully exercising generosity to persuade village members toward a desired course of action. Building these talents, ogimaag gained influence through marriage connections, consulted community and council opinion, and had assistants such as giigidowininiwag, miishinoog, and oshkaabewisag to assist them in their duties. Manidoog power enhanced the authority and influence ogimaag obtained through other sources.

Ogimaag faced with the responsibility of building coalitions and making decisions that affected the fate of the community needed strong and reliable sources of outside assistance. They achieved this not only through successfully becoming mayosewininiwag or gechi-midewijig, but also through the consistent successful decision making that led to mino-bimaadiziwin—living well—for oneself and for the whole community. Because of this constellation of requirements, influential ogimaag skillfully and successfully wielded charismatic authority. The strict dichotomy some have held between peace and war leaders in Ojibwe communities does not stand up to scrutiny and needs to be reexamined.

The scholarly characterization of charismatic leadership as aberrant, irrational, and distinctive to societies in transition ignores the many societies that had orderly and stable charismatic leadership structures over long periods. Societies reliant upon such structures for group decision making would hardly have maintained them if they had not proven successful in meeting people's needs. The sources of prestige and respect stemmed not only from organizational positions of authority but also from the participation of leaders in activities that continued and strengthened confidence in societal centers. Religion and politics are the most logical institutional abodes of charismatic qualities and symbols. In societies like that of the Anishinaabeg and other Native American peoples who do not sharply differentiate religious and political spheres, charismatic authority was a stabilizing institution. This means that the fluidity of Anishinaabeg leadership had more structure than has previously been recognized.

Despite the inherent temptations and dangers of seeking enhanced connections to manidoog power, many chose this route to improve social status and authority. The Anishinaabeg not only encouraged but also expected such ambitions on a moderate level, since no one could survive without manidoog help to make crops grow, to call game, to protect one from enemies, and to heal the sick. Even if the Midewiwin did not always offer a successful route to leadership over the village, it did expand the influence of those hereditary ogimaag who attained high degrees in the society. The intervillage integrative functions of the Midewiwin also increased political cooperation among villages and enhanced the role of those leaders who officiated at these intervillage events. Just as opportunities to lead war parties democratized access to prestige and authority, so the Midewiwin also constructed a procedure by which power, otherwise attainable only through heredity or physical prowess, could be redistributed throughout the community. This important source of charismatic authority offered opportunity on a broad democratic basis to all within Ojibwe society, and it was also a means for ambitious hereditary leaders to expand their influence or at least hold their own against religious practitioners within their communities who tested the bounds of their authority.

Often, leaders inherited access to spiritual power through their families, either in the form of sacred bundles passed down from parent to child or via specialized ceremonial knowledge practiced within certain lineages. While Ojibwe ogimaag did not have the kind of absolute religious power that the leaders of chiefdoms of the southeastern United States asserted, supernatural assistance supported all skills in an Ojibwe world view. In other words, everything happened for a reason and everything had a specific cause. Ojibwe leaders were successful because they derived spiritual support from the manidoog and the ceremonies of their clan and lineage, from the successful chiefs from whom they descended, from their personal spiritual connections made while fasting or dreaming, and from the spiritual power and knowledge gained through Midewiwin membership. Indigenous prophets and Christian missionaries opened up additional avenues to attain the spiritual counterpart of the chief's temporal authority.

Many of the most influential Anishinaabeg leaders, such as Eshkibagikoonzh and Bagone-giizhig II of Leech Lake, also held charismatic leadership roles at one time or continued to hold them simultaneously with their other civic responsibilities. The responsibilities and authority of Midewiwin leaders and war leaders augmented the influence of these men and had deep ties to the manidoog community. Anishinaabeg society evaluated the quality of candidates for hereditary chiefly offices according to their ability to obtain and hold other charismatic leadership roles. As a result, charismatic leadership provided stability and authority rather than chaos to Anishinaabeg governance. The Anishinaabeg world view institutionalized charismatic authority in such a way that community members easily recognized who had it and who did not. All of the most prominent hereditary leaders of Ojibwe communities in northern Wisconsin and Minnesota in the early nineteenth century demonstrated their charismatic authority through becoming skilled mayosewininiwag during their youth or through attainment of gichi-midewijig status or both. These avenues to leadership were open to anyone in the community regardless of hereditary qualifications. Those who gained prestige through these avenues at times successfully challenged the authority of hereditary leaders. But those who exerted the strongest influence in Anishinaabeg society were those who combined hereditary and charismatic leadership.

That many ogimaag chose to bolster their authority through the pursuit of additional connections to manidoog power also deepens our understanding of the nature of chiefly conversion to Christianity. Because the Ojibwe world view recognized dreams and visions as not only modes of communication with manidoog power but conduits along which new songs, ceremonies, and rituals could be communicated to the people, new ceremonies and religious ideas commonly found their way into Ojibwe communities. Therefore, as the new religious tradition of Christianity expanded into Ojibwe communities, some Ojibwe leaders sought to join the church and use its authority in a similar manner. Ogimaag, who had inheritance to fall back on, felt less threatened by Christianity than did other leaders since it did not challenge the foundation of their authority. Those leaders whose social rank depended entirely upon their reputation as religious leaders were more likely to support the movement wholeheartedly in search of new sources of prestige, or they resisted Christian influence much more strongly than ogimaag and attempted to prevent fellow community members from joining the Christian faction and leaving their own. This meant that the choice between Midewiwin and Christianity opened up a new field for the contestation of chiefly authority. The expansion of bases for claims to authority allowed new grounds for potential successors to the hereditary ogimaag at Fond du Lac to argue their case for authority before the community. Certainly the career of Maangozid demonstrates the various avenues open to ambitious individuals in Anishinaabeg society.

Because Anishinaabeg communities did not make a distinction between religious and political power, the ABCFM missionaries challenged not only the religious authorities of Anishinaabeg communities but their political authorities as well. Conversely, by presenting an alternative image of religious authority, they provided another route to charismatic religious leadership for ambitious community members. Missionaries did indeed increase factional tensions in communities, but often these tensions preceded missionary intervention and continued to exist in spite of it. Most studies have examined missionaries in the period between the American Revolution and the signing of the Ojibwe treaties as either religious or political actors, reflecting Western assumptions about the nature of religious authority and the separation of church and state. Ojibwe society in this era did not make these distinctions or sharply differentiate the religious and political roles of the missionaries. Similarly, nativist and accommodationist Ojibwe leaders were not exclusively political: both had strong religious feelings and experiences. Power came from many sources, and leaders exercised authority in many arenas at once. Although various political factions in Ojibwe communities did hearken to missionaries at various times for their own purposes, they did so not in spite of but because of the missionaries' religious claims.

Beyond reflecting misunderstandings of one another's cultures by Maangozid, Nindipens, and the missionary Ely, the conflict over land usage rights at Fond du Lac reveals a great deal about leadership among Ojibwe communities in the late eighteenth and early nineteenth centuries. Further, the confrontation shows the centrality of religious experience to Anishinaabeg leadership without suggesting any of this adherence to be merely superficial. Anishinaabeg religious expression had always been inclusive rather than exclusive. The choice of Christianity or Midewiwin did not always negate belief in the other. Religious experience with either source of power potentially expressed charismatic authority that could be used to bolster leadership. Missionaries lived in Anishinaabeg communities oblivious to the temporal responsibilities their claims to religious authority entailed and found themselves at the center of community controversies concerning expressions or uses of power that they did not fully comprehend. While missionaries and other American observers in the early nineteenth century did not comprehend the sources, nature, and expectations of power in Anishinaabeg communities, understanding them today will help scholars discern the motives behind decisions Anishinaabeg leaders made in difficult circumstances.

Charismatic leadership positions provided some individuals in the community a chance for advancement, authority, and prestige, but charismatic credentials alone could not trump the credentials of local hereditary ogimaag. Despite their lack of coercive power, only ogimaag from hereditary lineages had the authority to designate land usage rights in the village community fisheries, hunting grounds, maple stands, and garden plots and to use social pressures to force compliance with community norms governing the redistribution of resources. Age, spiritual authority, and chiefly medals played important roles, but they were not determining factors. Not only did extraordinary leaders like Eshkibagikoonzh use religion as a unifying force in Native communities, but at least among the Anishinaabeg, all leaders employed ceremony, ritual, and religious symbols to promote unity and enhance their authority.

Notes

INTRODUCTION

1. Nichols, "Red Gentlemen and White Savages," 34.

2. *Anishinaabe* (plural, *Anishinaabeg*) is the Indigenous name for the peoples of the Three Fires Confederacy of the western Great Lakes. This confederacy consisted of the Ojibwe (also known as Chippewa, Missisauga, Saulteurs, and Nipissings), the Bodewatomi (Potawatomi), and Odawa (Ottowa). Throughout this work I use *Anishinaabe* and *Anishinaabeg* to refer to customs, traditions, and practices common to all three of these groups, and *Ojibwe* to refer to those that are common only to that group within the confederacy. All Ojibwe language terms used in this text use the double-vowel orthography standard in Ojibwe scholarly literature. The western dialect is used as many of the historical examples are from Minnesota and western Wisconsin. Special thanks to Anton Treuer for his help to transition various spellings in the original sources to the double-vowel system.

3. For a discussion of the social (as opposed to economic) context of gifts, see Murray, *Indian Giving*, 33–39. Anthropologist Marcel Mauss recognized that exchanges converting the outsider from potential enemy to friend must be examined as part of a dynamic whole; Pierre Bourdieu expanded the concept of economy to include symbolic as well as material value; Johnathan Parry suggested that only with the market do economic relations become differentiated from other types of social relationship; and C. A. Gregory proposed that gift exchange in pre-capitalist societies establishes a relationship between the partners (not between the objects exchanged). In a gift-oriented economy the goal is to expand social relations, and social relationships affirmed represent the true value of the exchange. The world view of the Anishinaabeg made this concept manifest.

4. John Tosh states that "the salient feature of the acephalous society can readily be defined. In societies of this kind, political authority is widely diffused; such authority positions as exist touch only a limited area of the lives of those subject to them; the unit within which disputes can peacefully be settled is small, and it tends to lack constant membership and fixed boundaries." Tosh, *Clan Leaders and Colonial Chiefs*, 3.

5. Sahlins, "Poor Man, Rich Man," 77; Tosh, *Clan Leaders and Colonial Chiefs*, 91–92. Junker, *Raiding, Trading, and Feasting*, 58–59.

6. Barnouw, *Wisconsin Chippewa Myths*; Grim, *The Shaman*; Hallowell, *Culture and Experience*; Landes, *Ojibwe Sociology*.

7. Grim, *The Shaman*, 94, 97–98; Schenck, *Voice of the Crane*, 106.

8. Although Ruth Landes and others have articulated atomism in detail, Victor Barnouw has provided perhaps the most concise definition of atomism as referring to "a loose form of social organization in which corporate organization and political authority are weak." Further, he stated: "It is not difficult for the component units to break away from the larger society of which they are a part," and "there are not many mechanisms for reinforcing larger-group social solidarity." Barnouw's research led him to believe that in Ojibwe society "there was no economic cooperation outside of the family unit . . . no communal hunting . . . no camp circle, no organized council of chiefs, no policing system, no regularly constituted military societies and no symbols of group integration."

The atomistic description of Ojibwe social organization so closely mirrors the social theories of such men as Sir Thomas More, John Locke, and Jean-Jacques Rousseau concerning the postulated "state of nature" prevailing before governed societies emerged that it is difficult not to interpret this theory as another incarnation of the "noble savage" trope. Locke suggested that while Native people enjoyed ownership of the meat they labored to procure, they had only a loose claim to land since Indian people did not improve it. In Locke's view this meant that Indians never left the state of nature and therefore also had never developed any form of social organization or government. In fact he equated North America and the state of nature so closely that he was able to conclude: "In the beginning, all the world was America" (Locke, *Second Treatise*, 17, 23, 26, 66). Like Locke, Barnouw and other atomist scholars perceived an Indian culture in which the individual is self-interested, separated from government, and in general, separated from society with little territorial claim. This similarity finds its origins not in Locke's impact on Barnouw's intellectual culture but rather in the enormous influence of Locke's political theories during the eighteenth and early nineteenth centuries when North America was being colonized. Locke's *Second Treatise* was popular in England and France, where the text formed part of university instruction, and by the mid-eighteenth century it was a standard element of curriculum in the American colonies as well. As a result the missionaries and officials who left us their accounts of American Indian life were informed long before they came to North America or ventured west from the colonies what they would see when they arrived in Indian country—and their expectations then shaped their observations.

9. White, *Middle Ground*. Richard White suggests that negotiated interactions between Europeans and Native peoples defined a political, cultural, and religious middle ground in the Great Lakes country from the seventeenth to early nineteenth centuries. In order to trade and build alliances with Native peoples, European powers found that they had to operate within the cultural conventions of the Native peoples or be considered enemies. This meant establishing kinship connections through marriage or adoption within Native communities and regularly giving gifts to community leaders. They may not have understood these relationships in the same manner— (both used the term "father" for the French governor in Quebec, the Europeans seeing an authoritative patriarch who kept order, while Indians perceived one who gave gifts to his children and mediated disputes between them)—but their perceptions overlapped enough to function smoothly. However, members of the group with the most political clout sought to establish their own cultural definitions more firmly on this "middle ground."

10. Kugel, *To Be the Main Leaders*, 6–7; Kugel, "Leadership within the Women's Community," 166–200.

11. Wallace, *Death and Rebirth of the Seneca*; Dowd, *A Spirited Resistance*.

12. Theresa S. Smith, *Island of the Anishinaabeg*, 24.

13. Hallowell, "Some Empirical Aspects of Northern Saulteux Religion," 392–93.

14. Berger and Luckmann, *Social Construction of Reality*, 135.

15. Sapir, "Linguistics as a Science."

16. Sapir "Conceptual Categories in Primitive Languages"; Nichols, "Red Gentlemen and White Savages," 515.

17. Dewdney, *Sacred Scrolls*, 37.

18. Johnston, *The Manitous*, 1–2.

19. Johnston, *The Manitous*, xxi.

20. Overholt and Callicott, *Clothed-in-Fur*, 5.

21. Overholt and Callicott, *Clothed-in-Fur*, 7.

22. Overholt and Callicott, *Clothed-in-Fur*, 9.

23. Berkhofer, *Salvation and the Savage*.

24. Hall and Boutwell, "Communication . . . Feb. 7th, 1833," 372.

25. Hämäläinen, *Comanche Empire*.

26. Schoolcraft, "Memoirs" (CD-ROM), 248–49, 306; Nicollet, *Journals of Joseph N. Nicollet*, 198.

27. Zebulon M. Pike to Hugh M'Gills, NW Establishment on Leech Lake, February 6, 1806, in Pike, *Expeditions*, 247–48.

28. John C. Calhoun to General Jacob Brown, Department of War, October 17, 1818, "Letters and Documents Relating to the Problems of the Frontier," in *Schoolcraft's Narrative Journal of Travels*, 281–82.

29. Murray, *Indian Giving*, 29.

30. Article 8 of the Treaty of Fond du Lac, August 5, 1826, states that the Chippewa agree to "disclaim all connexion with any foreign power." Lowrie and Franklin, eds., *American State Papers* 5:677.

31. Covering the dead: "consoling the mourners with gifts of brandy, and rewarding Indian emissaries active in the negotiations." Presents could also turn back war parties and reward those who had refused to organize war parties. White, *Middle Ground*, 140–41.

32. William Clark, August 19, 1825, Journal of the Proceedings of the Treaty of Prairie du Chien, August 1825, under William Clark and Louis Cass, William Clark Miscellaneous Papers, Archives, Wisconsin Historical Society, Madison (hereafter cited as Clark Papers).

33. Lawrence Taliaferro, Daily Journal for the Agency 1827–1829,

n.d. 1827, Lawrence Taliaferro Papers, Archives, Minnesota Historical Society, St. Paul. Thirty-nine Anishinaabeg chiefs signed an undated letter to the president of the United States requesting to be attached to an agency in Minnesota. Taliaferro's entry for May 7, 1827, reports the speeches from a council with Anishinaabeg chiefs at St. Peter's Agency. At this council, Bezhig of the St. Croix band stated: "Mr. Schoolcraft and Mr. Johnson are too far off—we have too many portages to make and we have to remain too long from our families."

34. Henry Rowe Schoolcraft did a census of Anishinaabeg territories in northern Wisconsin and Minnesota in 1832. In that year he suggests that 14,279 Native people, 1,553 mixed-bloods, and 259 Americans lived in the region. Schoolcraft, "Reports and Letters of Henry Rowe Schoolcraft on the Expedition of 1832," 152.

35. Berkhofer, *Salvation and the Savage*.

36. Hallowell, "Myth, Culture, and Personality," 551.

1. POWER IN THE ANISHINAABEG WORLD

1. Johnston, *The Manitous*, 2. In the Ojibwe language the third person pronoun is the same for both genders. The male/female gender of Gichi-Manidoo is not identified in the language and it is discussed as a truly balanced being. Basil Johnston also refers to Gichi-Manidoo as neither male nor female.

2. Johnston, *The Manitous*, xxi, 2–4.

3. Vecsey, *Traditional Ojibwa Religion*, 164.

4. Barnouw, *Wisconsin Chippewa Myths*, 253–54.

5. Black-Rogers, "Algonquin Gender Revisited," 63.

6. Hallowell, "Myth, Culture, and Personality," 551.

7. Overholt and Callicott, *Clothed-in-Fur*, 141.

8. Johnston, *The Manitous*, 13.

9. Smith, *Island of the Anishinaabeg*, 168–69.

10. Smith, *Island of the Anishinaabeg*, 51.

11. Hallowell, *The Ojibwa of Berens River*, 64.

12. Hallowell, "Ojibway World View and Disease," 272.

13. Overholt and Callicott, *Clothed-in-Fur*, 143.

14. Peers, *The Ojibwe of Western Canada*, 25.

15. Barnouw, *Wisconsin Chippewa Myths*, 247.

16. Grim, *The Shaman*, 90–91.

17. Overholt and Callicott, *Clothed-in-Fur*, 141.

18. Boatman, *My Elders Taught Me*, 9.

19. Overholt and Callicott, *Clothed-in-Fur*, 151.

20. Smith, *Island of the Anishinaabeg*, 183.

21. Black-Rogers, "Starving and Survival," 367.

22. Densmore, "The Belief of the Indian," 220.

23. Dewdney, *Sacred Scrolls*, 38.

24. White, *Middle Ground*, 129.

25. Smith, *Island of the Anishinaabeg*, 59. Smith, who did her research in the east on Manitoulin Island, spells this term *naabndanwin*.

26. Overholt and Callicott, *Clothed-in-Fur*, 148.

27. Cleland, *Rites of Conquest*, 65.

28. Overholt and Callicott, *Clothed-in-Fur*, 161.

29. Overholt and Callicott, *Clothed-in-Fur*, 144, 146–47.

30. Boatman, *My Elders Taught Me*, 9.

31. Hallowell, "Ojibwa Ontology, Behavior," 172–73.

32. Hallowell, "Ojibwa Ontology, Behavior," 152.

33. Barnouw, *Wisconsin Chippewa Myths*, 160.

34. Hallowell, "Ojibway World View and Disease," 272.

35. Smith, *Island of the Anishinaabeg*, 6–7. Smith spells this term *atisokan*.

36. Hallowell, "Ojibwa Ontology, Behavior," 149–50; Grim, *The Shaman*, 74.

37. Hallowell, "Ojibwa Ontology, Behavior," 144–45.

38. Overholt and Callicott, *Clothed-in-Fur*, 149–50.

39. Overholt and Callicott, *Clothed-in-Fur*, 76–77.

40. It must be noted that some gifted individuals do not always need modes of amplification to understand the information passed to them through the senses of the soul. They perceive either visually or audibly, or in both ways, the spirits that they understand to be around them in the course of normal routine waking life.

41. Shkilnyk, *Poison Stronger than Love*, 75; Hallowell, *Culture and Experience*, 232.

42. There is really no difference between dreams and visions,

other than that visions tend to be sought and dreams tend to be spontaneous. There is certainly no qualitative difference in the messages they deliver. Both are equally valid.

43. Hallowell, *Culture and Experience*, 99.

44. Cleland, *Rites of Conquest*, 55.

45. White, "The Woman Who Married a Beaver," 111.

46. Cleland, *Rites of Conquest*, 55–56.

47. Overholt and Callicott, *Clothed-in-Fur*, 151.

48. Landes, *Ojibwe Sociology*, 142. "Non-perishable gifts are keepsakes; it is considered offensive to have them circulate in a round of exchanges as the Dakotas do," Miller, "Gifts as Treaties," 221–45.

49. Whelan, "Dakota Indian Economics," 256–57.

50. Cleland, *Rites of Conquest*, 57.

51. Some scholars have suggested that the Anishinaabeg originally lived in uni-clan villages, but the Ojibwe oral tradition indicates that the doodemag were both a pre-European and a pre-migration development (Warren, *History of the Ojibway People*, 43–44; Benton-Banai, *Mishomis Book*, 74–78, 94–102). Anthropologists representing an atomist perspective argue that doodemag and multi-clan villages developed post-contact (Rogers, *Round Lake Ojibwa*; Angel, *Preserving the Sacred*; Schenck, *Voice of the Crane*). Harold Hickerson and Charles Bishop, however, argue that like other central Great Lakes groups, the Ojibwe would have had doodemag. "A system of such importance . . . could not possibly have arisen in post-contact times," suggests Bishop, citing widespread evidence that Ojibwe communities "fissioned and coalesced for subsistence and trade," relying on the kin of both mother and father. He considers it "unlikely that groups in early records were single patrilineal patrilocal clans" (Bishop, "The Question of Ojibwa Clans," 53, 58).

52. Tanner, *The Falcon*, 207–8.

53. Edmund F. Ely, Thursday 12 November 1835, Diaries of Edmund F. Ely, no. 9, 1835–1836, 5, Edmund F. Ely Papers, 1833–1904, Archives, Wisconsin Historical Society, Madison (hereafter cited as Diaries and Ely Papers); Edmund F. Ely, Friday 27 January 1837, Diaries nos. 11–20, 1836–1854, 91–92, Ely Papers. Ely identifies a distance of five encampments as equivalent to one day's march.

54. Hickerson, "Land Tenure of the Rainy Lake Chippewa," 54.

55. Bishop, *Northern Ojibwa*, 7–8, 10; Rogers "Band Organization," 21–50, 26; Rogers, *Round Lake Ojibwa*, B15.

56. Rogers "Band Organization," 25. Rogers spells this term *nintipencikewin*.

57. Rogers, *Round Lake Ojibwa*, B82.

58. Rogers, *Round Lake Ojibwa*, B83; Rogers conducted his ethnographic studies in the 1960s, and his informants asserted that in the past the nintipencikewin unit was an important and active political, religious, and economic division of the community.

59. *Minnesota Daily Pioneer* (St. Paul), June 20, 1850, quoted in Diedrich, *Ojibway Chiefs*, 21, spelling the name Buginogayshig.

60. Barnouw, *Wisconsin Chippewa Myths*, 178.

61. Cleland, *Rites of Conquest*, 61.

62. Carver, *Travels through the Interior*, 259–60.

63. Schoolcraft, *Schoolcraft's Narrative Journal of Travels*, 145; Baraga, *Short History*, 82–83. Nicollet, *Journals of Joseph N. Nicollet*, 51–52, 144, 266–68, 271; Copway, *Indian Life and Indian History*, 134.

64. Copway, *Indian Life and Indian History*, 134.

65. Nicollet, *Journals of Joseph N. Nicollet*, 144.

66. Tanner, *The Falcon*, 165.

67. Trowbridge, "Sketches of a Tour to the Lakes," 337.

68. Symbolic Petition of the Chippewa Chiefs, Wisconsin Historical Society.

69. Carver, *Travels through the Interior*, 242–43; 361–63.

70. Warren, *History of the Ojibway People*, 45–46.

71. Ziibiwing Cultural Society, *Ziibiwing Center*, 23.

72. Cleland, *Rites of Conquest*, 50.

73. Cleland, *Rites of Conquest*, 50.

74. Benton-Banai, *Mishomis Book*, 74–76.

75. Warren, *History of the Ojibway People*, 45–53.

76. Baraga, *Chippewa Indians*, 10.

77. Hickerson, "The Southwestern Chippewa," 41.

78. Villages were associated with specific tracts of land to which they had preeminent right that was respected by other groups, and they could even charge tolls for others to pass through, depending

on their kinship standing with members of the village community. Bohaker, "Nindoodemag," 42–43.

79. Bohaker, "Nindoodemag," 42–43.

80. James G. E. Smith, "Leadership among the Indians," 309.

81. Schoolcraft, "Reports and Letters of Henry Rowe Schoolcraft on the Expedition of 1832," 152. Schenck, *Voice of the Crane*, 68; Witgen, "Rituals of Possession," 648.

82. Smith, "Leadership among the Southwestern Ojibwa," 14–15.

83. Doty, "Journal and Letters of James Duane Doty," 436.

84. Smith, "Leadership among the Southwestern Ojibwa," 14–15. Smith's numbers are derived from population data Henry Rowe Schoolcraft recorded during his 1831 and 1832 trips to Wisconsin and Minnesota. Schoolcraft, "Reports and Letters of Henry Rowe Schoolcraft on the Expedition of 1832," 151–62.

85. Schenck, *Voice of the Crane*, 55.

86. Hickerson, "The Southwestern Chippewa," 62.

87. Grim, *The Shaman*, 97–98.

88. Hickerson, "The Southwestern Chippewa," 62–63.

89. Hickerson, "The Southwestern Chippewa," 62–63; Grim, *The Shaman*, 97–98.

90. Hickerson, "The Southwestern Chippewa," 50–51.

91. Hickerson, "The Southwestern Chippewa," 33–34, 61–62.

92. Schoolcraft, *Personal Memoirs of a Resident*, 367–68.

93. Frederick Ayer, letter to David Green, May 15, 1834, American Board of Commissioners for Foreign Missions, North American Indian Missions Records, ABC:18.3.7, Houghton Library, Harvard University, Boston, Massachusetts.

94. Baraga, *Chippewa Indians*, 10; Edmund F. Ely, Monday 20 June 1836, Diaries no. 10, January–February 1836, 65, Ely Papers; Edmund F. Ely, Wednesday 21 August 1833, Diaries no. 2, September 28–December 7, 1833, 18, Ely Papers.

95. Charlevoix, *Journal of a Voyage to North America*, 2:27, quoted in White, *Middle Ground*, 147–48.

96. William Clark, August 9, 1825, Journal of the Proceedings of the Treaty of Prairie du Chien, August 1825, under William Clark and Louis Cass, Clark Papers.

97. White, *Middle Ground*, 441.

98. Benton-Banai, *Mishomis Book*, 94–102.

99. Fixico, "The Alliance of the Three Fires," 2–3.

100. Proceedings of the Treaty at Chicago 1821, Group 75 NIS-203, National Archives.

101. Fixico, "The Alliance of the Three Fires," 10–11.

102. William Clark, August 9, 1825, Journal of the Proceedings of the Treaty of Prairie du Chien, August 1825, under William Clark and Louis Cass, Clark Papers.

103. Curot, "A Wisconsin Fur-Trader's Journal," 401, 421, 423, 426–27, 429, 436, 466.

104. Densmore, *Chippewa Customs*, 123.

105. Peers, *The Ojibwa of Western Canada*, 54.

106. Hickerson, "William T. Boutwell," 5, 17.

107. Densmore, "Uses of Plants by the Chippewa Indians," 123.

108. Densmore, "Uses of Plants by the Chippewa Indians," 310.

109. Densmore, *Chippewa Customs*, 124. William T. Boutwell, May 3, and May 16, 1833, Journal Kept While at Leech Lake, 1832–1837, William T. Boutwell Papers, Archives, Minnesota Historical Society, St. Paul (hereafter cited as Boutwell Papers, with date of entry only).

110. Densmore, "Uses of Plants by the Chippewa Indians," 312–13.

111. Peers, *The Ojibwa of Western Canada*, 80–81.

112. Peers, *The Ojibwa of Western Canada*, 54.

113. Curot, "A Wisconsin Fur-Trader's Journal," 401, 421, 423, 426–27, 429, 436, 466.

114. Cleland, *Rites of Conquest*, 243.

115. Densmore, *Chippewa Customs*, 122.

116. Allen, "Journal and Letters of Lieutenant James Allen," 181.

117. Peers, *The Ojibwa of Western Canada*, 22–23; Schoolcraft, *Schoolcraft's Narrative Journal of Travels*, 85.

118. Allen, "Journal and Letters of Lieutenant James Allen," 181.

119. Schoolcraft, *Schoolcraft's Narrative Journal of Travels*, 120.

120. Peers, *The Ojibwa of Western Canada*, 22–23, 54–55, 81.

121. Frederick Ayer, "Extract from a Letter of Mr. Ayer Dated at Yellow Lake Dec. 1, 1833," *Missionary Herald* 30 (April 1834): 137.

122. Schoolcraft, *Schoolcraft's Narrative Journal of Travels*, 169,

173–74; Gartner, "Four Worlds without an Eden," 336. Evidence of all these fishing methods is found in pre-contact archeological records in Wisconsin.

123. Allen, "Journal and Letters of Lieutenant James Allen," 209.

124. Densmore, *Chippewa Customs*, 122–25.

125. Schoolcraft, "Schoolcraft's Narrative of an Expedition through the Upper Mississippi to Itaska Lake," 20–21.

126. Densmore, *Chippewa Customs*, 122, 124.

127. Densmore, *Chippewa Customs*, 122–23.

128. Gartner, "Four Worlds without an Eden," 332–34.

129. Pike, *Expeditions*, 108.

130. Gartner, "Four Worlds without an Eden," 339.

131. Allen, "Journal and Letters of Lieutenant James Allen," 201.

132. Allen, "Journal and Letters of Lieutenant James Allen," 201.

133. I have been shown these beds by a local resident.

134. In the mission records of the ABCFM, missionaries at La Pointe frequently complain that the Indians left the island every summer to plant their gardens on the mainland near Bad River. Eventually a missionary station was opened at Bad River (Odanah) to be with the community year-round.

135. Gartner, "Four Worlds without an Eden," 339.

136. Schoolcraft, "Text of the Narrative Journal," 137.

137. Densmore, *Chippewa Customs*, 127.

138. Densmore, *Chippewa Customs*, 127.

139. Schoolcraft, "Text of the Narrative Journal," 177.

140. Schoolcraft, "Text of the Narrative Journal," 166. Schoolcraft observed this on July 20, 1820.

141. Densmore, *Chippewa Customs*, 127.

142. Densmore, "Uses of Plants by the Chippewa Indians," 313–14.

143. Boutwell, "Journal and Letters of the Reverend William Thurston Boutwell," 342.

144. Vennum, *Wild Rice and the Ojibway People*, 82; Densmore, "Uses of Plants by the Chippewa Indians," 313–14.

145. Densmore, *Chippewa Customs*, 123, 128.

146. Densmore, "Uses of Plants by the Chippewa Indians," 316.

147. Densmore, "Uses of Plants by the Chippewa Indians," 314.

148. Densmore, *Chippewa Customs*, 128.

149. Doty, "Journal and Letters of James Duane Doty," 440; Densmore, "Uses of Plants by the Chippewa Indians," 315.

150. Densmore, "Uses of Plants by the Chippewa Indians," 316.

151. Lips, *Die Reisernte der Ojibwa-Indianer*, 238–39, 265 quoted in Vennum, *Wild Rice and the Ojibway People*, 72.

152. Vennum, *Wild Rice and the Ojibway People*, 69.

153. Vennum, *Wild Rice and the Ojibway People*, 72.

154. Benton-Banai, *Mishomis Book*, 100–101; Vennum, *Wild Rice and the Ojibway People*, 72.

155. Densmore, *Chippewa Customs*, 40.

156. Densmore, "Uses of Plants by the Chippewa Indians," 319.

157. Densmore, *Chippewa Customs*, 40.

158. Curot, "A Wisconsin Fur-Trader's Journal," 411–12, 413–14, 416–17, 440, 460, 467.

159. Peers, *The Ojibwa of Western Canada*, 24–25.

160. Curot, "A Wisconsin Fur-Trader's Journal," 409–10, 411–12.

161. Peers, *The Ojibwa of Western Canada*, 71.

162. Schoolcraft, "Schoolcraft's Narrative of an Expedition through the Upper Mississippi to Itaska Lake," 21.

163. Henry, *Travels and Adventures in Canada*, 53–54.

164. Henry, *Travels and Adventures in Canada*, 243–44.

165. Schoolcraft, *Schoolcraft's Narrative Journal of Travels*, 95–96.

166. Densmore, *Chippewa Customs*, 123, 125.

167. Densmore, *Chippewa Customs*, 120.

168. Densmore, *Chippewa Customs*, 120–21.

169. Doty, "On the Manners and Customs of the Northern Indians."

170. Densmore, *Chippewa Customs*, 121.

171. Densmore, *Chippewa Customs*, 121.

172. Densmore, *Chippewa Customs*, 121.

173. Schoolcraft, *Schoolcraft's Narrative Journal of Travels*, 127.

174. Allen, "Journal and Letters of Lieutenant James Allen," 209.

175. White, "A Skilled Game of Exchange," 236–37.

176. Densmore, *Chippewa Customs*, 128–29.

177. Trowbridge, "Journal and Letters," 492; Baraga, *Chippewa Indians*, 57.

178. Densmore, *Chippewa Customs*, 128, 131.

179. Johnston, *The Manitous*, 9–10.

180. Peers, *The Ojibwe of Western Canada*, 25.

181. Grim, *The Shaman*, 106.

182. White, *Middle Ground*, 115–16.

183. Grim and St. John, "The Northeast Woodlands," 118.

2. OGIMAAG

1. Copway, *Indian Life and Indian History*, 137–38; Schoolcraft, "Schoolcraft's Narrative of an Expedition through the Upper Mississippi to Itaska Lake," 11; Satz, *Chippewa Treaty Rights*, 9–10; Warren, *History of the Ojibway People*, 318, 320–21, 334–35; Grant, "The Saulteaux Indians about 1804," 349–50; Beltrami, *A Pilgrimage in Europe and America*, 437–39; Baraga, *Chippewa Indians*, 21–22; McKenney and Hall, *Indian Tribes of North America*, 345; Carver, *Travels through the Interior*, 257–58; Schoolcraft, "Memoirs" (CD-ROM), 252.

2. Densmore, *Chippewa Customs*, 131–32. Earlier scholars used *band* to designate a variety of levels of social organization in tribal societies. I have chosen to use *village* both because it more closely conforms to Ojibwe linguistic terminology and because the social body it defines is more specific.

3. Nichols, "Red Gentlemen and White Savages," 222.

4. Kugel, *To Be the Main Leaders*, 71.

5. Kugel, *To Be the Main Leaders*, 71.

6. Johnston, "Letters on the Fur Trade 1833," 180–81.

7. Kugel, "Leadership within the Women's Community," 175–76.

8. Kugel, "Leadership within the Women's Community," 171.

9. Kugel, "Leadership within the Women's Community," 170.

10. Henry, *Travels and Adventures in Canada*, 48–49.

11. Carver, *Travels through the Interior*, 300–1.

12. Schoolcraft, "Memoirs" (CD-ROM)M, 387.

13. Johnston, "Reminiscences," 610.

14. McKenney, *Sketches of a Tour to the Lakes*, 183.

15. McKenney, *Sketches of a Tour to the Lakes*, 314, 461.

16. Buffalohead, "Farmers, Warriors, Traders," 242–43.

17. Romero, "'Ranging Foresters,'" 304–5.

18. Kugel, "Leadership within the Women's Community," 175–76.

19. McKenney, *Sketches of a Tour to the Lakes*, 346.

20. Tanner, *The Falcon*, 73.

21. Henry, *Travels and Adventures in Canada*, 100–1.

22. Grant, "The Saulteaux Indians about 1804," 320–21.

23. Baraga, *Chippewa Indians*, 46.

24. Hickerson, "The Southwestern Chippewa," 48–49.

25. White, *Middle Ground*, 214.

26. Kugel, *To Be the Main Leaders*, 71.

27. Warren, *History of the Ojibway People*, 49.

28. William Johnston, letter to Jane Schoolcraft, Leech Lake, October 28, 1833, in Johnston, "Letters on the Fur Trade 1833," 197.

29. Kohl, *Kitchi-Gami*, 111.

30. Edmund F. Ely, Monday 11 November, 1833, Diaries no. 2, September 28–December 7, 1833, 18, Ely Papers; Kohl, *Kitchi-Gami*, 111.

31. White, "Give Us a Little Milk," 71.

32. Diedrich, *Ojibway Chiefs*, 51–52, 53.

33. White, "The Woman Who Married a Beaver," 130; White, "Give Us a Little Milk," 71.

34. White, "Give Us a Little Milk," 71.

35. Johnston, *The Manitous*, xix.

36. Peers, Schenck, and Brown, "'There is No End,'" n.p.

37. *Ogimaa* is the singular and *ogimaag* is the plural form of this word.

38. Baraga, *A Dictionary of the Ojibway Language*, 194.

39. "Maissewinini—he who marches at the head of his band of warriors." Baraga, *A Dictionary of the Ojibway Language*, 206.

40. White, *Middle Ground*, 37.

41. Thwaites, ed., *Jesuit Relations*, 38:265.

42. Onions, ed., *Shorter Oxford English Dictionary*, 324.

43. Johnston, *The Manitous*, 23.

44. Johnston, *The Manitous*, xix.

45. Johnston, *The Manitous*, 23.

46. Peacock and Wisuri, *Ojibway Waasa Inaabidaa*, 118–19.

47. Landes, *Ojibwa Sociology*, 2–3.

48. Carver, *Travels through the Interior*, 259–60.

49. Carver, *Travels through the Interior*, 259–60.

50. Densmore, *Chippewa Customs*, 131–32.

51. Kugel, "Leadership within the Women's Community," 170.

52. Carver, *Travels through the Interior*, 259–60.

53. Boutwell, "Extracts from Boutwell's Journal of 1832," 180.

54. Hall and Boutwell, "Communication . . . Feb. 7th, 1833," 316.

55. Baraga, *A Dictionary of the Ojibway Language*, 36. Baraga spells this term *anikeogima*.

56. Chapman, "The Historic Johnston Family of the 'Soo,'" 352.

57. Chapman, "The Historic Johnston Family of the 'Soo,'" 311–12.

58. "The old chief was not at home—you would distinguish his house from others by a flag floating high above it in the air, the sign of his rank." Florantha Sproat, letter to Cephas Thompson, September 12, 1838, Letters of Florantha Sproat written at La Pointe 1838–1845, Archives, Wisconsin Historical Society, Madison.

59. Baraga, *Chippewa Indians*, 66–67; Grant, "The Saulteaux Indians about 1804," 349–50.

60. Baraga, *Chippewa Indians*, 66–67.

61. Grenville Sproat, postscript to letter of Florantha Sproat to Cephas Thompson, October 10, 1842, Letters of Florantha Sproat written at La Pointe 1838–1845, Archives, Wisconsin Historical Society, Madison.

62. Van Antwerp, quoted in Cleland, "The Western Chippewa," 33.

63. Baraga, *Chippewa Indians*, 66–67.

64. Schoolcraft, "Schoolcraft's Narrative of an Expedition through the Upper Mississippi to Itaska Lake," 56.

65. William Johnston, letter to Jane Schoolcraft, Leech Lake, October 8, 1833, in Johnston, "Letters on the Fur Trade 1833," 186.

66. White, "Give Us a Little Milk," 63–64.

67. William T. Boutwell, October 19, 1836, Journal Kept While at Leech Lake, 209, Boutwell Papers.

68. Baraga, *Chippewa Indians*, 47; William T. Boutwell, "Extracts from the Journal of Mr. Boutwell: Voyage through Lake Superior, Ascent of the St. Louis River," *Missionary Herald* 30 (April 1834): 133.

69. Diedrich, *Ojibway Chiefs*, 13; "Proceedings of a Council with

the Chippewa Indians July 1837," 416, 417, 418; Cleland, "The Western Chippewa," 33.

70. Edmund F. Ely, 9 March 1836 and 31 May 1836, Diaries nos. 11–20, 1836–1854, 33–34, 60–61, Ely Papers.

71. Trowbridge, "Journal and Letters," 331.

72. Baraga, *Chippewa Indians*, 31.

73. Baraga, *A Dictionary of the Ojibway Language*, 36. Baraga spells this Anikeshkagewin.

74. Smith, "Leadership among the Indians," 311.

75. Thwaites, ed., *Jesuit Relations*, 135–37.

76. Henry Rowe Schoolcraft, quoted in Smith, "Leadership among the Southwestern Ojibwa," 17.

77. Johnston, *Ojibwe Heritage*, 63–64.

78. Hall, "Extracts from the Journal of Mr. Hall . . . 25 Sept 28, 1833," 25.

79. Grant, "The Saulteaux Indians about 1804," 349–50.

80. Hickerson "The Southwestern Chippewa," 47.

81. Hickerson, "The Southwestern Chippewa," 46–47; Baraga, *A Dictionary of the Ojibway Language*, 239, 335. Baraga uses the spellings *gigitowinini* and *oshkabewiss*.

82. Grant, "The Saulteaux Indians about 1804," 349–50; William T. Boutwell, "Extracts from Boutwell's Journal of 1832," *Missionary Herald* 30 (June 1834): 222; Schoolcraft, "Schoolcraft's Narrative of an Expedition through the Upper Mississippi to Itaska Lake," 65.

83. Warren, *History of the Ojibway People*, 318. Warren spells the name of the chief Giishkimin as Keesh-ke-mun.

84. Nicollet, *Journals of Joseph N. Nicollet*, 157, 202.

85. Angel, *Preserving the Sacred*, 90.

86. Baraga, A Dictionary *of the Ojibway Language*, 236. Baraga spells this term *mijinawe*.

87. Grant, "The Saulteaux Indians about 1804," 349–50.

88. Pike, *Expeditions*, 133–34, note 46.

89. "Proceedings of a Council with the Chippewa Indians July 1837," 415–16.

90. Schoolcraft, "Schoolcraft's Narrative of an Expedition through the Upper Mississippi to Itaska Lake," 65.

91. Schoolcraft, "Schoolcraft's Narrative of an Expedition through the Upper Mississippi to Itaska Lake," 65.

92. Schoolcraft, "Schoolcraft's Narrative of an Expedition through the Upper Mississippi to Itaska Lake," 65.

93. Kohl, *Kitchi-Gami*, 161–62.

94. Densmore, *Chippewa Customs*, 131–32.

95. Pike, *Expeditions*, 133–34.

96. Densmore, *Chippewa Customs*, 60.

97. Johnston, *Ojibway Heritage*, 78–79.

98. Gunn, "Peter Garrioch at St. Peter's in 1837," 120.

99. Johnston, "A Reminiscence of George Johnston," 507.

100. "Proceedings of a Council with the Chippewa Indians July 1837," 413. Bezhig's name is spelled "Pay-a-jig" in the council proceedings.

101. Cleland, "The Western Chippewa," 33.

102. William T. Boutwell, May 29, 1835, Journal Kept While at Leech Lake, 197, Boutwell Papers; "Proceedings of a Council with the Chippewa Indians July 1837," 415–16.

103. "Proceedings of a Council with the Chippewa Indians July 1837," 415–16.

104. William T. Boutwell, May 29, 1835, and October 19, 1836, Journal Kept While at Leech Lake," 195–96, 196–97, 209, Boutwell Papers.

105. Cleland, "The Western Chippewa," 33.

106. Hickerson, *The Chippewa and the Neighbors*, 58–59; Houghton, "Journal, Letters and Reports of Dr. Douglass Houghton," 262.

107. Kugel, *To Be the Main Leaders*, 23–24.

108. Edmund F. Ely, Friday February 26, 1836, and Tuesday 31 May 1836, Diaries nos. 11–20, 1836–1854, 60–61, Ely Papers; Edmund F. Ely, letter to David Green, January 9, 1837, in Early Protestant Missionaries in the Lake Superior Country, vol. 1, 152, Archives, Wisconsin Historical Society, Superior.

109. Bieder, *Native American Communities in Wisconsin*, 24–25.

110. Baraga, *Chippewa Indians*, 52.

111. Kohl, *Kitchi-Gami*, 270.

112. Perrot, "Memoir on the Manners, Customs, and Religion," 136–37.

113. William T. Boutwell, Rev. William T. Boutwell's Reminiscences, Boutwell Papers.

114. Cleland, *Rites of Conquest*, 62–63.

115. Copway, *Indian Life and Indian History*, 138.

116. Copway, *Indian Life and Indian History*, 138.

117. Cleland, *Rites of Conquest*, 62–63.

118. Baraga, *Chippewa Indians*, 32.

119. Densmore, *Chippewa Customs*, 132; Grant, "The Saulteaux Indians about 1804," 350–51; Sherman Hall, letter to Richards and Tracy, July 10, 1834, Miscellaneous Letters of Sherman Hall and His Sisters 1831–1875, in Early Protestant Missionaries in the Lake Superior Country, vol. 3, 214–15, Archives, Wisconsin Historical Society, Superior. Baraga, *Short History*, 172; Nicollet, *Journals of Joseph N. Nicollet*, 255–56.

120. Baraga, *Short History*, 172; Tanner, *The Falcon*, 166.

121. Grant, "The Saulteaux Indians about 1804," 350–51.

122. Baraga, *Chippewa Indians*, 24.

123. Copway, *Indian Life and Indian History*, 138; Baraga, *Short History*, 172.

124. Curot, "A Wisconsin Fur-Trader's Journal," 464.

125. White, *Middle Ground*, 40.

126. William T. Boutwell, "Extracts from the Journal of Mr. Boutwell," *Missionary Herald* 30 (April 1834): 133.

127. Benton-Banai, *Mishomis Book*, 95–103; Peacock and Wisuri, *Ojibway Waasa Inaabidaa*, 45.

128. Peacock and Wisuri, *Ojibway Waasa Inaabidaa*, 45.

129. Benton-Banai, *Mishomis Book*, 95–103; Kugel, *To Be the Main Leaders*, 25.

130. Ojibwe Curriculum Committee et al., *Land of the Ojibwe*, 4; Baraga, *Chippewa Indians*, 31; Kugel, *To Be the Main Leaders*, 25.

131. Speck and Eiseley, "Significance of Hunting Territory Systems," 274–75.

132. Grant, "The Saulteaux Indians about 1804," 326.

133. Hickerson, "Land Tenure of the Rainy Lake Chippewa," 57–58.

134. Baraga, *Chippewa Indians*, 24–25.

135. Speck, "The Family Hunting Band," 298–99.

136. Brinkman, "Challenges of Wisconsin's Weather," 50.

137. William Johnston, letter to Jane Schoolcraft, Grand Portage, August 31, 1833, in Johnston, "Letters on the Fur Trade 1833," 166–67.

138. Waisberg, "Boreal Forest Subsistence," 183–84; Hickerson, "The Southwestern Chippewa," 35; Jenness, "The Indians of Canada," 124–25.

139. Waisberg, "Boreal Forest Subsistence," 182.

140. Hickerson, "The Southwestern Chippewa," 45, 49–50.

141. Hickerson, "Land Tenure of the Rainy Lake Chippewa," 54–55, 58–59.

142. "Annual Report," Missionary Herald 32 (January 1836): 25, 7; Frederick Ayer, letter to David Green, October 1835, American Board of Commissioners for Foreign Missions Papers, Archives, Minnesota Historical Society, St. Paul (hereafter cited as ABCFM Papers).

143. Hickerson, "Land Tenure of the Rainy Lake Chippewa," 60–61.

144. Speck and Eiseley, "Significance of Hunting Territory Systems," 277.

145. Carver, Travels through the Interior, 297–98.

146. Speck, "The Family Hunting Band," 289–305, 297–98.

147. Grim, The Shaman, 100; Doherty, "We Don't Want Them to Hold Their Hands over Our Heads," 58–59.

148. Grim, The Shaman, 100.

149. Hickerson, "The Southwestern Chippewa," 51.

150. Tanner, The Falcon, 31, 69, 207–8.

151. Speck, "The Family Hunting Band," 295–96.

152. Tanner, The Falcon, 31.

153. Tanner, The Falcon, 207–8.

154. Barnouw, Wisconsin Chippewa Myths, 41.

155. William T. Boutwell, May 24, 1835, Journal Kept While at Leech Lake, 193–94, Boutwell Papers.

156. Edmund F. Ely, Friday 26 February 1836, Diaries nos. 11–20, 29.

157. William Clark, August 8, 1825, Journal of the Proceedings of the Treaty of Prairie du Chien, August 1825, under William Clark and Lewis Cass, Clark Papers.

158. William Clark, August 6, 1825, Journal of the Proceedings of the Treaty of Prairie du Chien, August 1825, under William Clark and Lewis Cass, Clark Papers.

159. "Proceedings of a Council with the Chippewa Indians July 1837 with the Chippewa Indians July 1837," 412.

160. Schoolcraft, *Schoolcraft's Narrative Journal of Travels*, 165.

161. White, *Middle Ground*, 104.

162. Speck and Eiseley, "Significance of Hunting Territory Systems," 271–72.

163. White, *Middle Ground*, 341–42.

164. Frederick Ayer and Edmund Ely, letter to David Greene, October 31, 1838, ABCFM Papers; Edmund F. Ely, 7 August 1838, Diaries nos. 11–20, 1836–1854, 162, Ely Papers; Doherty, "We Don't Want Them to Hold Their Hands over Our Heads," 56–57.

165. Edmund F. Ely, 7 August 1838, Diaries nos. 11–20, 1836–1854, 162, Ely Papers.

166. Doherty, "We Don't Want Them to Hold Their Hands over Our Heads," 56.

167. Hall and Boutwell, "Communication . . . Feb. 7th, 1833," 316.

168. Schoolcraft, "Travels among the Aborigines," 100.

169. Peacock and Wisuri, *Ojibway Waasa Inaabidaa*, 118–19.

170. Sherman Hall, September 6, 1831, Journal of Rev. Sherman Hall, August 27, 1831–March 11, 1832, ABCFM Papers.

171. White, *Middle Ground*, 56.

172. Cleland, *Rites of Conquest*, 59–60.

173. Kohl, *Kitchi-Gami*, 273.

174. Leonard H. Wheeler to David Green, May 3, 1843, ABCFM Papers.

175. "Proceedings of a Council," 430.

176. Carver, *Travels through the Interior*, 259–60.

177. Isham, *Observations on Hudson's Bay, 1743*, 82–83.

178. Carver, *Travels through the Interior*, 259–60.

179. Johnston, *Ojibway Ceremonies*, 159.

180. Baraga, *Short History*, 170.

181. Baraga, *Short History*, 170.

182. Johnston, *Ojibway Ceremonies*, 159.

183. Trowbridge, "Journal and Letters," 329.

184. William Clark, Journal of the Proceedings of the Treaty of Prairie du Chien, August 1, 1825, under William Clark and Louis Cass, Clark Papers.

185. Cleland, *Rites of Conquest*, 60–61.

186. Henry, *Travels and Adventures in Canada*, 96–97.

187. Baraga, *Chippewa Indians*, 22.

188. In the example cited earlier, Boutwell indicated that he laid thirty plugs of tobacco at Elder Brother's feet when he made the request. Ely had less tact and social grace. The ogimaag at Fond du Lac usually had to request of him the food and tobacco needed to supply councils held on his behalf. See William T. Boutwell, 20 March, 1835, Journal Kept While at Leech Lake, Boutwell Papers; Edmund F. Ely, Thursday 16 June 1836, Diaries nos. 11–20, 64–65.

189. Frederick Ayer, letter to David Green, May 15, 1834, American Board of Commissioners for Foreign Missions, North American Indian Missions Records, ABC:18.3.7, Houghton Library, Harvard University, Boston, Massachusetts; William T. Boutwell, March 12, 1835, Journal Kept While at Leech Lake, 187–88, Boutwell Papers.

190. Nicollet, *Journals of Joseph N. Nicollet*, 117–18.

191. Leonard H. Wheeler to David Green, May 3, 1843, box 3, ABCFM Papers.

192. Fixico, "The Alliance of the Three Fires," 11–12.

193. Johnston, *Ojibwe Ceremonies*, 159–60; Cleland, "The Western Chippewa," 33.

194. Johnston, *Ojibwe Ceremonies*, 159–60.

195. Johnston, *Ojibwe Ceremonies*, 159–60; Benton-Banai, *Mishomis Book*, 94–102.

196. McNally, *Ojibwe Singers*, vii.

197. Henry Wheeler, letter to David Green, September 23, 1841, ABCFM Papers.

198. Cleland, "The Western Chippewa," 33. These statements of authority were also made in meetings on a smaller scale with missionaries and the like. It seems that whenever authority was exercised, the basis of this authority had to be established. Aishke-bugekosh on Sunday May 24, 1835, told W. T. Boutwell that he was

the authority to listen to in the community because "this Lake was first discovered by my ancestors, and if anyone has anything to say, I am the one." William T. Boutwell, May 24, 1835, Journal Kept While at Leech Lake, 193–94, Boutwell Papers. Nindipens made similar statements to Edmund F. Ely, Friday 4 March 1836, Diaries nos. 11–20, 31, Ely Papers.

199. Cleland, "The Western Chippewa," 33.

200. Landes, *Ojibwe Sociology,* 2–3.

201. William T. Boutwell, March 20, 1835, Journal Kept While at Leech Lake, 189–90, Boutwell Papers. Boutwell asked the ogimaa Elder Brother to call a council at which he would ask the young men to refrain from pulling out the tail hairs of his horse. Boutwell had to supply thirty plugs of tobacco, one for each man invited to the council, and Elder Brother made it clear that he made the request on Boutwell's behalf. Frederick Ayer, "Extracts from Various Communications: Station at Yellow Lake," *Missionary Herald* 30 (1834): 59. "On the first day of their [the Indians'] arrival, they met in a body to transact some business; after which I made known to them the object of our coming to Yellow Lake, and the design of the Board relative to the Ojibwas generally. . . . As the principal chief and many other Indians were not present, they made no definite answer to my remarks, and will not probably, till winter or spring."

202. Frederick Ayer, letter to David Green, October 1835, ABCFM Papers.

203. Johnston, *Ojibwe Heritage,* 78–79.

204. Grant, "The Saulteaux Indians about 1804," 349–50.

205. Smith, "Leadership among the Southwestern Chippewa," 18.

3. MAYOSEWININIWAG

1. Eisenstadt, Introduction to *Max Weber on Charisma,* xviii.

2. Eisenstadt, Introduction, xix.

3. Eisenstadt, Introduction, xxiv.

4. Densmore, "The Belief of the Indian in a Connection between Song and the Supernatural", Smithsonian Institution, *Bureau of American Ethnology,* Bulletin 151, 1953, 219.

5. Shils, "Charisma, Order, and Status," 201.

6. Shils, "Charisma, Order, and Status," 201.

7. Eisenstadt, Introduction, xxix, xxxiii–xxxiv.

8. Cleland, "The Western Chippewa," 25.

9. Kugel, "Religion Mixed with Politics," 128–29.

10. Copway, *Indian Life and Indian History*, 140.

11. Nicollet, *Journals of Joseph N. Nicollet*, 176.

12. Kohl, *Kitchi-Gami*, 343.

13. Johnston, *Ojibway Heritage*, 68.

14. Densmore, "Chippewa Music II," 61.

15. Henry, *Travels and Adventures*, 44–45.

16. Lawrence Taliaferro, January 13, 1826, Daily Journal for the Agency 1827–1829, Lawrence Taliaferro Papers, Archives, Minnesota Historical Society, St. Paul.

17. Densmore, "Chippewa Music II," 61.

18. Densmore, "Chippewa Music II," 87–88.

19. Densmore, "Chippewa Music II," 67.

20. Kohl, *Kitchi-Gami*, 125–26.

21. Densmore, "Chippewa Music II," 131.

22. Frances Densmore's informant concerning Ojibwe war traditions was eighty-nine in 1909 and so must have been born in about 1820. He died in April 1911. He was a parallel cousin (brother) of Buginogayshig, who was assassinated in 1868. During his life the informant led many war parties before his community was moved to the reservation. Densmore, "Chippewa Music II," 59–61.

23. Densmore, "Chippewa Music II," 67.

24. Densmore, "Chippewa Music II," 67, 59–61.

25. Densmore, "Chippewa Music II," 67.

26. Landes, *Ojibwe Sociology*, 119.

27. Densmore, "Chippewa Music II," 68.

28. Hickerson, "The Southwestern Chippewa," 56–57, 59–60, 63.

29. Hickerson, "The Southwestern Chippewa," 56–57.

30. Hickerson, "The Southwestern Chippewa," 56–57, 63.

31. Frederick Ayer, "Letter of Mr. Ayer dated at Fond du Lac Oct. 8, 1838," *Missionary Herald* 35 (1839): 315.

32. William T. Boutwell, October 18, 1836, Journal Kept While at Leech Lake, 206–7, Boutwell Papers.

33. William T. Boutwell, October 18, 1836, Journal Kept While at Leech Lake, 208–9, Boutwell Papers.

34. Warren, *History of the Ojibway People*, 301–2.

35. Johnston, "A Reminiscence of George Johnston," 507.

36. Johnston, "Reminiscences," 610–11.

37. William T. Boutwell, letter to David Green, March 26, 1835, ABCFM Papers.

38. Boutwell, "Letter of Mr. Boutwell at Fond du Lac Post, June 25, 1832."

39. Allen, "Journal and Letters of Lieutenant James Allen," 192.

40. William Johnston, letter to Jane Schoolcraft, Leech Lake, October 21, 1833, in Johnston, "Letters on the Fur Trade 1833," 192–93.

41. Hickerson, "The Southwestern Chippewa," 60–61.

42. Densmore, "Chippewa Music II," 68.

43. Landes, *Ojibwe Sociology*, 119–20.

44. Nicollet, *Journals of Joseph N. Nicollet*, 165, 174.

45. Densmore, "Chippewa Music II," 84–85.

46. Kohl, *Kitchi-Gami*, 343–44.

47. Densmore, "Chippewa Music II," 84–85.

48. Baraga, *Short History*, 157.

49. Kohl, *Kitchi-Gami*, 341–43; Landes, *Ojibwe Sociology*, 118–19.

50. Landes, *Ojibwe Sociology*, 118–19.

51. Kohl, *Kitchi-Gami*, 341–42.

52. Kohl, *Kitchi-Gami*, 342–43.

53. Kohl, *Kitchi-Gami*, 342–43; Hall and Boutwell, "Communication . . . Feb. 7th, 1833," 316.

54. Kohl, *Kitchi-Gami*, 342–43.

55. Landes, *Ojibwe Sociology*, 118–19.

56. Landes, *Ojibwe Sociology*, 118–19.

57. Densmore, "Chippewa Music II," 87–88.

58. Densmore, "Chippewa Music II," 89–90.

59. Johnston, *Ojibway Heritage*, 78–79.

60. Densmore, "Chippewa Music II," 90–92.

61. Densmore, "Chippewa Music II," 89–90; Kohl, *Kitchi-Gami*, 342–43.

62. Densmore, *Chippewa Customs*, 134.

63. Densmore, "Chippewa Music II," 90; Boutwell, "Letter of Mr. Boutwell at Fond du Lac Post, June 25, 1832." Chief White Crow abandoned a Fond du Lac war party due to death of a child.

64. Densmore, *Chippewa Customs*, 134.

65. Kohl, *Kitchi-Gami*, 342–43.

66. Densmore, "Chippewa Music II," 93–94.

67. Kohl, *Kitchi-Gami*, 343.

68. Densmore, "Chippewa Music II," 110–11.

69. Edmund F. Ely, Thursday June 1842, Diaries nos. 11–20, 1836–1854, 258, Ely Papers.

70. Densmore, "Chippewa Music II," 110–11.

71. Densmore, "Chippewa Music II," 134.

72. Edmund F. Ely, Diaries nos. 11–20, 1836–1854, 258, Ely Papers.

73. Kohl, *Kitchi-Gami*, 344.

74. Edmund F. Ely, Diaries nos. 11–20, 1836–1854, 258, Ely Papers; Densmore, *Chippewa Customs*, 134–35.

75. Densmore, *Chippewa Customs*, 134–35; Densmore, "Chippewa Music II," 93–94.

76. Densmore, "Chippewa Music II," 126–29.

77. Kohl, *Kitchi-Gami*, 344; Densmore, "Chippewa Music II," 91–92.

78. Kohl, *Kitchi-Gami*, 344.

79. Densmore, "Chippewa Music II," 63, 99, 101, 111–12.

80. Kohl, *Kitchi-Gami*, 343–44.

81. Kohl, *Kitchi-Gami*, 343–44.

82. Landes, *Ojibwe Sociology*, 119–20.

83. Kohl, *Kitchi-Gami*, 344–45.

84. Densmore, "Chippewa Music II," 85–86.

85. Densmore, "Chippewa Music II," 86.

86. Densmore, "Chippewa Music II," 94–95.

87. Nelson, *My First Years in the Fur Trade*, 175.

88. Densmore, "Chippewa Music II," 106–7.

89. Edmund F. Ely, Thursday June 1842, Diaries nos. 11–20, 1836–1854, 258, Ely Papers.

90. Densmore, "Chippewa Music II," 111–12.

91. Densmore, "Chippewa Music II," 70–71.

92. Densmore, "Chippewa Music II," 106–9.

93. Densmore, "Chippewa Music II," 134–35.

94. Henry, *Travels and Adventures in Canada*, 203–4, quoted in Schenck, *Voice of the Crane*, 93.

95. Schenck, *Voice of the Crane*, 93.

96. Kohl, *Kitchi-Gami*, 345.

97. Densmore, "Chippewa Music II," 115–16.

98. Densmore, "Chippewa Music II," 118, 134–35.

99. Boutwell, "Extracts from Boutwell's Journal of 1832," *Missionary Herald* 30 (May 1834): 179.

100. Densmore, "Chippewa Music II," 118.

101. Boutwell, "Journal and Letters of the Reverend William Thurston Boutwell," 328.

102. Densmore, "Chippewa Music II," 118.

103. Densmore, *Chippewa Customs*, 134–35.

104. Schoolcraft, "Schoolcraft's Narrative of an Expedition through the Upper Mississippi to Itaska Lake," 26.

105. Densmore, "Chippewa Music II," 126.

106. Boutwell, "Journal and Letters of the Reverend William Thurston Boutwell," 328, 332.

107. Densmore, Chippewa Music II, 126.

108. Densmore, *Chippewa Customs*, 134–35.

109. Kohl, *Kitchi-Gami*, 380.

110. Densmore, "Chippewa Music II," 68–70.

4. GECHI-MIDEWIJIG

1. Angel, *Preserving the Sacred*, 59.

2. Hickerson, "Notes on the Post-Contact Origin of the Midewiwin," 404–23; Hickerson, "The Sociohistorical Significance of Two Chippewa Ceremonials," 67–85; Grim, *The Shaman*, 115, 117; Barnouw, *Wisconsin Chippewa Myths*, 9; Schlesier, "Rethinking the Midewiwin"; Bishop, *Northern Ojibwa*, 9.

3. Benton-Banai, *Mishomis Book*, 61–74, 95–103.

4. Warren, *History of the Ojibway People*, 67.

5. Densmore, "Chippewa Music," 14–15.

6. Densmore, "Chippewa Music," 18.

7. Hickerson, *The Chippewa and the Neighbors*, 142–43; Kigoshi, Aizawa, and Suzuki, "Gakushuin Natural Radiocarbon Measurements VII," 320; Kidd, "Birch-Bark Scrolls in Archaeological Contexts."

8. Peers, *The Ojibwe of Western Canada*, 23; Hickerson, *The Chippewa and the Neighbors*, 142–43.

9. Johnston, *Ojibway Ceremonies*, 93.

10. Ziibiwing Cultural Society, *Ziibiwing Center*, 5.

11. Grim, *The Shaman*, 68, 70.

12. Deleary, "The Midewiwin, an Aboriginal Spiritual Institution," 78.

13. Densmore, "Chippewa Music," 13; Densmore, *Chippewa Customs*, 86–87; Hoffman, "The Midewiwin or 'Grand Medicine Society,'" 197–203; Angel, *Preserving the Sacred*, 47–76; Hallowell "Ojibwe Ontology, Behavior," 171.

14. Peers, *The Ojibwa of Western Canada*, 23–24.

15. Smith, *Island of the Anishinaabeg*, 183.

16. Densmore, *Chippewa Customs*, 86–87.

17. Johnston, *Ojibway Heritage*, 93.

18. Benton-Banai, *Mishomis Book*, 64.

19. Grim, *The Shaman*, 75–76.

20. Densmore, *Chippewa Customs*, 86–87.

21. Peers, *The Ojibwa of Western Canada*, 167–68.

22. Vennum, *Wild Rice and the Ojibway People*, 72.

23. The mission at Fond du Lac was not opened until 1833. The years 1835 and 1836 at Fond du Lac represent a period in which the primary missionary there, Sherman Hall, spent most of his time translating books into Ojibwe for use at the school and seldom interacted with the Indian community. The dates for the village at Yellow Lake, which later moved to Pokegoma, are less precise as Frederick Ayer left only infrequent letters and no diaries. The few occasions when the Midewiwin was held in the winter were the result of organizing special ceremonies for the sick.

24. Densmore, "Chippewa Music," 13.

25. Copway, *Indian Life and Indian History*, 161–62.

26. Angel, *Preserving the Sacred*, 155.

27. Warren, *History of the Ojibway People*, 264–65.

28. Nicollet, *Journals of Joseph N. Nicollet*, 196. Nicollet relates that the medewijig cannot open their *pinjigoosan* (medicine bags) without performing a sweat lodge ceremony.

29. Nicollet, *Journals of Joseph N. Nicollet*, 195.

30. Edmund F. Ely, Manners and Customs of the Ojibuey, Ely Papers.

31. Baraga, *Chippewa Indians*, 41–42.

32. Rogers, *Round Lake Ojibwa*, D10.

33. Nicollet, *Journals of Joseph N. Nicollet*, 220–21; Edmund F. Ely, Manners and Customs of the Ojibuey, Ely Papers.

34. Edmund F. Ely, Manners and Customs of the Ojibuey, Ely Papers.

35. William T. Boutwell, November 9, 1833, Journal Kept While at Leech Lake, 141–42, Boutwell Papers; Ruth Landes, *Ojibwa Sociology*, 139.

36. William T. Boutwell, November 9, 1833, Journal Kept While at Leech Lake, 142, Boutwell Papers.

37. Huron H. Smith, "Ethnobotany of the Ojibwe Indians."

38. Densmore, *Chippewa Customs*, 121.

39. Nicollet, *Journals of Joseph N. Nicollet*, 211–12; 214.

40. Nicollet, *Journals of Joseph N. Nicollet*, 211–12; Edmund F. Ely, Diaries nos. 11–20, 57–58, 99–100, Ely Papers.

41. Brown and Brightman, *Orders of the Dreamed*, 61–62; 68–69.

42. Tanner, *The Falcon*, 32, 47–48, 51, 91, 164–65, 180, 202; 251–52.

43. Baraga, *Chippewa Indians*, 41–42.

44. Copway, *Indian Life and Indian History*, 128–31.

45. Copway, *Indian Life and Indian History*, 132; Densmore, "Chippewa Music," 16. "The drawings of mide songs are universally understood by members of the Midewiwin. A large number of drawings have been tested in the following manner: A song has been phonographically recorded and the picture drawn on one reservation and later the phonograph record has been played to a member of the Midewiwin living on a distant reservation. The song has been recognized at once and a picture drawn without hesitation. This pic-

ture, on comparison with the first, has been found identical in symbolism, differing only as one person draws better than another. By an inverse test, a song picture has been shown to a member of the Midewiwin and she has sung the song which was sung on a distant reservation by the person who drew the picture" (Densmore, "Chippewa Music," 16).

46. Lewis, "Maps, Mapmaking," 82.

47. *Diba Jimooyung*, 12.

48. Kohl, *Kitchi-Gami*, 43.

49. Vecsey, *Traditional Ojibwa Religion*, 184–85.

50. Bieder, *Native American Communities in Wisconsin*, 101–2. Bieder states that the Midewiwin spread among the Menominee, Winnebago, Sauk, Fox, Potawatomi, Dakota, Miami, and Iowa, allowing it to "function as both a spiritual and integrative force." See also White, *Middle Ground*, 217: White likewise discusses this intertribal dispersion.

51. White, *Middle Ground*, 217–18; Lawrence Taliaferro, February 20 and May 17, 1826, Daily Journal for the Agency 1827–1829, Lawrence Taliaferro Papers, Archives, Minnesota Historical Society, St. Paul.

52. Angel, *Preserving the Sacred*, 75–76.

53. Deleary "The Midewiwin, an Aboriginal Spiritual Institution," 75.

54. Nicollet, *Journals of Joseph N. Nicollet*, 210.

55. Warren, *History of the Ojibway People*, 100.

56. Densmore, "Chippewa Music II."

57. William T. Boutwell, May 28, 1835, Journal Kept While at Leech Lake, 194–95, Boutwell Papers.

58. Nicollet, *Journals of Joseph N. Nicollet*, 221.

59. Angel, *Preserving the Sacred*, 12–13.

60. Densmore, "Chippewa Music," 13–14.

61. Anton Treuer, personal communication, October 27, 2008.

62. William T. Boutwell, May 28, 1835, Journal Kept While at Leech Lake, 194–95, Boutwell Papers.

63. Densmore, "Chippewa Music," 13–14.

64. Angel, *Preserving the Sacred*, 180.

65. Landes, *Ojibwa Religion and the Midewiwin*, 44.

66. Vecsey, *Traditional Ojibwa Religion*, 188.

67. Vecsey, *Traditional Ojibwa Religion*, 184–85.

68. Frederick Ayer, "Extract from a letter of Mr. Ayer dated at Yellow Lake, Dec. 1, 1833," *Missionary Herald* 30 (April 1834): 137.

69. Ayer, "Extract from a letter of Mr. Ayer dated at Yellow Lake, Dec. 1, 1833," 137.

70. Schoolcraft, *History, Condition and Prospects of the Indian Tribes of the United States*, 144.

71. Tanner, *The Falcon*, 169–70.

72. Tanner, *The Falcon*, 186–93. Ais-kaw-ba-wis in western dialect is spelled Oshkaabewis. However, because I discuss the office of oshkaabewis extensively, I left Tanner's spelling of the name for clarity.

73. Nicollet, *Journals of Joseph N. Nicollet*, 198.

74. Hickerson, *The Chippewa and the Neighbors*, 57.

75. Nicollet, *Journals of Joseph N. Nicollet*, 198.

76. Nicollet, *Journals of Joseph N. Nicollet*, 198.

77. Nicollet, *Journals of Joseph N. Nicollet*, 198.

78. Smith, "Leadership among the Southwestern Chippewa," 19.

79. Smith, "Leadership among the Southwestern Chippewa," 19.

80. Baraga, *Chippewa Indians*, 23.

81. Baraga, *Chippewa Indians*, 41–42.

82. Baraga, *A Dictionary of the Ojibway Language*, 194.

83. Grim, *The Shaman*, 114–15.

84. Beltrami, *A Pilgrimage in Europe and America*, 403.

85. Fixico, "The Alliance of the Three Fires," 11–12.

86. Kohl, *Kitchi-Gami*, 84–85.

87. Kohl, *Kitchi-Gami*, 84–85.

88. William Johnston, letter to Jane Schoolcraft, Leech Lake, September 20, 1833, in Johnston, "Letters on the Fur Trade 1833," 179–80.

89. Hallowell, *The Ojibwa of Berens River*, 11.

90. Kohl, *Kitchi-Gami*, 85–86, 344–45; Densmore, "Chippewa Music II," 94–95.

91. Diedrich, *Ojibwe Chiefs*, 33.

92. Diedrich, *Ojibway Chiefs*, 24–25, 33.

93. Bieder, *Native American Communities in Wisconsin*, 102; Grim, *The Shaman*, 91–92.

94. Edmund F. Ely, Wednesday 17 August 1836 and Thursday February 16, 1837, Diaries nos. 11–20, 69, 104, Ely Papers; William T. Boutwell, August 27, 1833, Journal Kept While at Leech Lake, 112, Boutwell Papers; Diedrich, *Ojibway Chiefs*, 51–53.

95. William T. Boutwell, August 27, 1833, Journal Kept While at Leech Lake, 112, Boutwell Papers.

96. Edmund F. Ely, Diaries nos. 11–20, 1836–1854, 99–100, 105, Ely Papers.

97. Diedrich, *Ojibway Chiefs*, 24–25.

98. Diedrich, *Ojibway Chiefs*, 43.

99. Warren, *History of the Ojibway People*, 269–70.

100. Lund, *Lives and Times*, 16.

101. Nicollet, *Journals of Joseph N. Nicollet*, 199.

102. Diedrich, *Ojibway Chiefs*, 43.

103. Diedrich, *Ojibway Chiefs*, 25.

104. Nicollet, *Journals of Joseph N. Nicollet*, 200.

105. William T. Boutwell, January 17, 1833, Journal Kept While at Leech Lake," 84–86, Boutwell Papers.

106. William T. Boutwell, October 10, 1832, "Journal Kept While at Leech Lake," 77–78, Boutwell Papers. In October of 1832 Boutwell was visiting the La Pointe mission to confer with Sherman Hall and therefore had the opportunity to observe Bizhiki perform this ceremony.

107. Schoolcraft, "Memoirs" (CD-ROM), 110, 306; Kohl, *Kitchi-Gami*, 380.

108. Kohl, *Kitchi-Gami*, 380.

109. Grim, *The Shaman*, 118.

110. Grim, *The Shaman*, 118.

111. White, *Middle Ground*, 217–18.

112. Smith, "Leadership among the Southwestern Chippewa," 15.

113. Cited in White, *Middle Ground*, 339.

114. Hall, "Extracts from a Communication . . . Oct. 17, 1834," 118: "To give you some idea of the artifices resorted to, to prevent the Indians from listening to the gospel, I will mention an instance

which occurred not long since. One day an Indian, of whom we entertain some hope that he has not listened in vain to the gospel invitation, came to our house, and said that the chiefs had reported the case of a pious, or in their dialect a Praying Indian, who died far away to the north. He had prayed a long time. On his death he went to heaven, but was refused on the ground that no praying Indians were admitted there. He then went to the place where the white people go, but was there told that he had been a praying Indian, and had forsaken the customs of his fathers, and they would not receive him and ordered him away. After these repulses, he came back again to this world and assumed the body he had before inhabited." See also Peers, *The Ojibwe of Western Canada*, 168: "Midewiwin leaders were forced to campaign to retain members."

115. Peers, *The Ojibwa of Western Canada*, 168.

5. THE CONTEST FOR CHIEFLY AUTHORITY AT FOND DU LAC

1. Andrew, *Rebuilding the Christian Commonwealth*, 19–23.

2. McLoughlin, *Champions of the Cherokees*; McLoughlin, *Cherokees and Missionaries*; Kidwell, *Choctaws and Missionaries*.

3. "Statistical View of the Board and Its Missions."

4. La Pointe was an Ojibwe and fur trade community on Madeline Island, the Native population of which was removed across the bay to join their relatives at the mainland reservation of Bad River under the 1854 treaty. There was an ABCFM station at Bad River as early as 1846, but after the treaty, the mission staff from La Pointe followed their parishioners to Bad River. Bad River and La Pointe are no more than forty miles apart.

5. "Ojibwas," *Missionary Herald* 64 (1868): 11. The final record for the Bad River mission appears in the 1870 edition of the *Missionary Herald* (vol. 66): "Mr. Blatchford, native preacher, reports favorably in regard to the church members at Odanah. He says that they are punctual in attending the services of the sanctuary, and that, while living in the midst of a perverse people, they are as 'a city set on a hill.' But the pagans still cling to their heathenism."

6. Odawa speak the same language as Ojibwe with some dialectical differences. Some might equate it to a "southern drawl" in

English, since Odawa speakers speak more slowly and tend to drop some syllables, relying more on the rhythm of the language.

7. Anderson, *Memorial Volume*, 444.

8. Kugel, "Of Missionaries and their Cattle," 162.

9. Kugel, *To Be the Main Leaders*, see especially chapters 1 and 2.

10. Meyer, *White Earth Tragedy*, 42, 50, 141.

11. Boutwell, "Letter of Mr. Boutwell dated at Leech Lake, January 22, 1835."

12. Kohl, *Kitchi-Gami*, 146–48.

13. Diedrich, *Ojibwe Chiefs*, 6–7, 25, 33–35.

14. Diedrich, *Ojibway Chiefs*, 33–35

15. Diedrich, *Ojibway Chiefs*, 51.

16. Cameron, "A Sketch of the Customs," 251–52.

17. Cameron, "A Sketch of the Customs," 251–52.

18. Edmund F. Ely, Saturday 27 February 1836, Diaries no. 10, 29–30, Ely Papers; Diedrich, *Ojibway Chiefs*, 13.

19. Kugel, "Religion Mixed with Politics," 131; Edmund F. Ely, Tuesday 31 May 1836, Diaries nos. 11–20, 60–61, Ely Papers; Edmund F. Ely, letter to David Green, January 9, 1837, in Early Protestant Missionaries in the Lake Superior Country, vol. 1, 152, Archives, Wisconsin Historical Society, Superior.

20. Edmund F. Ely, Tuesday 23 February 1836, Diaries no. 10, 27–28, Ely Papers.

21. Edmund F. Ely, Tuesday 23 February 1836, Diaries no. 10, 27–28. Ely observed that prior to Nindipens's assertion of authority concerning his building project, this man had "no more authority in the band than any other man. This is the 1st time that I have known of his pretensions to the dictatorship."

22. Edmund F. Ely, 28 August 1834, Diaries nos. 5, 9, Ely Papers.

23. Edmund F. Ely, Monday 15 September 1834, Diaries no. 5, 11.

24. Edmund F. Ely, letter to David Green, December 31, 1835, Letters of Ely to Green 1833–1837, in Early Protestant Missionaries in the Lake Superior Country, vol. 1, 139–40, Archives, Wisconsin Historical Society of Wisconsin, Superior.

25. Edmund F. Ely, Tuesday 23 February 1836, Diaries no. 10, 27–28, Ely Papers.

26. Schoolcraft, "Reports and Letters of Henry Rowe Schoolcraft on the Expedition of 1832," 144–62. At each Ojibwe community Schoolcraft introduced Boutwell and asked the chiefs to allow him to speak to the community.

27. Edmund F. Ely, Tuesday 11 September 1838, Diaries nos. 11–20, 166, Ely Papers.

28. Ely, Tuesday 11 September 1838, Diaries nos. 11–20, 166.

29. Ely, Monday 22 February 1836, Diaries no. 10, 27; Brabant's first name is not disclosed in Ely's diary.

30. Ely, Saturday 20 February 1836 and Monday 22 February 1836, Diaries no. 10, 26.

31. Ely, Tuesday 23 February 1836, Diaries no. 10, 27–28.

32. Kugel, "Religion Mixed with Politics," 137–38.

33. Ely, Wednesday 24 February 1836, Diaries no. 10, 28.

34. Ely, Friday 26 February 1836, Diaries no. 10, 29.

35. Ely, Saturday 6 December 1834, Diaries no. 5, 25.

36. Ely, Friday 29 February 1836, Diaries no. 10, 29.

37. Ely, Friday 29 February 1836, Diaries no. 10, 29.

38. Ely, 8 March 1836, Diaries nos. 11–20, 33.

39. Ely, Friday, 26 February 1836, Diaries no. 10, 29.

40. Bieder, *Native American Communities in Wisconsin*, 96.

41. Ely, Saturday 27 February 1836, Diaries no. 10, 29–30.

42. Ely, Friday 26 February 1836, Diaries no. 10, 29.

43. Ely, Saturday 27 February 1836, Diaries no. 10, 29–30.

44. Ely, Saturday 27 February 1836.

45. Ely, Saturday 27 February 1836.

46. Ely, Saturday 27 February 1836.

47. Diedrich, *Ojibway Chiefs*, 51.

48. Ely, Friday 4 March 1836, Diaries nos. 11–20, 31.

49. Ely, Friday 4 March 1836.

50. Ely, Friday 4 March 1836.

51. Ely, Friday 4 March 1836.

52. Ely, Saturday 5 March 1836, Diaries nos. 11–20, 31–32.

53. Ely, 8 March 1836, Diaries nos. 11–20, 33.

54. Ely, 8 March 1836.

55. Ely, 9 March 1836, Diaries nos. 11–20, 33–34.

56. Ely, 9 March 1836.

57. Ely, 9 March 1836.

58. Ely, 9 March 1836.

59. Ely, 10 March 1836, Diaries nos. 11–20, 34.

60. Ely, 10 March 1836.

61. Ely, 12 March 1836, Diaries nos. 11–20, 34.

62. Ely, Saturday 19 March 1836, Diaries nos. 11–20, 36.

63. Ely, Saturday 19 March 1836.

64. Ely, Sunday 20 March 1836, Diaries nos. 11–20, 37–38.

65. Ely, Sunday 20 March 1836, 38.

66. Ely, Sunday 20 March 1836, 38; Ely, Saturday 21 November 1835, Diaries no. 9, 6.

67. Ely, Sunday 15 May 1836, Diaries nos. 11–20, 51–52.

68. Ely, Sunday 15 May 1836, 51–52.

69. Diedrich, *Ojibway Chiefs*, 25; Ely, 8 March 1836, Diaries nos. 11–20, 33.

70. Ely, Friday 20 May 1836, Diaries nos. 11–20, 53.

71. Ely, Friday 20 May 1836.

72. Ely, Friday 20 May 1836.

73. Ely, Tuesday 9 August 1836, Diaries nos. 11–20, 66–67.

74. Ely, Friday 20 May 1836, Diaries nos. 11–20, 54.

75. Ely, Saturday 21 May 1836, Diaries nos. 11–20, 54.

76. Frederick Baraga, letter to Leopoldine Stiftung, June 17, 1836, Grace Lee Nute Papers, Archives, Minnesota Historical Society, St. Paul.

77. Frederick Baraga, Letters of Frederick Baraga, Grace Lee Nute Papers, Archives, Minnesota Historical Society, St. Paul.

78. Ely, Saturday 15 September 1838, Diaries nos. 11–20, 166–67.

79. Ely, Saturday 21 May 1836, Diaries nos. 11–20, 55. The English had not actively missionized in the region with the exception of Lord Selkirk's community.

80. Ely, Friday 19 August 1836, Diaries nos. 11–20, 70.

81. Ely, Saturday 20 August 1836, Diaries nos. 11–20, 65.

82. Ely, Monday 23 May 1836, Diaries nos. 11–20, 56–57.

83. Ely, Tuesday 24 May 1836, Diaries nos. 11–20, 57–58.

84. Ely, Tuesday 24 May 1836, Diaries nos. 11–20, 57–58.

85. Ely, Tuesday 31 May 1836, Diaries nos. 11–20, 60–61.

86. Florantha Sproat, letter to Mrs. Cephas Thompson (mother), June 23, 1839, Letters of Florantha Sproat written at La Pointe 1838–1845, Archives, Wisconsin Historical Society, Madison.

87. Ely, Tuesday 31 May 1836, Diaries nos. 11–20, 60–61.

88. Ely, Tuesday 31 May 1836.

89. Ely, Tuesday 31 May 1836.

90. Ely, Tuesday 31 May 1836. This concern about Ely's associates probably resulted from a recent visit of Miss Cook and Mr. Sproat of the La Pointe mission to the Fond du Lac mission. Though Ely gives no details in his letters or diaries, he mentioned that Gandanonib and Inini and the visitors had "a very disagreeable meeting" at Bears Island on their way in to Fond du Lac. Ely, Wednesday 25 May 1836, Diaries nos. 11–20, 59.

91. Edmund F. Ely, letter to David Green, January 9, 1837, Letters of Ely to Green 1833–1837, in Early Protestant Missionaries in the Lake Superior Country, vol. 1, 152–53, Archives, Wisconsin Historical Society, Superior. Report on council of May 31, 1836.

92. Ely, Friday June 1836, Diaries nos. 11–20, 62–63. Ely does not give a numerical date—the entry is labeled Friday and occurs between entries for June 2 and Sunday June 12.

93. Ely, Thursday 2 June, 1836, Diaries nos. 11–20, 62–63.

94. Ely, Thursday 2 June, 1836.

95. Ely, Saturday June 1836, Diaries nos. 11–20, 64. Ely does not give a numerical date—the entry is labeled Saturday and occurs between entries for June 2 and Sunday June 12.

96. Ely, Saturday June 1836.

97. Ely, Sunday 12 June 1836, Diaries nos. 11–20, 64.

98. Ely, Thursday 16 June 1836, Diaries nos. 11–20, 64–65.

99. Ely, Thursday 16 June 1836.

100. Ely, Thursday 17 August 1836, Diaries nos. 11–20, 69.

101. Kugel, "Religion Mixed with Politics," 142.

102. Ely, Wednesday 24 August 1836, Diaries nos. 11–20, 71.

103. Ely, Thursday 8 September 1836, 72.

104. Ely, Thursday 8 September 1836.

105. Ely, Saturday 10 September 1836, 74.

106. Ely, Saturday 12 November 1836, 83–84.
107. Ely, Saturday 12 November 1836.
108. Ely, Tuesday 27 December 1836, 86.
109. Ely, Tuesday 27 December 1836, 87.
110. Ely, Saturday 1 October 1836, 77.
111. Ely, Saturday 1 October 1836.
112. Ely, Sunday 16 October 1836, 80.
113. Ely, Wednesday 19 October 1836, 81.
114. Ely, Sunday 4 December 1836, 84.
115. Ely, Sunday 4 December 1836.
116. Ely, Sunday 4 December 1836.
117. Ely, Wednesday 8 February 1837, 95–96.
118. Ely, Monday 13 February 1837, 98.
119. Ely, Tuesday 14 February 1837, 99–100.
120. Ely, Thursday 16 February 1837, 101–2.
121. Ely, Thursday 16 February 1837.
122. Ely, Saturday 6 May 1837, 119.
123. Ely, Saturday 21 May 1837, 121.
124. Ely, Saturday 21 May 1837.
125. Ely, Friday 26 May 1837, 124.
126. Ely, Friday 26 May 1837.
127. Ely, Sunday 5 June 1837, 126–27.
128. Ely, Sunday 5 June 1837.
129. Ely, Thursday 9 June 1837, 127.
130. Ely, Thursday 9 June 1837.
131. Ely, Thursday 9 June 1837.
132. Ely, Thursday 9 June 1837.
133. Ely, Thursday 9 June 1837.
134. Ely, Thursday 9 June 1837.
135. Ely, Thursday 24 August 1837, 137.
136. Ely, Thursday 24 August 1837.

CONCLUSION

1. Nicollet, *Journals of Joseph N. Nicollet*, 184–85.
2. Schenck, *Voice of the Crane*, 106.
3. Hickerson, "The Southwestern Chippewa," 49–50.

4. Smith, "Leadership among the Indians," 309.
5. Hickerson, "The Southwestern Chippewa," 51.
6. Smith, "Leadership among the Indians," 305.
7. Murray, *Indian Giving*, 33–34; Cleland, *Rites of Conquest*, 55.
8. Smith, "Leadership among the Indians," 305.

Glossary

aadizookaan, *pl.* **aadizookaanag:** A more respectful term than *grand-father* for those manidoog with whom one has established a special relationship, according to Theresa Smith in *Island of the Anishinaabeg*. It is also used as the word for sacred stories.

aaniikanootaagewinini, *pl.* **aaniikanootaagewininiwag:** Speaker.

aanike-ashangewin: Feast to install a chief.

aanike-ogimaa: Second chief, underchief.

anishinaabe, *pl.* **anishinaabeg:** The people: Ojibwe, Potawatomi, and Odawa collectively.

bizhikiiwaak: Cattle herb medicine, a medicine commonly carried by warriors.

doodem, *pl.* **doodemag:** Clan.

gechi-midewid, *pl.* **gechi-midewijig:** Mide elder, high degree mide (see also *medewid*).

gichi-anishinaabe, *pl.* **gichi-anishinaabeg:** Headmen of each lineage in a village, elders.

Gichi-Manidoo: Great Spirit.

giigidowinini, *pl.* **giigidowininiwag:** Speaker.

inaabandamowin: A term used for both dreaming and waking experiences; Minnesota–Wisconsin–North Dakota dialect conversion of the eastern dialect term *naabndanwin*.

indinaakonigewin *or* **genawendamaan:** That of which I am in charge, a term used by a head man to refer to the lineage group he represents in council; Minnesota–Wisconsin–North Dakota dialect conversion. Edward S. Rogers in "Band Organization among the Indians of the Eastern Subarctic" spells this term *nintipencikewin*.

jaasakiid, *pl.* **jaasakiijig;** *also* **jiisakiiwinini,** *pl.* **jiisakiiwininiwag:** A person who can perform the shaking tent ceremony.

madwe'ikewinini: Drum man.

makak, *pl.* **makakoon:** Birch bark container.

manidoo, *pl.* **manidoog:** Spirit.

manidookaazowin: A ceremony that hunters use to find or call game.

mayosewinini, *pl.* **mayosewininiwag (archaic):** War chief.

medewid, *pl.* **medewijig:** A person who is a member of the Midewiwin. Medewid is a participle of the verb *midew*, the first vowel shifting to *e* in such a use; in *gechi-midewid* the vowel shift is in the prefix.

Midewiwin: Grand Medicine Society, religious organization of the Ojibwe people.

mide-mashkikiwinini: Herbal specialist.

midenaabe: Spirit man.

miishinoo, *pl.* **miishinoog (archaic):** Ambassador, secretary, apprentice.

minisinoowaak: Island herb medicine, a medicine commonly carried by warriors.

mino-bimaadiziwin: Good life, live well.

mitigwaakik: Water drum.

nanaandawiʼiwewin: A healing ceremony done by a medewid; Minnesota–Wisconsin–North Dakota dialect conversion.

ogimaa, *pl.* **ogimaag:** Hereditary Ojibwe leader responsible for mediation and resource use in village communities.

ogimaakwe, *pl.* **ogimaakweg:** Leader woman, woman chief.

ogichidaa, *pl.* **ogichidaag:** Warriors.

oshkaabewis, *pl.* **oshkaabewisag:** Lieutenant, assistant, pipe bearer.

waabanoowaak: Eastern herb medicine (used as a war medicine).

zagaswe'idiwin: To hold a council, or the smoking of the pipe; Minnesota–Wisconsin–North Dakota dialect conversion of the term *Zuguswediwin*.

Bibliography

UNPUBLISHED SOURCES

American Board of Commissioners for Foreign Missions, Correspondence, 1827–78. Archives, Minnesota Historical Society, St. Paul.

American Board of Commissioners for Foreign Missions, North American Indian Missions Records. Houghton Library, Harvard University, Boston, Massachusetts.

Boutwell, William T., Papers, 1832–81. Archives, Minnesota Historical Society, St. Paul.

Clark, William, Miscellaneous Papers. Archives, Wisconsin Historical Society, Madison.

Ely, Edmund F., Papers, 1833–1904. Archives, Wisconsin Historical Society, Madison.

Hall, Sherman. Miscellaneous Letters of Sherman Hall and His Sisters 1831–1875, in Early Protestant Missionaries in the Lake Superior Country, vol. 3. Archives, Superior Public Library, Superior.

Journal of the Treaty Concluded at Chicago on the 26th and 27th of September, 1883. NAM T494 R:3:60–87, National Archives.

Johnston, George, Papers, 1819–58. Archives, Minnesota Historical Society, St. Paul.

Letters and Journals of Missionaries at the Head of the Lakes 1832–43, in Early Protestant Missionaries in the Lake Superior Country, vol. 1. Archives, Superior Public Library, Superior.

Nute, Grace Lee, Papers, 1924–45, 1957. Archives, Minnesota Historical Society, St. Paul.

Proceedings of the Treaty at Chicago 1821. Group 75 NIS-203, National Archives.

Stevens, Jedediah D., Papers, 1827–76. Archives, Minnesota Historical Society, St. Paul.

Sproat, Florantha, Letters, 1838–45. Archives, Wisconsin Historical Society, Madison.

Taliaferro, Lawrence. Daily Journal for the Agency 1827–1829, Lawrence Taliaferro Papers, 1813–68. Archives, Minnesota Historical Society, St. Paul.

Treuer, Anton. Personal communication, October 27, 2008.

PUBLISHED SOURCES

Allen, Lieutenant James. "Journal and Letters of Lieutenant James Allen." In *Schoolcraft's Expedition to Lake Itaska*, ed. Philip Mason, 163–241. East Lansing: Michigan Historical Society Press, 1993.

Anderson, Rufus. *Memorial Volume of the First 50 Years of the American Board of Commissioners for Foreign Missions*, 5th ed. Boston: American Board of Commissioners for Foreign Missions, 1862.

Andrew, John A. *Rebuilding the Christian Commonwealth: New England Congregationalists and Foreign Missions, 1800–1830*. Lexington: Kentucky University Press, 1976.

Angel, Michael. *Preserving the Sacred: Historical Perspectives on the Ojibwa Midewiwin*. Winnipeg: University of Manitoba Press, 2002.

"Annual Report." *Missionary Herald* 32 (January 1836): 26.

Ayer, Frederick. "Extract from a Letter of Mr. Ayer Dated at Yellow Lake, Dec. 1, 1833." *Missionary Herald* 30 (April 1834): 137–39.

————. "Extracts from Various Communications: Station at Yellow Lake." *Missionary Herald* 30 (1834): 58–60.

————. "Letter of Mr. Ayer dated at Fond Du Lac, Oct. 8, 1838." *Missionary Herald* 35 (1839): 314–15.

Baraga, Frederic. *Chippewa Indians: As Recorded by Rev. Frederick Baraga in 1847*. New York: Studia Slovenica League of Slovenian Americans, 1976.

————. *A Dictionary of the Ojibway Language*. St. Paul: Minnesota Historical Society Press, 1992.

————. *Short History of the North American Indians*, trans. and ed. Graham MacDonald. Calgary: University of Calgary Press, 2004.

Baily, F. G. *Stratagems and Spoils*. Oxford: Blackwell, 1969.

Barnouw, Victor. "Acculturation and Personality among the Wisconsin Chippewa." *American Anthropological Association Memoir* 72 (1950): 1–152.

———. *Wisconsin Chippewa Myths and Tales and Their Relation to Chippewa Life: Based on Folktales Collected by Victor Barnouw.* Madison: University of Wisconsin Press, 1977.

Beltrami, Giacomo Constantino. *A Pilgrimage in Europe and America, Leading to the Discovery of the Sources of the Mississippi and Bloody River; with a Description of the Whole Course of the Former and of the Ohio.* London: Hunt and Clarke, 1828; reprint, Chicago: Quadrangle Books, 1962.

———. "Travels among the Aborigines: The Chippewa Indians." *North American Review* 27 (July 1828): 89–114.

Benton-Banai, Edward. *Mishomis Book.* St. Paul: Red School House, 1988.

Berger, Peter, and Thomas Luckmann. *The Social Construction of Reality.* Garden City NY: Doubleday, 1967.

Berkhofer, Robert F. *Salvation and the Savage: An Analysis of Protestant Missions and American Indian Response, 1787–1862.* Lexington: University of Kentucky Press, 1965.

Bieder, Robert E. *Native American Communities in Wisconsin, 1600–1960: A Study of Tradition and Change.* Madison: University of Wisconsin Press, 1995.

Bishop, Charles A. *The Northern Ojibwa and the Fur Trade: An Historical and Ecological Study.* Toronto: Holt, Rinehart, and Winston, 1974.

———. "The Question of Ojibwa Clans." In *Actes du vingtieme Congres des Algonquinistes,* 43–61. Hull, Quebec: 20th Algonquian Conference, 1988.

Black, Mary B. "Ojibwa Power Belief System." In *The Anthropology of Power,* ed. Raymond Fogelson and Richard Adams, 141–51. New York: Academic Press, 1977.

Blackbird, Andrew J. *History of the Ottawa and Chippewa Indians of Michigan.* Ypsilanti: Ypsilantian Job Printing House, 1887.

Black-Rogers, Mary. "Algonquin Gender Revisited: Animate Nouns and Ojibwa Power—an Impasse?" *Papers in Linguistics* 15, nos. 1–4 (1982): 59–76.

———. "Varieties of Starving: Semantics and Survival in the Subarctic Fur Trade, 1750–1850." *Ethnohistory* 33 (Fall 1986): 353–83.

Boatman, John. *My Elders Taught Me: Aspects of Great Lakes American Indian Philosophy*. Lanham MD: University Press of America, 1992.

Bohaker, Heidi. "Nindoodemag: The Significance of Algonquian Kinship Networks in the Eastern Great Lakes Region, 1600–1701." *William and Mary Quarterly*, 3rd series, vol. 63, no. 1 (January 2006): 23–52.

Boutwell, William T. "Extracts from the Journal of Mr. Boutwell: Voyage through Lake Superior, Ascent of the St. Louis River." *Missionary Herald* 30 (April 1834): 132–36.

————. "Extracts from the Journal of Mr. Boutwell, on a Tour to the Sources of the Mississippi." *Missionary Herald* 30 (May 1834): 177–80.

————. "Extracts from the Journal of Mr. Boutwell, on a Tour to the Sources of the Mississippi." *Missionary Herald* 30 (June 1834): 222–23.

————. "Journal and Letters of the Reverend William Thurston Boutwell." In *Schoolcraft's Expedition to Lake Itaska*, ed. Philip Mason, 306–51. East Lansing: Michigan State University Press, 1993.

————. "Letter of Mr. Boutwell at Fond du Lac Post, June 25, 1832." *Missionary Herald* 28 (1832): 293.

————. "Letter of Mr. Boutwell dated at Leech Lake, January 22, 1835." *Missionary Herald* 31 (1835): 342.

Brinkman, Waltrund A. R. "Challenges of Wisconsin's Weather and Climate." In *Wisconsin Land and Life*, ed. Robert C. Ostergren and Thomas R. Vale, 49–64. Madison: University of Wisconsin Press, 1977.

Brown, Jennifer S. H., and Robert Brightman. *The Orders of the Dreamed. 1823: George Nelson on Cree and Northern Ojibwa Religion and Myth*. Winnipeg: University of Manitoba Press, 1987.

Buffalohead, Priscilla K. "Farmers, Warriors, Traders: A Fresh Look at Ojibway Women." *Minnesota History* 48, no. 6 (1983): 236–44.

Cameron, Duncan. "A Sketch of the Customs, Manners, and Way of Living of the Natives in the Barren Country about Nipigon." In *Les Bourgeois de la Compagnie du Nord-Ouest*, vol. 2, ed. Louis François Rodrique Masson, 230–300. Quebec: A. Cote et Cie., 1890.

Carver, Jonathan, Esq. *Travels through the Interior Parts of North America in the Years 1766, 1767, and 1768*, London: J. Walter and S. Crowder, 1778; reprint, Toronto: Coles Publishing, 1974.

Chalevoix, Pierre de. *Journal of a Voyage to North America*. London: R. and J. Dodsley, 1761.

Chapman, Charles H. "The Historic Johnston Family of the 'Soo.'" *Michigan Pioneer and Historical Society Collections* 32 (1902): 305–53.

Cleland, Charles E. *Rites of Conquest: The History and Culture of Michigan's Native Americans*. Ann Arbor: University of Michigan Press, 1992.

———. "The Western Chippewa in the Early Nineteenth Century." In *Fish in the Lakes, Wild Rice, and Game in Abundance*, ed. James M. McClurken, 1–35. East Lansing: Michigan State University Press, 2000.

Copway, George. *Indian Life and Indian History: By an Indian Author Embracing the Traditions of the North American Indians Regarding Themselves, Particularly of That Most Important of All Tribes, the Ojibways*. Boston: Albert and Company, 1860; reprint, New York: AMS, 1978.

Curot, Michel. "A Wisconsin Fur-Trader's Journal, 1803–4." *Wisconsin State Historical Society Collections* 20 (1911): 396–471.

Deleary, Nicholas. "The Midewiwin, an Aboriginal Spiritual Institution. Symbols of Continuity: A Native Studies Culture-Based Perspective." Master's thesis, Carleton University, Ottawa, 1990.

Densmore, Francis. "The Belief of the Indian in a Connection between Song and the Supernatural." *Bureau of American Ethnology Bulletin* 151, no. 37 (1953): 217–23.

———. *Chippewa Customs*. St. Paul: Minnesota Historical Society Press, 1979.

———. "Chippewa Music." *Bureau of American Ethnology Bulletin* 45 (1910): 1–216.

———. "Chippewa Music II." *Bureau of American Ethnology Bulletin* 53 (1913): 1–341.

———. "Uses of Plants by the Chippewa Indians." *Bureau of American Ethnology Annual Report* 44 (1928): 275–397.

Dewdney, Selwyn. *The Sacred Scrolls of the Southern Ojibway.* Toronto: University of Toronto Press, 1967.

Diba Jimooyung, Telling Our Story: A History of the Saginaw Ojibwe Anishinabek. Ed. Charmaine M. Benz and R. Todd Williamson. Mount Pleasant: Saginaw Chippewa Indian Tribe of Michigan and Ziibiwing Cultural Society, 2005.

Diedrich, Mark F. *Ojibway Chiefs: Portraits of Anishinaabe Leadership.* Rochester MN: Coyote Books, 1999.

Doherty, Robert. "We Don't Want Them to Hold Their Hands over Our Heads: The Economic Strategies of the L'Anse Chippewas, 1830–1860." *Michigan Historical Review* 20, no. 2 (1994): 47–70.

Doty, James D. "The Journal and Letters of James Duane Doty." In *Schoolcraft's Narrative Journal of Travels,* ed. Mentor L. Williams, 401–60. East Lansing: Michigan State University Press, 1992.

———. "On the Manners and Customs of the Northern Indians." *Detroit Gazette,* January 19, 1821.

Dowd, Gregory E. *A Spirited Resistance: The North American Indian Struggle for Unity, 1745–1815.* Baltimore: Johns Hopkins University Press, 1992.

Eisenstadt, S. N. Introduction to *Max Weber on Charisma and Institution Building,* by Max Weber, ed. S. N. Eisenstadt. Chicago: University of Chicago Press, 1968.

Fixico, Donald L. "The Alliance of the Three Fires in Trade and War, 1630–1812." *Michigan Historical Review* 20, no. 2 (1994): 1–23.

Gartner, William Gustav. "Four Worlds without an Eden: Pre-Columbian Peoples and the Wisconsin Landscape." In *Wisconsin Land and Life,* ed. Robert C. Ostergren and Thomas R. Vale, 331–50. Madison: University of Wisconsin Press, 1997.

Graham, Andrew. *Andrew Graham's Observations on Hudson's Bay, 1767–91,* ed. G. Williams. London: Hudson's Bay Record Society, 1969.

Grant, Peter. "The Saulteaux Indians about 1804." In *Les Bourgeois de la Compagnie du Nord-Ouest,* ed. Louis François Rodrique Masson, 303–66. Quebec: A. Cote et Cie., 1890.

Grim, John A. *The Shaman: Patterns of Religious Healing among the Ojibway Indians.* Norman: University of Oklahoma Press, 1983.

Grim, John A., and D. P. St. John. "The Northeast Woodlands." In *Native American Religions: North America*, ed. L. E. Sullivan. New York: Macmillan, 1989.

Gunn, George Henry. "Peter Garrioch at St. Peter's in 1837." *Minnesota History* 20 (June 1939): 119–28.

Hall, Sherman. "Extracts from a Communication of Mr. Hall, Dated at La Pointe, Oct. 17th, 1834." *Missionary Herald* 31 (March 1835): 118–20.

————. "Extracts from a Communication of Mr. Hall, Dated at La Pointe, Feb. 8th, 1835." *Missionary Herald* 31 (June 1835): 227–28.

————. "Ojibwas: Extracts from the Journal of Mr. Hall: Visit to Lac du Flambeau." *Missionary Herald* 30 (January 1834): 24–27.

Hall, Sherman, and William T. Boutwell. "Communication from Messrs. Hall and Boutwell, Dated at La Pointe, Feb. 7th, 1833." *Missionary Herald* 29 (September 1833): 314–17.

————. "Communication from Messrs. Hall and Boutwell, Dated at La Pointe, Feb. 7th, 1833." *Missionary Herald* 29 (October 1833): 371–74.

Hallowell, A. I. *Culture and Experience.* Philadelphia: University of Pennsylvania Press and Schocken Books, 1967.

————. "Myth, Culture, and Personality." *American Anthropologist* 49 (1947): 544–56.

————. *The Ojibwa of Berens River, Manitoba: Ethnography into History.* New York: Harcourt Brace Jovanovich College Publishers, 1992.

————. "Ojibwa Ontology, Behavior, and World View." In *Teachings from the American Earth: Indian Religion and Philosophy*, ed. Dennis Tedlock and Barbara Tedlock, 141–78. New York: Liverwright, 1975.

————. "Ojibway World View and Disease." In *Man's Image in Medicine and Anthropology*, ed. Iago Galdson, 258–315. New York: International Universities Press, 1963.

————. "The Role of Conjuring in Saulteux Society." *Publications of the Philadelphia Anthropological Society* 2 (1942): 1–96.

————. "The Role of Dreams in Ojibwa Culture." In *The Dream and Human Societies*, ed. Gustav E. Grunebaum and Roger Callois, 267–92. Berkeley: University of California Press, 1966.

—————. "Some Empirical Aspects of Northern Saulteux Religion." *American Anthropologist* 36 (1934): 389–404.

Hämäläinen, Pekka. *Comanche Empire*. New Haven: Yale University Press, 2008.

Havard, Gilles. *The Great Peace of Montreal of 1701: French Diplomacy in the 17th Century*. Montreal: McGill-Queens University Press, 2001.

Henry, Alexander. *Travels and Adventures in Canada and the Indian Territories between the Years 1760 and 1776* [1809]. Ann Arbor: University Microfilms, 1966.

Hickerson, Harold. *The Chippewa and the Neighbors*, rev. and expanded ed. Prospect Heights IL: Waveland Press, 1988.

—————. "Land Tenure of the Rainy Lake Chippewa at the Beginning of the 19th Century." *Smithsonian Contributions to Anthropology* 2 (1967): 41–63.

—————. "Notes on the Post-Contact Origin of the Midewiwin." *Ethnohistory* 9 (1962): 404–23.

—————. "The Sociohistorical Significance of Two Chippewa Ceremonials." *American Anthropologist* 65 (1963): 67–85.

—————. "The Southwestern Chippewa: An Ethnohistorical Study." *American Anthropological Association* 64, no. 3, pt. 2 (1962): 1–110.

—————. "William T. Boutwell of the American Board and the Pillager Chippewa: The History of a Failure." *Ethnohistory* 12 (1965): 1–29.

Hoffman, W. J. "The Midewiwin or 'Grand Medicine Society' of the Ojibwa." *Bureau of American Ethnology Annual Report* 7 (1885–86): 143–300.

Holzkamm, Tim E. "Ojibwa Horticulture in the Upper Mississippi and Boundary Waters." In *Papers of the Seventeenth Algonquin Conference* (1985), ed. William Cowan, 143–54. Ottawa: Carleton University, 1986.

Houghton, Douglas. "Journal, Letters and Reports of Dr. Douglass Houghton." In *Schoolcraft's Expedition to Lake Itaska*, ed. Philip Mason, 242–305. East Lansing: Michigan State University Press, 1993.

Isham, James. *Observations on Hudson's Bay, 1743*. Toronto: Champlain Society, 1949.

Jenness, Diamond. "The Indians of Canada." *National Museum of Canada Bulletin* 65, 3rd ed. (1955): 1–452.

Johnston, Basil. *The Manitous: The Spiritual World of the Ojibway.* Toronto: Key Porter Books, 1995.

———. *Ojibway Ceremonies.* Lincoln: University of Nebraska Press, 1982.

———. *Ojibway Heritage.* Lincoln: University of Nebraska Press, 1976.

Johnston, George. "A Reminiscence of George Johnston: The Incident at Sault de Ste Marie, June 16, 1820." In *Schoolcraft's Narrative Journal of Travels,* ed. Mentor L. Williams, 505–8. East Lansing: Michigan State University Press, 1992.

———. "Reminiscences." *Michigan Pioneer and Historical Society Collections* 18 (1908): 605–11.

Johnston, William. "Letters on the Fur Trade 1833 by William Johnston," ed. J. Sharpless Fox. *Michigan Pioneer and Historical Collections* 37 (1909–10): 132–207.

Junker, Laura Lee. *Raiding, Trading, and Feasting: The Political Economy of Philippine Chiefdoms.* Honolulu: University of Hawaii Press, 1999.

Kidd, Kenneth E. "Birch-Bark Scrolls in Archaeological Contexts." *American Antiquity* 30, no. 4 (1965): 480.

Kidwell, Clara Sue. *Choctaws and Missionaries in Mississippi, 1818–1918.* Norman: University of Oklahoma Press, 1995.

Kigoshi, K., Aizawa, H., and Suzuki, N. "Gakushuin Natural Radiocarbon Measurements VII." *Radiocarbon* 11, no. 2 (1969): 295–326.

Kohl, Johann Georg. *Kitchi-Gami: Life among the Lake Superior Ojibway* [1860], trans. Lascelles Wraxall, intro. by Robert Bieder, and additional translations by Ralf Neufang and Urlike Bocker. Reprint, St. Paul: Minnesota Historical Society Press, 1985.

Kugel, Rebecca. "Leadership within the Women's Community: Susie Bonga Wright of the Leech Lake Ojibwe." In *Native Women's History in Eastern North America before 1900: A Guide to Research and Writing,* ed. Rebecca Kugel and Lucy Eldersveld Murphey, 166–200. Lincoln: University of Nebraska Press, 2007.

———. "Of Missionaries and Their Cattle: Ojibwa Perceptions of a Missionary as Evil Shaman." In *American Encounters: Natives and Newcomers from European Contact to Indian Removal, 1500–1850*, ed. Peter Mancal and James Merrell, 162–75. New York: Routledge, 2000. First published in *Ethnohistory* 41, no. 2 (1994): 227–44.

———. "Religion Mixed with Politics: The 1836 Conversion of Mang'osid of Fond du Lac." *Ethnohistory* 37, no. 2 (Spring 1990): 126–57.

———. *To Be the Main Leaders of Our People: A History of Minnesota Ojibwe Politics, 1825–1898*. East Lansing: Michigan University Press, 1998.

Landes, Ruth. *Ojibwa Religion and the Midewiwin*. Madison: University of Wisconsin Press, 1968.

———. *Ojibwa Sociology*. New York: Columbia University Press, 1937.

Lavender, David. "Some American Characteristics of the American Fur Company." *Minnesota History* 40 (Winter 1966): 178–87.

"Letters and Documents Relating to the Problems of the Frontier." In *Schoolcraft's Narrative Journal of Travels*, ed. Mentor L. Williams, 275–97. East Lansing: Michigan State University Press, 1992.

"Letters and Reports Relating to the Organization of the Expedition in 1831 and 1832." In *Schoolcraft's Expedition to Lake Itaska*, ed. Philip Mason, 107–43. East Lansing: Michigan State University Press, 1993.

Lewis, G. Malcolm. "Maps, Mapmaking and Map Use by Native Americans." In *The History of Cartography*, vol. 2, book 3: *Cartography in the Traditional African, American, Arctic, Australian and Pacific Societies*, ed. J. B. Harley and David Woodward. Chicago: University of Chicago Press, 1998.

Lips, Eva. *Die Reisernte der Ojibwa-Indianer: Wirtschaft und Recht eines Erntevolkes*. Berlin: Akademie Verlag, 1956.

Locke, John. *The Second Treatise of Government*. New York: Liberal Arts Press, 1952.

Lowrie, Walter, and Walter S. Franklin, eds. *American State Papers: Documents, Legislative and Executive of the Congress of the United*

States, vol. 5: *Indian Affairs*. Washington DC: Gales and Seaton, 1834.

Lund, Duane R. *The Lives and Times of Three Powerful Ojibwe Chiefs*. Brainerd MN: Nordell Graphic Communications, 2003.

Mauss, Marcel. *The Gift: Forms and Functions of Exchange in Archaic Societies*. New York: W. W. Norton, 1967.

McClurken, James M., ed. *Fish in the Lakes, Wild Rice, and Game in Abundance: Testimony on Behalf of Mille Lacs Ojibwe Hunting and Fishing Rights*. East Lansing: Michigan State Historical Society Press, 2000.

McKenney, Thomas L. *Sketches of a Tour to the Lakes, of the Character and Customs of the Chippeway Indians, and of Incidents Connected with the Treaty of Fond du Lac*. Baltimore, 1827; reprint Minneapolis: Ross and Haines, 1959.

McKenney, Thomas L., and James Hall. *The Indian Tribes of North America with Biographical Sketches and Anecdotes of the Principal Chiefs*. Edinburgh: John Grant, 1933.

McLoughlin, William. *Champions of the Cherokees, Evan and John B. Jones*. Princeton NJ: Princeton University Press, 1990.

——. *Cherokees and Missionaries, 1789–1839*. New Haven: Yale University Press, 1984.

McNally, Michael D. *Ojibwe Singers: Hymns, Grief, and a Native Culture in Motion*. New York: Oxford University Press, 2000.

Meyer, Melissa L. *The White Earth Tragedy: Ethnicity and Dispossession at a Minnesota Anishinaabe Reservation, 1889–1920*. Lincoln: University of Nebraska Press, 1994.

Miller, Cary. "Gifts as Treaties: The Political Use of Received Gifts in Anishinaabeg Communities, 1820–1832." *American Indian Quarterly* 26, no. 2 (2003): 221–45.

Miller, Cary. "Rethinking Tradition: The Anishinaabe Perception of Time and the Jingle Dress Dance as a Traditional Practice." Master's thesis, University of North Carolina–Chapel Hill, 1995.

Miller, Frank C. "Problems of Succession in a Chippewa Council." In *Political Anthropology*, ed. Marc J. Swartz, Victor Turner, and Arthur Tuden, 173–85. Chicago: Aldine Publishing Company, 1966.

Minnesota Daily Pioneer (St. Paul), June 20, 1850.

Moodie, D. W., and Barry Kaye. "The Northern Limit of Indian Agriculture in North America." *Geographical Review* 59, no. 4 (1969): 513–29.

More, Thomas. *Utopia* [1516]; available online from the Oregon State University Philosophy Department, http://oregonstate.edu/instruct/phl302/texts/more/utopia-contents.html.

Murray, David. *Indian Giving: Economies of Power in Indian-White Exchanges.* Amherst: University of Massachusetts Press, 2000.

Nelson, George. *My First Years in the Fur Trade: The Journals of 1802–1804,* ed. Laura Peers and Theresa Schenck. St. Paul: Minnesota Historical Society Press, 2002.

Nicholas, Ralph W. "Segmentary Factional Political Systems." In *Political Anthropology,* ed. Marc J. Swartz, Victor W. Turner, and Arthur Tuden, 49–59. Chicago: Aldine Publishing Company, 1966.

Nichols, David. "Red Gentlemen and White Savages: Indian Relations and Political Culture after the American Revolution, 1784–1800." PhD diss., University of Kentucky, 2000.

Nicollet, Joseph N. *The Journals of Joseph N. Nicollet: A Scientist on the Mississippi Headwaters with Notes on Indian Life, 1836–7.* Ed. Martha Coleman-Bray, trans. Andre Fertey. St. Paul: Minnesota Historical Society Press, 2004.

Nichols, John D. "The Translation of Key Phrases in the Treaties of 1837 and 1855." In *Fish in the Lakes, Wild Rice, and Game in Abundance,* ed. James McClurken. Lansing: Michigan State University Press, 2000.

"Ojibwas," *Missionary Herald* 64 (1868): 11.

The Ojibwe Curriculum Committee, American Indian Studies Department, University of Minnesota and Minnesota Historical Society Educational Services Division. *The Land of the Ojibwe.* St. Paul: Minnesota Historical Society Press, 1973.

Onions, C. T., ed. *The Shorter Oxford English Dictionary,* 3rd ed., vol. 1. New York: Oxford University Press, 1952.

"Ordination and Departure of Missionaries." *Missionary Herald* 27 (July 1831): 298.

Overholt, Thomas W., and J. Baird Callicott. *Clothed-in-Fur and Other Tales: An Introduction to an Ojibwa World View.* Lanham: University Press of America, 1982.

Peacock, Thomas, and Marlene Wisuri. *Ojibwe Waasa Inaabidaa: We Look in All Directions.* Afton MN: Afton Historical Society Press, 2002.

Pearson, Thomas E. "The Wild Rice Harvest at Bad River: Natural Resources and Human Geography in Northern Wisconsin." In *Wisconsin Land and Life,* ed. Robert C. Ostergren and Thomas C. Vale, 505–20. Madison: University of Wisconsin Press, 1997.

Peers, Laura. *The Ojibwa of Western Canada: 1780–1870.* Manitoba Studies in Native History, vol. 8. St. Paul: Minnesota Historical Society Press, 1994.

Peers, Laura, Theresa Schenck, and Jennifer S. H. Brown. "'There Is No End to Relationship among the Indians': Ojibwa Families and Kinship in Historical Perspective." *History of the Family* 4, no. 4 (1999): 529–55.

Perrot, Nicholas. "Memoir on the Manners, Customs, and Religion of the Savages of North America." In *The Indian Tribes of the Upper Mississippi Valley & Region of the Great Lakes,* ed. Emma Helen Blair. Cleveland OH: Arthur H. Clark Company, 1911; reprint, Lincoln: University of Nebraska Press, 1996.

Pike, Zebulon M. *The Expeditions of Zebulon M. Pike to the Headwaters of the Mississippi River, through Louisiana Territory, and in New Spain, during the Years 1805–7. A New Edition Now First Reprinted in Full from the Original of 1810, with Copious Critical Commentary, Memoir of Pike and Complete Index,* ed. Elliot Coues. New York: F. P. Harper, 1895.

"Proceedings of a Council with the Chippewa Indians July 1837." *Iowa Journal of History and Politics* 9 (1911): 408–37.

Ritzenthaler, Robert. "Southwestern Chippewa." *Handbook of North American Indians,* vol. 15, ed. Bruce Trigger, 743–59. Washington DC: Smithsonian Institution, 1978.

Rogers, Edward S. "Band Organization among the Indians of the Eastern Subarctic, Canada." *Contributions to Anthropology: Band Societies.* Ottawa: Conference on Band Organization, 1965.

———. *The Round Lake Ojibwa.* Ottawa: Ontario Department of Lands and Forests for Royal Ontario Museum, 1962.

———. "Southeastern Chippewa." *Handbook of North American*

Indians, vol. 15, ed. Bruce Trigger, 760–771. Washington DC: Smithsonian Institution, 1978.

Romero, R. Todd, "'Ranging Foresters' and 'Women-Like Men': Physical Accomplishment, Spiritual Power and Indian Masculinity in Early 17th Century New England," *Ethnohistory* 53, no. 2 (2006): 281–329.

Sahlins, Richard. "Poor Man, Rich Man, Big-Man, Chief." In *Culture in Practice*. New York: Zone Books, 2005.

Sapir, Edward. "Conceptual Categories in Primitive Languages." *Science* 74 (1931): 578.

———. "The Status of Linguistics as a Science." In *Culture, Language, and Personality*, ed. David G. Mandelbaum. Berkeley: University of California Press, 1964. First published in *Language* 5 (1929): 207–214.

Satz, Ronald. *Chippewa Treaty Rights*. Madison: Wisconsin Academy of Sciences, Arts and Letters, 1991.

Schlesier, Karl. "Rethinking the Midewiwin and the Plains Ceremonial Called the Sun Dance." *Plains Anthropologist* 35, no. 127 (1989): 1–27.

Schenck, Theresa. *The Voice of the Crane Echoes Afar: The Sociopolitical Organization of the Lake Superior Ojibwa 1640–1855*. New York: Garland Publishing, 1997.

Schoolcraft, Henry Rowe. *History, Condition and Prospects of the Indian Tribes of the United States*. Philadelphia: Lippincott, Grambo and Company, 1852.

——— "Memoirs," *The American Indian* (CD-ROM). Carmel: Guild Press of Indiana, 1998.

———. *Personal Memoirs of a Resident of Thirty Years with the Indian Tribes on the American Frontiers: With Brief Notices of Passing Events, Facts, and Opinions, AD 1812 to AD 1842*. Philadelphia: Lippincott, Grambo, and Company, 1851.

———. "Reports and Letters of Henry Rowe Schoolcraft on the Expedition of 1832." In *Schoolcraft's Expedition to Lake Itaska*, ed. Philip Mason, 144–62. East Lansing: Michigan State University Press, 1993.

———. "Schoolcraft's Narrative of an Expedition through the

Upper Mississippi to Itaska Lake." In *Schoolcraft's Expedition to Lake Itaska*, ed. Philip Mason, 1–75. East Lansing: Michigan State University Press, 1993.

———. "Text of the Narrative Journal." In *Schoolcraft's Narrative Journal of Travels*, ed. Mentor L. Williams, 33–273. East Lansing: Michigan State University Press, 1992.

———. "Travels among the Aborigines: The Chippewa Indians." *North American Review* 27 (July 1828).

Sheehan, Bernard. *Seeds of Extinction: Jeffersonian Philanthropy and the American Indian*. Chapel Hill: University of North Carolina Press, 1973.

Shils, Edward. "Charisma, Order, and Status." *American Sociological Review* 30, no. 2 (April 1965): 199–213.

Shkilnyk, Anastasia M. *A Poison Stronger than Love*. New Haven: Yale University Press, 1985.

Smith, Huron H. "Ethnobotany of the Ojibwe Indians." *Bulletin of the Public Museum of the City of Milwaukee* 4, no. 3 (1932): 327–525.

Smith, James G. E. "Leadership among the Indians of the Northern Woodlands." In *Currents in Anthropology: Essays in Honor of Sol Tax*, ed. Robert Hinshaw, 305–24. The Hague: Mouton, 1979.

———. "Leadership among the Southwestern Chippewa." *National Museums of Canada Publications in Ethnology* 7 (1973): 1–36.

———. "Leadership among the Southwestern Ojibwa." *National Museums of Canada Publications in Ethnology* 7, Ottawa: National Museums of Canada, 1973.

Smith, Theresa S. *Island of the Anishinaabeg: Thunderers and Water Monsters in the Traditional Ojibwe Life-World*. Boise: University of Idaho Press, 1995.

Speck, Frank. "The Family Hunting Band as the Basis of the Social Organization of the Algonkian." *American Anthropologist* 17, no. 2 (1915): 289–305.

———. "Kinship Terms and the Family Band among the Northeastern Algonkian." *American Anthropologist* 20, no. 2 (1918): 143–61.

Speck, Frank, and Lauren C. Eiseley. "Significance of Hunting Territory Systems of the Algonkian in Social Theory." *American Anthropologist* 41, no. 2 (1939): 269–80.

"Statistical View of the Board and Its Missions." *Missionary Herald* 36 (1840): 34–35.

Symbolic Petition of the Chippewa Chiefs, Wisconsin Historical Society, http://www.wisconsinhistory.org/whi/fullRecord.asp?id=1871&qstring=

Tanner, John. *The Falcon* [1830]. New York: Penguin Books, 1994.

Tedlock, Dennis, and Barbara Tedlock, eds. *Teachings from the American Earth: Indian Religion and Philosophy.* New York: Liveright Publishing Corporation, 1975.

Thwaites, Ruben Gold, ed. *The Jesuit Relations and Allied Documents.* New York: Pageant, 1959.

Tosh, John. *Clan Leaders and Colonial Chiefs in Lango: The Political African Stateless Society ca. 1800–1939.* Oxford: Clarendon Press, 1978.

Trowbridge, Charles Christopher. "The Journal and Letters of Charles Christopher Trowbridge, Expedition of 1820." In *Schoolcraft's Narrative Journal of Travels,* ed. Mentor L. Williams, 461–500. East Lansing: Michigan State University Press, 1992.

Vecsey, Christopher. *Traditional Ojibwa Religion and Its Historical Changes.* Philadelphia: American Philosophical Society, 1983.

Vennum, Thomas. *Wild Rice and the Ojibway People.* St. Paul: Minnesota Historical Society Press, 1988.

Waisberg, Leo. "Boreal Forest Subsistence and the Windigo: Fluctuation of Animal Populations." *Anthropologica* 17 (1975): 169–85.

Wallace, Anthony F. C. *The Death and Rebirth of the Seneca.* New York: Vintage Books, 1972.

Warren, William Whipple. *History of the Ojibway People.* St. Paul: Minnesota Historical Society Press, 1984.

Whelan, Mary K. "Dakota Indian Economics and the Nineteenth-Century Fur Trade." *Ethnohistory* 40, no. 2 (Spring 1993): 246–76.

White, Bruce. "'Give Us a Little Milk': The Social and Cultural Significance of Gift Giving in the Lake Superior Fur Trade." *Minnesota History* 48, no. 2 (1982): 60–71.

———. "A Skilled Game of Exchange: Ojibway Fur Trade Protocol." *Minnesota History* 50, no. 6 (1987): 229–40.

———. "The Woman Who Married a Beaver: Trade Patterns and

Gender Roles in the Ojibwa Fur Trade." *Ethnohistory* 46, no. 1 (Winter 1999): 109–47.

White, Richard. *The Middle Ground: Indians, Empires, and Republics in the Great Lakes Region, 1650–1815.* New York: Cambridge University Press, 1991.

Widder, Keith R. *Battle for the Soul: Métis Children Encounter Evangelical Protestants at Mackinaw Mission, 1823–1837.* East Lansing: Michigan State University Press, 1999.

Williams, Mentor L. Introduction to *Schoolcraft's Narrative Journal of Travels*, by Henry Rowe Schoolcraft, ed. Mentor L. Williams, 1–24. East Lansing: Michigan State University Press, 1992.

Witgen, Michael. "The Rituals of Possession: Native Identity and the Invention of Empire in Seventeenth-Century Western North America." *Ethnohistory* 54, no. 4 (Fall 2007): 639–68.

Ziibiwing Cultural Society. Ziibiwing Center of Anishinabe Culture and Lifeways. Barrien Center: Penrod/Hiawatha, 2005.

Index

Aadizookaanag, 28

ABCFM. *See* American Board of Commissioners for Foreign Missions (ABCFM)

absolute monarchy, 2

acephalous societies, 3–4, 238n4

administrative structure of Anishinaabeg society, 76–77

adoption: of captives to fulfill revenge obligations, 118; by childless hereditary chiefs, 84–85, 179; as establishment of kinship ties, 32; renamed convert considered to be adopted by Ely, 204; role of women in, 70. *See also* fictive kinship

adultery, punishments for, 90

agricultural year: fall, 55–58; spring, 49–52; summer, 52–55; winter, 59–60

Ais-kaw-ba-wis, 171–72

Aitkin, Alfred, 191

Aitkin, William, 190, 193, 209, 214

Algonquian-speaking tribes, 45, 163

Allen, James, 51, 54, 127

alliances and alliance kinship, 46, 79–80

American Board of Commissioners for Foreign Missions (ABCFM): considered as representatives of U.S. government, 210; failures of among Ojibwe, 186; founding of, 183–85; obligations to compensate for land use, 101; on policing functions of warrior society, 124; role of villages in establishing missions, 43; suspicions of, 212. *See also* missionaries

American Fur Company (AFC), 186–87, 190, 192

American response to Anishinaabeg society. *See* European and American response to Anishinaabeg society; U.S. Government

Andanonib (Gandanonib), 195–96, 198, 219, 220, 224

Angel, Michael, 83, 149, 167

animals, 23–24, 27, 29, 59–60. *See also* hunters and hunting

atomism, 4–5, 228–30, 238n8, 243n51

authority: based on religious and hereditary sources, 2–3, 65–66, 110, 111, 115, 148, 172, 174, 181,

295

authority (*cont.*)
231, 233, 234; based on religious power, 3, 5–6, 8, 9, 32, 110, 173, 180, 193, 213, 218, 232–33, 235; based on right actions, 76, 111; as demonstrated through clothing, 78, 80; European and American misinterpretations of, 74, 216, 235; extension of through marriage, 70–71, 188; and missionaries, 10; and recitation of hereditary claims, 80, 109–10, 188, 257n198; transfer of to next generation, 81–82; of women, 67–68. *See also* charismatic leadership; hereditary leadership

Ayer, Frederick: and Fond du Lac controversy, 214; on leadership, 95, 101, 110; on opposition to missionaries, 52, 101, 147, 167–69; on war parties, 124

Badabi, 193
Bagone-giizhig I (Hole-in-the-Day the elder), 71, 84, 86
Bagone-giizhig II (Hole-in-the-Day the younger), 71, 233
Baraga, Frederic: and Fond du Lac controversy, 211–12, 213–14; on hereditary leadership, 66, 77–78, 81, 83–85, 90, 94, 107; on Indian society, 41, 44; on Midewiwin, 159, 174, 175; on warfare, 130

Barnouw, Victor, 148, 238n8
"Begging Dance," 126–28
Beltrami, Giacomo, 66, 176
Benton-Banai, Edward 40, 152
Berkhofer, Robert, 10
berry season, 54–55
Bezhig (The One Who Stands Alone), 87, 99, 241n33, 253n100
Biauswah II, 178
Bicaganab, 120–21
birch bark: collection of, 55; used for food storage, 50, 55, 57; used for messages, 37, 99, 188; used for Midewiwin scrolls, 149, 162, 179; used in hunting, 61; used in ricing, 56
Bishop, Charles, 148
Bizhiki (Buffalo), 1, 38, 70, 109, 179, 267n106
bizhikiiwaak, 137
Bourdieu, Pierre, 237n3
Boutwell, William T.: considered as U.S. representative, 9–10, 193; on Indian society, 10, 43, 56, 85, 99; on Midewiwin, 80, 110, 164–65, 166–67, 179; on ogimaag, 76, 90; support from American Fur Company, 187; on tobacco, 257n188, 258n201; on warfare, 124, 126, 143, 144
Brabant (hired man for Ely), 194–95
bravery, demonstrations of, 129, 141
bride service, 188–89
Broken Tooth (Katawabeda), 71, 72, 99, 177–78, 188

coercion, lack of (*cont.*)
  domination, 82; by war leaders, 118. *See also* consensus building
community ratification of appointment of new ogimaa, 82
community sanction for war parties, 133
consensus building: and fact finding by community members, 101–2; in Fond du Lac leadership crisis, 202; and gichi-anishinaabeg, 104–6; giigidowininiwag's role in, 87; ogimaag required for, 110, 231; role of in society, 1–2; sought by gechimidewid, 170; in territorial disputes, 101–2; at treaty gatherings, 103–4; and village council, 75–77, 104–5; through visiting, 44–45, 102. *See also* egalitarianism or democracy in Anishinaabeg society
controlled burning in agriculture, 53–54
Copway, George, 37, 66, 90–91, 155, 162, 217
Cotte, Isabella, 196
Cotte, Pierre: as Catholic lay preacher, 193–94, 208, 212; in Ely controversy, 201–2, 209, 213, 214, 217; as fur trader, 191, 201; on healing by spiritual leaders, 178
councils: calling of, 105, 107, 110, 257n201; consultations with,

75–77, 104–5, 231; modeled after council of Gichi-Manidoo, 36; organization of, 104–7; rituals for, 46, 107–8; varying purposes of, 175–76. *See also* women's councils
criminal activities, responses to, 90–91, 125
cultural biases of sources, 12–13
Curly Head, 84, 86
Curot, Michel, 91

Dakotas: Anishinaabeg exchange of clothing with, 79–80; as enemy of Anishinaabeg, 17, 41–42, 84, 92, 113, 121, 131, 139, 142; negotiations with, 37–38, 43, 96; participation in Midewiwin, 163; treaty violations by, 17
dance: "Begging" or Ogitchidaa Dance, 126–28; and connection to manidoog, 11, 31, 113–14, 147, 227; and Midewiwin, 158, 165–68, 177; misinterpretation of by Western observers, 128, 177; scalp dance, 142, 143, 144; social dance, 136; victory dances, 142–45; village dance area, 52; war dances, 68, 124, 126–28, 133–34, 137
Davenport, Ambrose, 101
Daybashah, 179
Deleary, Nicholas, 150, 163
democracy or egalitarianism in Anishinaabeg society, 3–4, 72, 148, 233, 236. *See also* charis-

matic leadership; consensus building

Densmore, Frances: on Midewiwin, 149, 151, 160–61; on oshkaabewis, 86; on warfare, 114, 118, 121–23, 132–33, 135, 137, 139, 145

dependency, 19, 228

divorce, 70, 89

dog feasts, 123, 128–29, 135

doodemag (clan system): and civil disputes, 90; gichi-anishinaabeg as representatives of, 105; and kinship obligations, 38–39; as means of community messaging, 36–38, 162; origin of, 243n51; rights of in cases of murder, 91, 131, 142

Dowd, Gregory, 5

dreams and visions: authority from, 10, 174, 233; available to all, 147–48; of Christian Maangozid, 219–20; in communication with manidoog, 8, 25–28, 31, 114, 119–20, 151, 227, 234; community sanctions of, 170–72, 234; dangers in, 26–27; interpretation of, 30–31, 122–23, 242n42; by Midewiwin initiates, 147, 148, 155, 179; and naming, 24; and political actions, 174; and power, 63; and prophets, 169, 174; used to find game, 161; and warfare, 119–23, 130–32, 138

drums: and Midewiwin, 134, 150, 155, 157–58, 159, 166, 217, 221; and ogitchidaa, 126–27; and warfare, 131–34, 137, 140, 141

eagle feathers as war honor, 128, 141

education, missionary: as benefit for the community, 194, 200–201, 205; for children of fur traders, 187; for Maangozid's sons, 195; opposition to, 52, 192; requiring conversion, 168

egalitarianism or democracy in Anishinaabeg society, 3–4, 72, 148, 233, 236

Eggan, Fred, 230

Ely, Catherine Bissell, 191, 218, 220, 223

Ely, Edmund: on Anishinaabeg rights to land, 101; background of, 190–91; community attempts to instruct, 199–201, 201–3; council discussions on, 110, 209, 213–14; failure of mission, 225; failure to participate in food sharing or gift exchange, 191–92, 194, 212, 216, 223; failure to see conflict in political terms, 203–4, 216; failure to support Nindipens, 215–17; failure to understand land usage rights, 205–6; on Midewiwin, 157–58, 161, 213; negotiations with Nindipens, 206–7; on Nindipens's claims to

Ely, Edmund (*cont.*)
leadership, 269n21; oblivious
to protocol, 194; on Ojibwe visiting, 44; relations with Maangozid, 221–23; role of in leadership crisis, 226; theological
debate with Catholic, 208; on
tobacco, 257n188; on warfare,
126, 135, 140
Enami'egaabaw, 186
En'dusogi'jig, 66
English society, comparison of
Anishinaabeg leadership to,
73–74
Eninabondo, 193, 208–9, 213, 215,
216–17, 222–23
Episcopalian missionaries, 186
Eshkibagikoonzh: as charismatic
leader, 165, 172–73, 233; hereditary powers of, 178–79, 236;
marriage connections of, 71–72;
and miishinoog, 85, 84; negotiations with Americans, 14; on
pipe smoking, 107; on rights
to land, 98–100; travels of, 44;
use of clothing symbolism, 78
ethnohistory, techniques of, 12–13
European and American response
to Anishinaabeg society: confusion on role of giigidowinini in
building of, 87, 88–89; cultural
world view of, 7–8; effect of arrival on Anishinaabeg, 13–14,
169–70; misunderstanding
of Anishinaabeg leadership,
73–74; not attuned to Anishinaabeg religious practices,

174–76; pressuring ogimaag
to interfere with clan prerogatives, 92; relationships with
controlled by Indians, 13–14;
as wealthy to Anishinaabeg,
102–3, 125

family: and dependence on village, 36, 42, 96–98, 228; and
gichi-anishinaabeg, 34–36,
75, 77, 104–5, 111, 171; in gift
exchange, 24–25, 44, 62, 63,
228; and manidoog, 26–28, 32,
33, 228; and Midewiwin, 167;
showing peaceful intentions,
85; usage rights, 49, 52, 55–56,
93–98, 142, 195
farming season, 52–54
fasting: to build relationships with
manidoog, 11, 25, 28, 114, 119,
151, 180, 227, 233; as frugality,
58; to improve chances of finding game, 134; and overfasting,
27; to prepare for war parties,
132, 138; at puberty, 119–20,
180
feasting: as connective ritual between humans and manidoog,
165; dog feasts, 123, 128–29,
135; "feasting the Dakota" and
scalp feasts, 143; "first fruits"
of maple sugar production,
49–50; misinterpretation of by
Western observers, 177; by war
parties, 133–34. *See also* ceremonies and rituals

fictive kinship: Americans' withdrawal from, 15–16; bringing outsiders into Anishinaabeg network, 32, 100, 126–28, 228; cemented by membership in Midewiwin, 164; as compensation for use of resources, 183; Ely's failure to establish, 192, 195, 205–6; established by clothing exchange, 79–80; with Europeans, 239n9; between fur traders and Indians, 72, 197. *See also* adoption; alliances and alliance kinship

fishing, 58–59

fish spawning run season, 50–52

flags as symbol of authority, 77

fluidity of leadership: in Midewiwin, 167; and respect for manidoog power, 132; as strength of Anishinaabeg governance, 4–5, 116, 229–32; in war parties, 132

fluidity of social, political, and religious boundaries, 194

Fond du Lac community, 11, 42, 44, 71, 72, 83, 89, 99, 101, 126, 154, 161, 178; attempting to instruct Ely in community norms, 199–201, 202–3; debates about Ely in, 195, 213–14, 224; discouraging Maangozid from visiting Ely family, 222; establishing mission at, 190–94; fears of American land-use policy, 192, 209–10, 214; leadership crisis at, 188–90,

208–9; and Maangozid's conversion, 219–20; underlying issues in, 225, 235–36; visit of Baraga to, 211–12; and war parties, 135, 140

food production: and allocation of land and resources, 93–94; seasonality of, 48–49. *See also* scarcity; women in agricultural economy

food sharing: and Midewiwin ties, 164–65; missionary failures at, 101, 183, 187–88, 206, 215–16; reinforcement of kinship ties, 164–65, 230; in times of scarcity, as insurance, 33

French society, comparison of Anishinaabeg leadership to, 73–74

funeral ceremonies, 108, 155, 177, 179, 193, 214

fur trade: in Anishinaabeg economy, 60–61; and availability of stored food, 57; effect on networks of interdependence, 62–63; territories for determined by Indians, 95, 100

fur traders: gift exchanges with Indians, 183, 197; land use permissions for, 101; marriage connections with, 32, 72; medals given by, 82; and missionaries, 193–94; trading for food with women, 48, 50

Gaashkibaaz, 213, 221

game calling ceremonies, 160–61

Locke, John, 2, 238n8
logging industry, effect on Anishinaabeg, 17
Loon's Foot. *See* Maangozid (Loon's Foot)

Maajii-giizhig, 130, 139
Maangozid (Loon's Foot), 71, 72, 89, 177–78; as broker between community and missionary, 216–17; claims to leadership, 188–89, 197–98; conversion to Christianity, 217–20, 224; end of conflict with Nindipens, 215; as giigidowinini, 188, 214; as medal chief, 190, 195, 199, 217; as Medewid, 161; return to Medewid, 220–22; and role of Ely in leadership crisis, 203, 209, 218, 224
madoodiswan (sweat lodges), 138, 156–57, 172–73, 220
Majigaabaw, 71, 78, 80, 84–85, 87–88, 109
manidoog and manidoog power: access to demonstrated by right actions, 111; Anishinaabeg understanding of, 7; approval sought for councils, 107; and charismatic leaders, 113, 115, 177; connected to humans by feasting, 165; as force behind a giigidowinini's words, 88; gifts or blessings of, 8–9, 21, 25–26, 29, 61; importance of connections to, 179–80; as means of

improving social status, 172, 180, 232, 236; and medicines, 137; modes of continuous interaction with, 31–32; mutual obligations with, 27–28, 29, 62; as necessary for survival, 23; need for adolescents to learn to use, 130; ogimaag relationships with, 66, 72–73, 74, 77, 107, 111–12, 227, 231; recognition of by community, 179–80; in rituals of warfare, 117, 119, 129, 130–31, 138, 139–40, 142, 144. *See also* charismatic leadership
Manidoo-giizhig, 170–71
manidookaazowin (hunting ceremony), 134, 160–61
Manidoons, 209–10, 212–13
Manypenny, George, 104
Maosit. *See* Maangozid (Loon's Foot)
maple sugar production, 49–50, 58. *See also* sugarbush
marriage and kinship ties: Ely's failure to establish, 192, 195; fostering dependence, 229; fur traders' marriage into families, 32, 72; importance of, 69–72; of Maangozid, 188–89; and ogimaag authority, 112; ogimaag mediating marriage disputes, 89; in peace negotiations, 136; and spread of Midewiwin tradition, 163–64; and visitations between tribal leaders, 45
Masewapega, 169, 173

Mauss, Marcel, 237n3
mayosewininiwag (war leaders): assistants to, 83, 131; definition, 73; influence of, 112, 145; and manidoog, 134, 139–40, 144–45, 177; ogimaag as, 230, 231, 234; planning a war party, 131–35; as temporary leaders, 117, 229
McKenney, Thomas L., 66, 68–69, 70
McLoughlin, William, 185
McNally, Michael, 109
medals as signs of office or authority: as attempt to control Anishinaabeg, 82; given to giigidowininiwag instead of ogimaag, 176, 198; and Maangozid's claim to leadership, 190, 195, 197–98, 199, 217; to Nindipens at 1837 treaty, 225; worn by giigidowininiwag, 88; worn by women, 69
mediation of disputes as power of ogimaag, 44–45, 89–90, 117, 225–26
medicinal plants, 55
medicine. *See* healing; Midewiwin society
menstrual observances of young girls, 120; and similarities to first-time warriors, 129–30
Midewiwin ceremonies: in agricultural seasons, 52, 56–57, 153–54; food sharing at, 164–65; fostering dependence, 229;

at meetings of council chiefs, 46; village as locus for, 42. *See also* ceremonies and rituals
Midewiwin society: code of conduct, 57, 151–53; inheritance of leadership in, 167; and intertribal relations, 163, 180–81, 232; leadership in, 165–66; meaning of term, 150; political dimension of, 11–12, 229, 232; pre-contact origin of, 148–50; resistance to Christian influence, 147, 167–69, 181, 212–13, 234–35; role in Anishinaabeg life, 150–51; role of doodemag in, 40; testing authority against ogimaag, 181. *See also* charismatic leadership; gechi-midewijig (Midewiwin leaders)
migration of Anishinaabeg to western Great Lakes, 13, 46, 92–94, 162
miishinoog (secretary) in village politics, 83–85
Minnehwehna, 118
mino-bimaadiziwin (good life), 151, 175, 231
Miskwaa-giizhig, 196
missionaries: asking permission to set up missions, 102; as challenge to Midewiwin leadership, 167–69, 181, 187–88, 210–11, 234–36; effect on Anishinaabeg society, 17, 211; failure to participate in food sharing and gift exchange, 101, 183, 187–88, 206, 215–16; ignorance of An-

ishinaabeg religious leadership, 176; influence of Locke on, 238n8; on Midewiwin ceremonies, 153–54, 263n23; as persons of religious authority, 9–10, 193, 210, 233; as subagents of American government, 188, 193, 210, 212–13; territories of, 43, 95; on welcome of new arrivals, 126–28. *See also* American Board of Commissioners for Foreign Missions (ABCFM); Catholic missionaries; education, missionary; Episcopalian missionaries

Miteui (Midewiwin). *See* Midewiwin society

More, Thomas, 2, 238n8

mourning ceremonies, 155

murder, response to, 90–92, 125, 131, 142. *See also* revenge obligations

mutual obligations. *See* kinship obligations

Naagaanab, 200–202

Nelson, George, 140, 161

Nichols, David, 1–2

Nicollet, Joseph, 211; on birch bark writing, 37; on Midewiwin, 156–57, 161, 164, 172–73, 179; on naming ceremonies and power, 227–28; on oshkabewis and miishinoo, 83; on pipe smoking, 107; on war leaders, 117, 129

Niigaani-benesi, 178–79

Nindipens: on Anishinaabeg rights to land, 99; attempts to instruct Ely, 201–2; and Baraga, 211–12; Catholicism of, 217; claims to leadership by, 189–90, 194, 196–97, 214–15, 269n21; leadership struggle with Maangozid, 198, 207, 215; negotiations with Ely, 190, 193, 204–7, 215–17, 226; and role of Ely in leadership crisis, 203

"noble savage" concept, 238n8

Nodin (the Wind), 109–10

Noodinens, 160–61

Odawa, ii, 96–97, 237n2, 268n6; as part of migration stories, 13, 46; as part of Three Fires, 46, 163; as "younger brother" to Ojibwe, 46

Odjibwe, 121–23, 133, 135, 137, 141, 145

Ogichidaag. *See* warrior society (Ogichidaag)

ogimaag: in allocation of land and resources, 92–96, 98–100, 195–96, 201, 226, 231, 236; assistants to, 83–89, 112; and Christianity, 181–82, 234; consultations with gichi-anishinaabeg, 104–5; as emissary to external groups, both human and manidoog, 17, 44–45, 77, 81, 98, 102, 105–6, 117, 228–29, 231; enhanced power using

ogimaag (cont.)
outside assistance, 231; having
both hereditary and religious
power, 10–11, 110–11; as hereditary leaders, 66; and hereditary
Midewiwin ties, 167; holding
more authority than other community members, 76; influence increased by manidoog
powers, 148, 172, 180, 236; in-
stallations of, 81–82; intervening in clan prerogatives, 92;
intervening in family disputes,
75; in intervillage relationships,
44–45, 48–49; involvement in
murder cases, 91; limits of authority of, 109–11; in matters of
civil concern, 89–90; as Midewiwin leaders, 167, 172–74,
177–79, 208, 230–33; as per-
suaders, 74–75, 111, 231; pressured by Americans to make
quick decisions, 103–4; role in
consensus building, 231; role in
councils, 105–6, 110; sources of
power, gift exchange, and intermarriage, 71, 230; symbols of
rank and authority, 77–80; as
war leaders, 145–46; and well-
being of community, 175. *See
also* giigidowininiwag (speakers); hereditary leadership;
miishinoog; oshkaabewisag
(pipe bearers)
ogimaakwe (chief woman), 67,
68–69

Ojibwe, 4, 46, 237n2
Ojibwe ministers, religious authority of, 217
Omiskwawegijigokwe, 135
oral history as historical technique, 12, 13
oral tradition: on ancient origins
of Midewiwin society, 149; as
instruction in Midewiwin, 159;
and pipe ceremony, 108; power
as shape changing, 24; on role
of ogimaag in resource allocation, 98; in socialization of
people, 6
oratory skills and persuasion: as
basis of war leader authority,
118, 145; building consensus
by, 231; and extension of power
over regional populations, 111;
of giigidowininiwag, 87–89;
and leadership skills, 231; of
Ogichidaag in settling disputes,
126; by ogimaag, 74–75, 111; in
war leaders, 118
origin stories, 13, 46, 92–94, 162
oshkaabewisag (pipe bearers): as
assistant to war leader, 132–33;
as messengers, 83; multiple
roles of, 176–77; in organizing
a council, 105–6; in peace negotiations, 136–37; in pipe smoking rituals, 108; and scalp dances, 144; summoning people to
ceremonies, 173; in village politics, 83, 85–86
outsiders, fictive kinship with, 32,
100, 126–28, 228

ownership of land. *See* land and resources, allocation of; land usage rights

Ozaanaamikoons, 201–2

Ozhaagashkodewike, 68

peace negotiations, 136–37

Peers, Laura, 149, 151

Perrot, Nicholas, 90

personhood of plants, animals, and forces, 23–24, 25–26

persuasion. *See* oratory skills and persuasion

Peter (Ely's convert), 191, 194, 204, 206

Pike, Zebulon, 53–54

pipe bearers. *See* oshkaabewisag (pipe bearers)

pipe smoking: as connection with spiritual world, 105–6, 107; at councils, 105–6, 107, 108–9, 176; in installation ceremony, 82; in peace negotiations, 136; in warfare, 127, 132, 133, 138–39. *See also* tobacco

Pokegoma, ii, 110, 124, 154, 214, 263n23

plants, knowledge of, 159

policing of community: by Ogichidaag, 124–26, 199; by ogimaag, doodemag, and gichi-anishinaabeg, 90

political agreements and gift exchange, 33, 38, 245n48

political constituencies in Ojibwe society, 2, 66, 77, 93, 109, 231

political process. *See* consensus building

polycephalitic, 132, 230

Pontiac's Revolt (1763–66), 2, 45

population of villages, 41–42

Potawatami: as part of migration stories, 13, 46; as part of Three Fires, 46, 163; as "younger brother" to Ojibwe, 46

power: in Anishinaabeg system, 10, 18–19; consequences of using for harm, 153; as cultural construct, 5–6; enhanced by connection with manidoog, 227; judged by success, 10; as lack of dependence, 19, 23; as manifestly present, 63; moral obligation to help others, 29; and obligation to give gifts, 21–23, 35–36; as skills in warfare, hunting, and healing, 228. *See also* manidoog and manidoog power

preservation of food as survival strategy, 57–58

prestige as measure of access to manidoog power, 10, 72, 115–16, 119, 232

puberty and initiation rituals, 129–30, 147–48, 151, 155–61, 164–68, 179

public rituals and connection with manidoog, 107, 114, 147

reciprocal social relationships. *See* kinship obligations

redistribution of resources. *See* land and resources, allocation of

religious and political power, fluidity of, 3, 5, 8, 175–76, 213, 232, 235

religious power. *See* charismatic leadership

respect: accorded to gichi-anishinaabeg, 75; accorded to oshkabewis and giigidowininiwag, 86, 89; in Anishinaabeg interpretations of Christianity, 208; as basis for ogimaag authority, 36, 45, 66, 70, 76, 82, 112, 115, 207; earning of by gechi-midewijig, 148, 172, 221–22; earning of by mayosewininiwag, 145, 146; and gift exchange, 35, 100; and missionaries, 186, 187, 214, 217, 218, 222, 223; in politics, 104, 105, 132; in relations with manidoog, 21, 22, 26, 27, 28, 55, 108, 115, 119, 130, 132, 152; social expectations for, 32, 33, 67; sources of, 231–32; for women, 66, 68, 69, 119, 151, 208; *See also* charismatic leadership

revenge obligations: for loss of resources and territorial issues, 96, 142; against missionaries, 124–25; ogimaag intervened in at peril, 91; and restoration of deceased, 118; success of war leaders in fulfilling, 117–19. *See also* murder, response to; warfare and war parties

revitalization movements, 5, 9; and Midewiwin, 11, 148–49

rituals. *See* ceremonies and rituals

Rogers, Edward, 159

Rousseau, Jean-Jacques, 2, 238n8

sacred fire at opening of council, 108

Sandy Lake, ii, 41, 71, 72, 84, 178, 185, 188, 198

Sassaba, 125–26

Sault Ste. Marie, ii, 9, 14, 15, 17, 58, 68, 87, 125, 149, 179, 196

scalps as war honor (scalp dance), 142, 143, 144

scarcity: and allocation of land resources, 95; food sharing in, 33; relationships of mutual obligation as protection against, 62, 228; role of leaders in planning for, 48; role of medewid in calling game, 160–61; and use of food caches, 58. *See also* land and resources, allocation of

Schlesier, Karl, 148

Schoolcraft, Henry Rowe: on first encounter with Europeans, 169; on Indian agriculture, 51, 54, 55, 60; on Indian society, 37, 43, 85, 101, 179; and introduction of missionaries, 9–10, 193, 210, 270n193; meetings with Eshkibagikoonzh, 78, 85; on ogimaag, 66, 82, 92; on warfare, 126–27, 144

seasonal round of food production, 48–50, 93

seating at treaty gatherings, 103–4
seating in family lodges, 80
semi-nomadic lifestyle of Anishinaabeg, 93
sexual abstinence in preparation
for war parties, 132
shaking tent ceremonies, 177
Shils, Edward A., 115
side-streaming concept, 12–13
sin, alien to Anishinaabeg beliefs,
219
Smith, James, 174
Smith, Theresa, 151
Snake River, ii, 1, 87, 95, 154
social connections. *See* kinship
obligations
socialization by religious texts, 6
songs as communication with
manidoog, 114–15, 119, 122, 131,
134, 136–37, 141–42
sorcery, 90, 96, 224
speakers. *See* giigidowininiwag
(speakers)
Speck, Frank G., 96
spiritual power. *See* charismatic
leadership; manidoog and
manidoog power
spouse stealing as major crime, 90
Sproat, Grenville, 78
St. Peters, ii, 1, 15, 37, 38, 88, 99,
104, 124, 190, 224
sticks, uses of: in calling a large
council, 105–6; in invitations to
ceremonies, 173; in Nindipens's
negotiations with Ely, 207
Strong Ground, 84, 86

subsistence base and networks of
interdependence, 62
success: as evidence of religious
power, 10, 72, 110, 115–16, 232;
and right living, 153; by war
leaders combining military and
spiritual power, 117
succession, ceremonies for, 81–82
sugarbush, 12, 42, 43, 49, 50, 94,
95, 221, 228
sweat lodges (madoodiswan), 138,
156–57, 172–73, 220

Taliaferro, Lawrence, 118–19, 163
Tanner, John: community sanctions for dreams, 170–71; and
doodemag messages, 37; and
need for community, 34; on resource allocation, 96–98; on
women's roles, 70, 161
temporary leadership: by appointed chiefs, 72; among Midewiwin, 167; war leaders as, 117
territorial boundaries: consequences of violating, 96; of ogimaag power, 111–12; recognition of, 93; war over as revenge
for loss of resources, 142. *See
also* land and resources, allocation of
Three Fires Confederacy (Anishinaabeg peoples), 46–47, 163,
237n2
time, Anishinaabeg perception of,
31–32

political, and economic entity, 36, 40–46, 75–77, 95–98, 228–29, 231; missionaries and missions at, 18, 76, 99, 101, 193–96, 205, 210, 225; political disputes in, 72, 229; sovereignty of, 15; as unit in territorial negotiations, 17, 96, 99–100, 104, 106. *See also* gichi-anishinaabeg (village headmen); intervillage relationships

Waabojiig, 77–80, 179
Waisberg, Leo, 94
Wallace, Anthony F. C., 5
war banners, 133, 141
war dances, 133–34
warfare and war parties: importance of leaders for, 116; and peace negotiations, 136; and power of manidoog, 121–22, 130–31, 138–40; preparations for, 126–28, 130–36; role of women in, 67–68, 120–21, 134–35, 143–44; support of community for, 128; victory dances, 142–44; war expeditions, 136–41; and white residents, 124
war honors, 140–41
war leaders. *See* mayosewininiwag (war leaders)
Warren, William, 39, 66, 83, 149, 155
warriors (young men): pipe bearers as, 86; as political constituency, 66; role in maintaining

territorial boundaries, 93, 95; at treaty gatherings, 103–4; in village council, 76, 77
warrior society (Ogichidaag): and community policing, 124–26, 199; initiations of young men into, 128–30; and preparations for war, 123; role of, 123–25
weather conditions: ability to affect or predict in warfare, 139–40; manidoog aid in controlling, 177
Weber, Max, 112–13
Wemitigoozhikwe, 188–89
Wenabozho (Anishinaabeg mythology), 98, 163
Western religion and philosophy: assuming distinction between politics and religion, 174–75; human domination over natural world, 23
Wheeler, Leonard, 107, 109
Whipple, Henry, 186
White, Bruce, 46–47
White, Richard, 5, 163, 239n9
White Buffalo Calf Woman, 134–35
white residents, policing of by Ogichidaag, 124
wild rice collection, 17, 55–56
winter, 59–60, 131
woman of sacrifice in war preparations, 134–35
women: dreams and visions of, 119–20; healing roles of, 159–60; in hunting ceremonies, 161; as interpreters, 195; in

www.ingramcontent.com/pod-product-compliance
Lightning Source LLC
Chambersburg PA
CBHW030640270326
41929CB00007B/143